STORMS
THE NORMS

Anisha Motwani is a multifaceted business leader and the managing director of StN Ventures. She is also the author of the national bestselling book *Storm the Norm*. A speaker, avid blogger and podcaster, Anisha is also an advisor, mentor and independent director on the boards of several organizations.

In recognition of her achievements, she was voted as one of the '50 Most Powerful Women in Indian Business' by *Business Today* for three consecutive years, among many others.

Priyadarshini Narendra is a marketing, communications and strategy expert. She has worked for close to three decades across advertising, marketing, consumer research and consulting with organizations such as Lintas, Kantar, HT Media, Iconoculture, CK Birla Group and more. A TedX speaker, she is passionate about the cause of Women at the Workplace. She now consults with multiple brands on strategy, trendspotting and research.

She is a fiction writer of two books, *Two Chalet School Girls in India, and You Never Know When You'll Get Lucky*! She has also been a contributor to an anthology of short stories inspired by the pandemic, titled *Here Today, Here Tomorrow*. This is her first non-fiction book.

SHE

STORMS
THE NORMS

ANISHA MOTWANI
PRIYADARSHINI NARENDRA

RUPA

Published by
Rupa Publications India Pvt. Ltd 2024
7/16, Ansari Road, Daryaganj
New Delhi 110002

Sales centres:
Bengaluru Chennai Hyderabad
Jaipur Kathmandu Kolkata
Mumbai Prayagraj

P-ISBN: 978-93-90260-74-4
E-ISBN: 978-93-90260-85-0

First impression 2024

10 9 8 7 6 5 4 3 2 1

The moral right of the authors has been asserted.

Printed in India

'If I have seen far, it is by standing upon the shoulders of giants.'
—**Isaac Newton**

⁑

To all the wonderful, fierce, feisty and warm women who nurtured us, supported us and inspired us to storm the norms, and who would be very surprised to be described as giants!

⁑

With much love and admiration to Premalatha Narendra, Subhadra and Shanta Bai, Champa Rao, Vasanthi Rao and Brinda Narasimha, Aliya Hasan, Masooma Ali, Mrinalini Narendra Vittal, Moomal Mehta, Fatima Bhagwani, Anurupa Pal and Parvati—the pillars of my house; my giants, my tribe!
—**Priyadarshini Narendra**

⁑

To my three mothers: Champa Chandwani, my guiding light; Mohini Motwani, my beacon of support; Dr B.G. Kotwani, a remarkable 95-year-old gynaecologist. With immeasurable gratitude, this is a tribute to the three pillars of my life, my giants!
—**Anisha Motwani**

CONTENTS

PREFACE

As working women who have had to make many hard decisions, we often wish we had a repository of knowledge that would help us figure out what other successful women have done in similar situations. Role models play an enormous part in shaping our aspirations, values and behaviours.

India's population is constituted by nearly 677 million women out of 1.4 billion. However, India's female labour participation rate has declined over the past two decades from a high of 35 per cent in 2005. In 2023, the employability gender gap in India was 50.9 per cent with only 19.2 per cent of women in the labour force compared to 70.1 per cent of men. According to the Global Gender Gap Report 2023, India ranks near the bottom with 40 per cent parity in terms of access to economic participation and opportunity.

Fewer women in the workforce mean that an enormous number of girls grow up without working women in their immediate surroundings. How will they learn to negotiate the various crossroads that come with deciding to have a career? How will they learn to storm their own uncertainties, and shrug off the burden of social expectations or the structural beliefs that block their path?

We wanted to put together the narratives of a group of very diverse women who have each stormed the norms in their own unique ways. At the same time, we didn't want it to be academic or a series of anecdotes strung together. Throughout history, human beings have relied on stories to learn about each other and to make sense of the world. We interacted with these wonderful women to bring to life their struggles and triumphs, their vulnerable moments and the times when they took the reins of their narratives—both professional and personal—in their own hands.

We hope that you, like us, find their stories not just inspiring, but moving and relatable. We hope you find nuggets in each story that can help you when you come to significant crossroads in your life. And we hope that you find, through them, the strength to Storm the Norm!

THESE WOMEN NEED NO INTRODUCTION

This is an anti-introduction. Usually, books begin with a brief note that orients the reader towards the ideas that the author wants to explore. However, this book requires *disorientation*, an estrangement and for us to hold an inside-out mirror to the constructs we take for granted. When I was growing up, there was a popular joke about how a doctor and a nurse were stranded on a deserted island. Nine months later, they had a baby. But the doctor was not the father of the baby and the nurse was not the mother. How did that happen?

If you're still wondering, the doctor was the mother and the nurse was the father. Back in the day, it took anyone several minutes to work out this possibility—if they got there at all! And yet, once it is explained, it seems so obvious, so simple, so logical that we wonder how we could have missed it the first time.

There's a popular meme that shows how men can spot a sniper 400 metres away amidst a thicket of trees in a game of paintball, but are unable to see a bottle of ketchup that is right before their eyes in the fridge. In many ways, this is a fitting metaphor for the seen and the unseen that becomes the basis for this *invisible* reality. We're so disoriented from the reality under our noses that we end up unseeing it. More importantly, this invisible reality is so *normalized* that it translates into a set of norms that we don't question at all.

The doctor joke and sniper meme may not be news to you, but you will be surprised to know that we are still in the matrix. We still miss the obvious, the simple, the logical assumptions that shape our gendered realities. These assumptions are so ubiquitous that they are invisible. And, in turn, they shape *visible* realities. And one powerful way to re-see, re-view and re-examine them is to invert them.

What exactly do I mean? Let us examine what this means by studying five of the many norms that form part of this *invisible* reality. We're going on a journey together to see if any of these make sense to you. Ready?

ഇ

Norm #1: Men stay away from the corner office because of the stress and pressure it brings.

Think about it. When you consider all the responsibilities of setting up and maintaining a home while also juggling child-rearing responsibilities, how are men supposed to have the bandwidth or energy to even aspire to the corner office with all the accompanying stress and pressure? No wonder men shy away from C-suite roles even if they are well-suited to them from an experience or expertise perspective. Yes, they stay in the kitchen because they can take the heat, literally, of the cooking fire. But can they take the metaphorical heat of the corner office, which means facing the fire of competition, clients and corporate politics?

Norm #2: There is a confidence gap between men and women that constantly makes men feel like they are imposters.

For millennia, men's identities have been built around working at home, and it is only of late that they have ventured into boardrooms. It is natural, then, that they feel a little under-confident in such alien settings. You may wield a mean knife on a chopping board but holding your own in board, meetings is a different cup of tea altogether. Men's natural instincts in navigating around the home don't always translate into the requisite skill set for scaling to the upper echelons of the corporate ladder. And with good reason; confidence is not a transferable skill.

Norm #3: The primary role of being the breadwinner falls to the woman; men have the secondary job. Thus, they risk rejection in what they choose to do, but they have the option

to take their job less seriously or deprioritize it in favour of family needs.

Bread-making, now that's something men are familiar with. Breadwinning? Not so much. So, when they move away from their ovens, they find that they have to take their gloves off in order to survive and thrive in the workplace. Hence, they take the easy way out by either doing their jobs half-heartedly or using the excuse of having to raise a family to treat their work as a secondary priority (sometimes tertiary, after socializing with other home-bound men). After all, when they don't *have* to be the primary breadwinners, why place additional burden on themselves?

Norm #4: Men see each other as rivals and not colleagues in the workplace.

This norm might seem odd given how men usually bond well at home, swapping recipes, stories of each other's children, their travails with the in-laws and so on. But this camaraderie does not extend to the workplace, and rather than being collegial with each other, they see each other as rivals. This is perhaps unavoidable given how few men make it to the top in professional settings and how women leave very few opportunities open for men. This competition results in a professional rivalry akin to what men (especially married ones) experience at home with their fathers-in-law—trying to carve out their relevance in the household.

Norm #5: Working men are torn between two role models— the mother, who went out and earned a living, and the stay-at-home father, who ran the home smoothly and spent his time bringing up the children. Thus, they constantly feel guilty, like they are compromising one for the other.

Put yourself in a homemaker's shoes—imagine what he goes through when confronted with this norm. His own mother—not some stranger—has nurtured the spark of ambition in him through the professional successes she has achieved, and the financial security she has provided to the whole family. On the other hand, his father has nurtured him in the true sense of 'parvarish', always putting his son's needs before his own. Who is the better role model? Whose path should the son follow? This dilemma often yields an all-consuming guilt regardless of which path he pursues, making it seem like a lose-lose proposition.

⁓

Dear Reader,

I am guessing that every one of the five norms I have outlined above sounds ludicrous. And yet, I also hope that their very absurdity brings home the stark reality of these norms with just a simple transposition of gender.

All I did was transpose those norms into the lives and perspectives of men. And these norms form only a tiny subset of the challenges women face in terms of self-belief. Imagine having to live with these norms that make up the reality that women confront daily.

Let me now lay out some systemic/structural/societal norms.

I will use the same device to outline the same systemic/structural/societal norms in the *unlived* realities of men. I won't belabour the point this time.

Norm #6: Leaders should be strong and demanding, not friendly and empathetic.

It's an accepted fact that men's strengths lie in their innate empathy, a trait that is critical to bringing up children in the correct manner. But is there really a place for empathy and friendliness in the dog-eat-dog world of work? Men tend to vacillate between being soft and empathetic or aggressive and overbearing. They can't seem to find the middle ground of self-assured assertiveness.

Norm #7: Career-driven people need to be their own advocates and promote their achievements to be noticed.

For millennia, men have been raised to be self-effacing. They are taught to demonstrate humility rather than achievement. 'Men should be seen, not heard', is a refrain that echoes everywhere. How, then, are they to be noticed? This puts men at a significant disadvantage when competing against women.

Norm #8: Men take paternity leave, and after that, their primary attention is on the child. Thus, they must be put on a slower 'daddy' track.

Working men are a 'risk-free talent' proposition only as long as they don't have children. After the responsibilities of fatherhood weigh in, their priorities shift from their work and career to their child. It is in their best interest—as well as that of corporates—to have lesser expectations from men when they come back from paternity leave. That way, men won't need to feel guilty about neglecting their child, and, at the same time, corporations can use their services without curtailing opportunities for women to fast-track their growth journeys that may otherwise be lost to an 'equality' agenda.

Norm #9: Men in family businesses have it easy.

This one needs no explanation. In family businesses, men have the cushion of unstinting support from the family. Additionally, they can get into positions of authority and responsibility by bypassing merit pathways. While getting to the top is easy, getting bored of it and moving on to something else is also not frowned upon, since the women are there to handle things if the men move away.

≈

Dear Reader,

Did these norms make you cringe even further? Did they heighten the absurdity of these propositions? Or did they make you ponder about the equally absurd but very real nature of these norms when transposed into women's lives?

Now consider the crosses women have to bear merely to get these norms *acknowledged* in the first place. And then consider the sociocultural (often internalized) odds they have to surmount in order to storm these norms.

That, dear reader, is what you are holding in your hands. Not a mere narration of some people's journeys. Not just 'case studies' of business or life success. Not a collection of mini-biographies.

These are reimaginations of previously-unquestioned conventions by a range of courageous women. These are big 'What-ifs' asked by a set of women who did not accept the status quo. These taken-for-granted norms have been broken by women who refuse to be taken for granted.

While these women don't need a book to celebrate their achievements or champion them, the aim of this book is perhaps most eloquently stated by Oscar Wilde, 'It is the spectator, and not life, that art really mirrors.'

If the stories of these Norm-Storming Women can awaken even one person to the reality of the norms that constrain women daily (and are not applicable to men), then this book would have done its job.

This book adds to the pantheon of books celebrating the breaking of glass ceilings while showing a mirror to all of us.

My request to you is this.

Pick a chapter—any chapter from any part of the book—and observe what you see in the mirror. Then ask yourself a few questions. Are you helping perpetuate the norms? Or do you feel better equipped now to storm these norms yourself and become an ally to others trying to storm the norms in their own ways? Does it make you go, 'I know a Stormer like this!'? From elevating your consciousness about unconscious biases to enabling action and inspiration, this book hopes to serve many purposes.

Who are these Stormers, and how can you best draw from their wisdom and experiences? A good place to start, as Julie Andrews famously sang in *The Sound of Music*, is at the very beginning. Each story starts by tracing the origins of these women's lives. How did they embark on this road for their journeys? Did the road choose them, or did they choose the road? Were there pivotal factors—personal, interpersonal, sociocultural, structural—that nudged them in the direction they travelled?

As they entered adulthood and the realm of professional work, what shaped their career? Looking back from the vantage point of hindsight, how does the road appear now? Did they stick to the straight and narrow, or were there multiple forks in the road they had to choose from? And how did their gender play a role in these choices? What systemic or structural norms did they have to storm as they paved the path to their future?

A quintessential part of the myriad tussles in journeys like these is self-belief. What were the foundations upon which these stalwarts built their self-belief? What were the crests and troughs as they filled their reservoir of self-belief?

It's difficult to put these women into boxes, but method and structure can sometimes help in simplifying complex stories while still retaining their nuances.

To begin with, the stories of the 17 women featured here are from diverse worlds: family businesses, Bollywood (intended to capture more than just the traditional stereotype of the Hindi film industry), professionals, entrepreneurs and underdogs.

These are not mutually exclusive categories, and you will see many intersections in the stories.

Irrespective of their origins, status and accomplishments, these are women who battled many age-old, stubborn norms. And their optimism in the ordinary has been the guiding force behind some of their extraordinary accomplishments.

Their backstories vary immensely: from royalty to poverty, big city to rural origins, from the film industry to the corporate world, privileged to underprivileged, single to married to divorced to lesbian, from holding an MBA from Stanford to being illiterate.

What this book *does not do* is try to reduce these diverse and complex stories into simplistic narratives or find common threads that bind them together. Instead, the attempt is to celebrate the diversity, tease out the nuances and understand the underlying factors that both helped and hindered them.

Always with an eye to making the invisible visible.

Take Apurva Purohit, an IIM Bengaluru graduate, co-founder of Aazol Ventures, and a seasoned and celebrated leader in the media and marketing fields. During one of her visits to a leading management institute in 2015, she had the following experience.

'I asked the female students in the audience how many of them wanted to work after college. They were appalled by my question and expressed that they all planned to work. I asked the boys how many of them wanted working wives, and surprisingly, only 10 per cent put up their hands.'

What does that say about the enabling—or in this case, disabling— social and professional environment in which women have to pursue their ambitions?

Instances like these have pushed Apurva to continually find ways to level the playing field for women. She authored two books on the subject of women at work. She created Aazol: a network of women from self-help groups (SHGs) and microentrepreneurs at the village level. Financial empowerment, as she says, is one of the most powerful forms of emancipation, and the foundation for growth and success.

From a different background altogether, Ruma Devi from Barmer in Rajasthan, is a winner of the Nari Shakti Puraskar, India's highest civilian award for women. Her story spans a personal history of losing her mother at an early age, being brought up by her uncle and aunt, dropping out of school in Class 8, getting married when she was 17 and more personal travails. Ruma Devi turned a highly traditional pathway—being taught stitching and embroidery at a young age— into a means to empower not just herself but over 30,000 women to become fashion and crafts entrepreneurs. Her journey was littered with personal, social and systemic norms that constantly tried to hold her back. What started as an ordinary woman's efforts to live an ordinary life independently became the means for thousands of women to find that the extraordinary could also be within their reach. This also helped Ruma Devi shape her own destiny beyond the confines of limited resources and opportunities in far-flung Barmer.

Perhaps one of the best exemplars of making the invisible visible is Raga Olga D'Silva, speaker, author, LGBTQIA+ activist and entrepreneur. How does a successful, middle-aged, married mother of twins traverse the journey of coming out as gay? How does she then further not only her personal but also her professional aspirations? Imagine the social and systemic norms at play.

As you can see, the roads that each of these women travel wind through many twists and turns. They do have a few common markers, and they invite us as readers to become companions in their journey.

None of these women harboured any illusions of invincibility. Unsurprisingly, one of the richest veins of wisdom in this book, therefore, comes from their narratives of failure, of dealing with emotional conflicts, of norms around self-belief that threatened to shackle them, how they broke free and who their supporters and cheerleaders were in this journey.

Each story is rounded off with a section that focusses on one norm that stood out to us, along with nuggets of reflections and advice, and identity markers that tell the reader a timeless truism: if I can do 'it', so can you.

The 'it', here, can be interpreted as creating roads and journeys to success like any of these women. 'It' can also refer to creating self-awareness about the multitude of constraining norms and sustaining a mindfulness about the invisible realities that women confront and storm daily. 'It' nudges you to choose from and become one among the stormers, the champions and the allies in a larger, interconnected reality where ability trumps constraining norms on the road to success.

None of these women set out to be 'inspirational'. But they can't help being inspiring.

If this book inspires you to shift perspectives, make the invisible visible for yourself and for others, and ultimately helps you storm the norms in your life, it would have served its purpose.

Happy storming!

ADHUNA
Dil Chahta Hai

Introduction

Born to a British mother and an Indian father, Adhuna started her hairstyling career as an apprentice in the UK straight out of school. Participating in hairdressing competitions to help hone her skills, she got her first big break at 17 when she was awarded the National Junior Champion (under 21) for hairdressing. She went on to work at Wella as part of the technical team in London. On holiday in India, Adhuna found herself having so much fun that she light-heartedly decided to stay back. Together with her brother Ashoke Bhabani (fondly called Osh) and Avan Contractor, she founded BBlunt Salons, growing it into a national chain, as well as the BBlunt hairstyling academy and the shoot crew, which styled hair for over 50 films. BBlunt also launched a brand of hair care and styling products specially created for Indian hair and weather.

Having recently sold the brand to Honasa, Adhuna will remain involved on the creative side. She wants to continue giving back to the hairdressing industry through training and mentoring.

> I firmly believe in my core philosophies. I will not cut, copy, paste! I believe that everyone is unique.
>
> My top priorities are being a great mentor and maintaining extremely high standards within the team, inspiring other hairdressers to achieve their best and ensuring every client that visits the salons leaves feeling their best.

Why Adhuna?

Dil Chahta Hai was arguably a movie that changed the styling of film characters for the better. The iconic hairstyles sported by the cast, including Preity Zinta's bouncy curls and Aamir Khan's stylized hair and soul patch, were a revelation and a revolution. We were intrigued to learn about the duo responsible for this transformation, Adhuna and Avan, and followed Adhuna's career closely. Despite being a director's/star's wife, she continued to focus on her career and build a recognizable brand.

How does a hairstylist from the UK end up becoming a household name in India? Adhuna's life script defies many of the norms for women, and even some laid out for men. In India, life follows a set pattern: once your career takes off, you don't throw it all away and uproot your life to start over. Moreover, with our country's historical context, the norm is to opt for a 'practical' career and a steady income rather than gamble on following one's passion and setting up a business. However, Adhuna, who had everything lined up for a successful career in the UK, decided to start over from scratch in a country where everything was new to her. She and Farhan Akhtar married when he was at the beginning of his career, directing his first film. She continued to pursue her career and built a recognizable brand even after his meteoric rise, when she could have chosen to take it easy and focus on the kids, since his career was hectic and well-paying. And years later, they went on to have an amicable divorce in a country where divorce is still seen as taboo by most people. How was she able to not only storm all these norms but also do it without turning a hair?

In for a Penny, in for a Pound #Adhunik

Adhuna was ecstatic. She had just bagged a terrific job at her dream firm, Toni and Guy! Always adventurous, with three months of free time before she started her job, she decided to travel. She was still deciding where to go when an unexpected destination popped into her head. She had only been to India once before and didn't have good memories of that visit. While she had distant relatives in India, she knew no one in Mumbai. Yet, suddenly, the thought of coming to India had her all fired up. On a whim, she decided to go where her instincts took her. Short of cash, she sold off all her belongings from the dicky of her car and landed in Bombay with just a backpack, £500 and a pair of scissors. And she never left!

Growing Up Different

Adhuna's incredible warmth and friendliness come through even over Zoom interactions, and she is quite candid about her journey. Born in the UK to an English mother and Bengali father, she grew up in a close-knit family made up of her parents, her twin sister and a brother who was six years younger. Her mother was a nurse, and her father a doctor—that was how they had met. The family lived in the countryside in St Helen's near Liverpool, in a lovely family home surrounded by fields; walked to the local primary school; and rode horses—something that remains a passion for Adhuna till date. In some ways, it was an idyllic life.

However, St Helen's had hardly any 'brown' people at the time. Adhuna and her siblings were the only Indian kids. Their paternal grandmother was famous for coming up with interesting names for the children in the family, and had named the older twin Adhuna, meaning 'modern', while the younger one was named Nutana, meaning 'new'. The sisters detested their Indian names since they made them stand out from the crowd at an age when children usually prefer to blend in. They were not accustomed to their Indian side and didn't understand it too well. Every year at school, they had to not only spell their names out but, during roll call, tell each new teacher how to pronounce them. They regularly got picked on by a gang of boys, who used to wait for them at the school gate just to hurl taunts. While their mother had taught them how to handle prejudice and the kids dealt with it strongly, Adhuna always felt like she didn't quite fit in.

Adhuna's father, like most Indians, prized formal education and was keen that the kids follow academic pursuits. He would often compare the twins based on their schoolwork. Nutana was more studious, and he coerced her into opting for medicine. Adhuna, on the other hand, hated school and loved creative activities from the beginning.

Life suddenly changed for the family when Adhuna was 12. Her father died of a heart attack. At just 33, her mother, who had given up working when the kids came along, was left to cope with three children as a single parent. This was a tragedy for the young family. At the same time, in some ways, it allowed the kids the freedom to choose their own paths in life. Adhuna's mother was more understanding of the children as different individuals and encouraged them to follow their passions. For instance, rather than getting them identical gifts for Christmas, she would make it a point to get Adhuna something like a colouring set, while her sister received a science kit.

Luckily, Nana, the children's maternal grandmother, was a pillar of support. She was a feisty old lady and an inspiration. When Adhuna's parents were getting married, Nana, a Catholic, wanted the ceremony to be performed by a Catholic priest. Adhuna's father agreed. However, when the priest saw the couple, he refused to perform the ceremony. Nana was so angry at the bigotry that she threw the priest out of her house right then and there and told the couple they should get married at a registry office. She also insisted that they allow their children to choose their own religion.

Nana came over to help look after the kids, while Adhuna's mother went back to study for a degree as a career guidance counsellor for children with special needs. Once Adhuna's mother had completed her degree, she made sure she balanced her work and being a hands-on mother, something Adhuna would emulate later. Despite her hectic schedule, she would ensure that she gave the three siblings time individually and together so that each child got the attention they needed.

A Casual Visit to the Salon and a First Step in the Right Direction

Adhuna's mother had always been very particular about keeping her hair well-groomed and visited a salon, Worthington Hair, regularly. When Adhuna was 14, she accompanied her mother to the salon on one occasion. When she walked in, her mother's favourite hairstylist came up to them, exclaiming animatedly, 'What a pretty girl! What's your name, dear?'

Adhuna self-consciously said her name out loud.

'Oh, that's an interesting name. What does it mean?'

Adhuna said, 'It means Modern.'

'What an interesting name,' she said. She turned to Adhuna's mother, 'She has lovely hair. And what gorgeous skin colour!'

Adhuna was flattered and surprised. This was the first time she had been complimented for either her looks or her name. She looked around the salon. Everyone was busy running around, but they all looked happy and excited to be there. There was a hum of conversation between the salon staff and the customers. Adhuna could feel the electric spark of creativity in the air around her. She turned to her mother, her eyes lit up with excitement.

'Mum, do you think I could get an after-school job here?'

Adhuna's mother was happy that Adhuna seemed to have found something she would enjoy doing and gave her permission, joking that she would now have a hairstylist at home too.

It was the eighties and punk rock was a big thing. For a girl who came from a sedate childhood spent in the countryside, the staff at the salon was very diverse, with people of different races and sexual orientations working side by side. It was an accepting environment; as long as you were good at your job and a good person, that's all anyone cared about. People loved experimenting with unique looks; it was cool to be different. For the first time, Adhuna felt like she fit in. Not only that, but for the first time, everything about her was something that was appreciated and valued by people outside the family.

Adhuna worked part-time at the salon for the next two years. By the time she had finished her O-Levels, Adhuna knew she wanted to make this her career. The UK had a scheme where 16-year-olds could sign up for vocational training in various disciplines. They would receive payment from both the employer and the government. After her O-Levels, Adhuna signed up for a hairdressing apprenticeship along with 25 others. Five of them stayed on in the main salon, and the rest went to the smaller salons around the town. One day in the week, everyone would come together for the training session, and the rest of the days they spent working.

An apprentice's job included not only chores like cleaning the floor, making coffee, helping customers take their coats off or doing laundry but also assisting the stylists and learning alongside them—shampoo, blow-drying and so on. It was hard work but fun—being friends, working together and hanging out. The group got up to lots of harmless pranks, blowing off steam. The owner of the salon had a preference for playing classical piano music in the salon, which the apprentices found boring. They would change the music to their choice as soon as he stepped out while keeping a careful eye out for him. As soon as they saw him coming back to the salon, they would switch it back. When she was very new, one of Adhuna's jobs was to shampoo all the clients. One time, when she turned the tap on the sink, the faucet accidentally came off and splashed her customer with ice-cold water. There was never a dull moment!

Soon, the stylists at the salon recognized that Adhuna had a talent for hair styling. The chief stylist at the salon, Tony Connell, started mentoring Adhuna and training her. After a year of training, Adhuna began participating in hairstyling competitions. She travelled across the country with her chosen models, styling them and showing off her skills to an audience of thousands. With the youngsters spending days on the road together in a creative pursuit, the models and their stylist developed a close-knit *jugalbandi* and an emotional bond. At just 17, she won the National Junior Hairstyling Competition, an achievement that put her name on the map as a hairstylist to watch.

Adhuna credits participating in the competitions with making her the hairstylist she is today. 'Doing competition hairdressing makes you a whole other kind of animal. You are obsessed with your models, where each and every hair has to set and the colouring process. So these models become people whom you are taking care of, making the competitions really emotional.'

Alongside her apprenticeship, Adhuna sought to learn more and improve her skills—something that remains a practice for her. She signed up for night school classes, and, at 18, she was awarded NVQ (National Vocational Qualification) levels 1–3, which qualified her to be able to teach hairdressing.

After five years with the salon, Adhuna moved with her mentor to the salon he was setting up and learnt all about the business of setting up and running a salon. A few years later, wanting to spread her wings, she moved to London for a job with Wella. That got her the exposure that led to her meeting some of her idols in the field—Vidal Sassoon, Toni and Guy, etc. This was also the start of a new phase in her life where she learnt to live by herself.

'It was my first experience of living alone. I shared a flat with a couple. I was 25 and living in London so I went crazy. Worked hard, partied hard.' As part of the technical team, she also got to travel across the country, training people and styling shows. Some years later, she got headhunted for her dream job. It was all going great. Then life took an unexpected turn.

Surprising Visit to India

Back when she was 12, soon after their father had died, Adhuna and her family had come to India to visit her father's family following his death. It was their first visit to the country, since their father had never wanted to go back. The extended family lived in a large joint-family home in Calcutta. Adhuna found India overwhelming—it was stickily hot, the large family home was crowded with innumerable relatives and the food was unfamiliar and spicy. In addition, the visit revived the extended family's mourning for her father. There was an overhanging atmosphere of bereavement that coloured the entire visit in sepia tones. While the kids made friends with their cousins, they couldn't wait to go back home to the comfort and familiarity of the UK. India never featured again in the family's discussions as a place to visit.

But now, as an adult, Adhuna was suddenly intrigued by the thought of coming back to India. Armed with £500, a backpack and her trusty pair of scissors, she made the bold decision to come to India. Once she landed in Mumbai, Adhuna realized that her money would not go far. She put her qualifications and UK experience to use, and began approaching salons for work. The salons were delighted! She landed a part-time job at the Oberoi salon as a visiting hairstylist.

One of her clients, Suzanne Caplan, was an Englishwoman who had settled in India many years earlier. She soon became a friend. As an advertising professional, she began getting Adhuna into the agency office to give people haircuts. People in the agency then started giving Adhuna assignments to style hair for ad shoots.

Suzanne introduced her to fashion photographer Rafique Syed, who got Adhuna to start styling fashion shoots. Adhuna then met the famous hair-styling duo Nalini–Yasmin, who asked her to start training stylists at their salon. She even got an opportunity with Channel V and did a show called Fashion Police, though she didn't have any experience in television! Soon, she was having so much fun that she took a giant leap of faith and bid her secure job at Toni and Guy in the UK goodbye. Without any regrets!

Six months later, Osh joined her in India.

'I always told him that he cashed in on my talent,' she says, adding that this is an old family joke. By this time, Adhuna had gained a steady stream of hair styling clients. She and her brother got to know some fairly influential people in the worlds of advertising, fashion and the entertainment industry through a mix of luck, their personalities and their skill sets; they offered something new to the social scene.

'Because we had this Indian connection but also had that Western accent, it was an unfair advantage as the way people received us was something different. Doors opened for us as a result.'

On a whim, the siblings decided to open a salon at Worli in Mumbai. They painted the salon themselves, and it had a giant lobby, almost big enough to be a dance floor. Extravagantly styled with just four seats for paying customers, the salon became a buzzy hang-out zone for their friends from advertising, fashion and entertainment. Every evening, their friends would congregate there and the team would conduct crazy experiments with their friends' hair late into the night. Adhuna admits with a grin that they only realized much later what a huge business error they had made in under-using Mumbai's criminally expensive real estate so poorly.

Adhuna was the only hairstylist at the salon and was keen to bring another one on board. She had gotten to know Zoya Akhtar through Nalini and Yasmin. Zoya invited her home to a party, to which Avan was also invited. Avan had been hearing about this British stylist making waves in Mumbai and wanted to meet her. As it turned out, Avan and Adhuna were the only two girls at the party who had short hair. Even though that was the smallest thing they had in common, a lifetime relationship and business collaboration were formed out of these insignificant coincidences! The chance meeting would go on to have another lasting impact on Adhuna's life.

At the time, Avan worked for an agency called Script Shop, where she was dating Farhan Akhtar's best friend. One evening, Avan and Adhuna were at J 29, a popular Mumbai nightclub. Avan waved across the crowded club, and a young, curly-haired man came across to greet her with a hug. Avan turned to Adhuna and said, 'This is Farhan, Zoya's brother. He's working on his first film script.'

Adhuna waved casually since it was too loud to attempt an actual conversation, grabbed a sip of water and went back to the dance floor. Dance had always been a passion, and the music was calling to her.

She got the tightly-packed crowd to clear a little floor space and broke into her favourite move—turning cartwheels. The circle of party-goers around her clapped and hooted in appreciation as she whirled across the dance floor. Farhan's interest was piqued by this gorgeous, exuberant, uninhibited woman.

A couple of days later, the door of the salon opened, and who should walk in but Farhan! Avan had set up a haircut appointment for him as a way of introducing him properly to Adhuna.

Dil Chahta Hai

The two of them found each other's company refreshing and began seeing each other. Although Adhuna was seven years older, they were always on the same wavelength. A couple of years later, they decided to get married. Adhuna found quick acceptance when she moved into a joint family set-up after marriage. While she was already friends with Zoya, she found her mother-in-law, Honey Irani, modern and very welcoming. Everyone respected her career as much as Farhan's. Farhan, too, was very proud of her success so far, so Adhuna had complete backing from the family to pursue her career.

'Honey—I am very close to her—is an amazing grandmother. She has been very instrumental in making me a mother. In fact, everyone in the family was proud that I did something on my own and the impact we made with BBlunt. They were very supportive.'

Soon, Farhan started directing his first film, while Adhuna was expecting their first child. Creating their first child and first film together cemented their bond. It was a manic phase.

Adhuna and Avan were involved in styling the actors' hair. The detailing of the characters was very intricate. At the time, the custom was that actors had a certain hairstyle that they believed worked for them, and would keep that across films, regardless of whether or not it suited the character they were playing. After Adhuna and Avan got involved, for the first time, the styling reflected the characters the actors were playing.

'When we were doing the styles, we didn't really set out to do something very different. We set out to create characters. We took the lead from the director, with the wardrobe department and everybody coming together to make this film very different. I had never experienced Indian cinema before, so it gave me a fresh outlook.'

Adhuna enjoyed spending time on the sets, even when her growing belly meant she couldn't get close enough to the chair to style hair anymore.

'I was literally on the set of *Dil Chahta Hai* when, in the morning, I started having contractions. And it also happened that the schedule of the film had a break for the weekend. We had the baby and then came back to set. It could not have been timed more perfectly; it was like a really organized thing.'

Dil Chahta Hai was a sensation for many reasons with its fresh, contemporary outlook on modern relationships. The success of the film led to many more such collaborations.

Meanwhile, the salon ran into a bit of trouble. One morning, Adhuna and Osh found that the landlord had suddenly sold the property. Overnight, they were out of their space. Luckily, their employees were extremely loyal and decided to stick it out till the duo were back in action.

They say that crisis is another name for opportunity. Working with the forward-thinking team at Olive, the siblings decided to innovate by creating a mini-salon at the restaurant. A popular new eatery for the hip Bollywood crowd, Olive attracted the right clientele, and the salon was packed with customers who would come in for a quick beauty treatment before heading next door for a meal.

'Every day we would put in furniture, plug in a sink and operate at Olive Salon. It was a pop-up before pop-ups were even a thing. The clients absolutely loved it. You think of hair and food, and they don't really go together, but it went really well.'

Sometime later, after a few missteps, they found a new property within which BBlunt began as a brand. Between the film-styling business and the salon, Adhuna had a packed schedule. At the same time, she was managing two young daughters. While her mother-in-law was supportive, Adhuna wanted to be a hands-on mum as much as possible, like her mother. Not used to domestic help in the UK, Adhuna found that an agreeable luxury and a great help in finding quality time with her kids.

'I would be the one who did the bath, the one who did the massage, the one who changed the diapers, but I could just drop those diapers and somebody else would wash them for me and that was really wonderful.'

She would often take the kids to the salon, and, on many occasions, do her work with baby Shakya strapped to her back. Having a brother and friend as business partners also helped to give Adhuna a certain amount of flexibility in how she spent her time at work.

In the early days, she, Osh and Avan knew each and every employee and had a personal relationship with them. Adhuna brought in several new practices from the UK, including hygiene, health and safety, etc., that were new for the industry. She also brought in training programmes and career path development for hairstylists. Their employees were given a healthy level of freedom, and, in return, grew very loyal to the BBlunt team. Even when they were offered more money, many continued to stay with BBlunt. The company managed to have low employee attrition levels, which is one of her strengths as a leader.

Over time, quite a few copycat salons sprang up around the country.

'I remember there was a person who had worked with and trained with us, and then went away and created his own company with almost the same name and logo. Over the years, it has happened that a salon will show up, somebody will send me a picture and ask me if it is BBlunt. Initially, I had a problem with it and found it irritating, but later I thought this was probably the best compliment you could get.'

The Role of Serendipity

A few years later, a group of four gentlemen from the UK walked into the salon one morning. They were investors and had begun studying the company because they thought it had untapped potential to create more impact. As it happened, the foursome walked into the salon on a day when Adhuna, Osh and Avan were all in office at the same time. They began discussing their vision for expansion and how BBlunt could grow.

The original team at BBlunt had always had the dream of creating their own line of hairstyling products. One of the UK investors had worked in marketing hair care products. This helped the team put together a concrete proposal for this project. They took the idea to Nisaba Godrej at Godrej Consumer Products, who immediately loved it.

BBlunt wanted to make products that were great value for money but in the professional range. Their many salons around the country and the multiple shoots they had styled meant they had the experience to be able to pull it off. Initially, their plan had been to create a line of styling products similar to those used in the UK, but for Indian hair and India's climatic conditions. But they realized that hair care was much more basic in India, with most people not even using conditioner.

It took three years of painstaking research before they launched a range of 26 shampoos, conditioners, styling products and a few hair accessories. Their salon's reputation and their expertise came together to give them a luxury brand that was unique. The team also realized that Indian consumers at the time had low awareness of what to do beyond the traditional habits of hair care. BBlunt started an online consultancy to educate consumers right from the basics: a consumer could enter his or her hair type and hair concerns and receive personalized recommendations for what to use. The brand became a huge success.

By this time, the business had expanded from one to three salons in Mumbai, and, later, in Bengaluru. But now they needed a different approach to continue expansion. Adhuna and the team decided to use the franchise model and appointed a CEO to lead this part of the business. For the first time, they began hiring people from outside. This was when they realized what a differentiator their in-house academy had created. There was an appreciable gap between the knowledge and expertise of the BBlunt team and that of others.

The academy was something Adhuna had started years ago. With her background in training hairstylists, she had created a structured academy training programme, and as she started working with different members of the team, she would continuously update the curriculum. While they never formalized the training by recognizing it with an international examination board, the standard of training was recognized by the industry.

'People have gone off and started their own businesses, and done different things within the hairdressing industry, based on the foundation at BBlunt. We have managed to get this reputation of being very thorough with our training; that contributed to creating the team, the standards and the quality control.'

Adhuna loved working with young people; they brought a new street cred and innovation to what they did.

'As a blade-wielding hairdresser, you have all these sharp tools all the time, and so when you try to do something new, it is scary. But you are constantly pushed in this profession to do exactly that.'

New Beginnings

Meanwhile, after over 15 years, Adhuna and Farhan's marriage began unravelling. Farhan was younger than Adhuna by seven years, and while that had never affected to their relationship, perhaps he had been too young to settle down when they got married. With his film career taking him to shoots far away over extended periods of time while she was tied down to Mumbai, the two of them began growing apart.

'I think we grew to have a very centred connection with our children, but we had very individual careers. His career took him around the world. We met different people. We experienced different things. The children were with me most of the time because of the nature of their dad's work.'

Reflecting on the situation, Adhuna feels that they should have worked on better communication and honesty between the two of them. Her advice to women is to always foster trust, honesty and good communication between partners in a relationship.

They decided that they would get a divorce but continue to jointly parent their daughters. The biggest concern in both their minds was to ensure that their daughters would not be hurt by the situation. Had she not had children, Adhuna would have preferred to move away and start afresh elsewhere. But with the well-being of the daughters in mind, Adhuna continued to stay on in the family home while Farhan visited them as much as he could. Both Adhuna and Farhan were as honest as possible with their children about the unfolding situation, something she hopes has helped them understand why they made the decisions they did.

'Our children have been the centre of our world. And we were not prepared, both of us, to sacrifice that. I wanted them to be close to their dad, and he wanted them to be close to him. It was a compromise for me, but my worldly wisdom said it would be better for the girls.'

One of the things that helped Adhuna bounce back was her flourishing career. Quite apart from the support she received from Osh, Avan and her immediate family, the fact that she had a career freed her financially, emotionally and mentally. So, even as she spent a lot of time with her daughters, making sure they were doing fine, she continued to focus on her work at the salon.

The franchise model had taken the salon to all corners of India, and the hair product range was expanding. And then, the Covid-19 pandemic hit! The team had to figure out what to do. Keeping it profitable was not the priority; the game was about survival. They tried to hang on to the core team and not let go of people who had been with them for the long haul.

By 2022, as the pandemic receded, footfalls began increasing again. And then, the team received confirmation of a big move they had been working on for a while. The brand was being acquired by Honasa Consumer Pvt Ltd, the conglomerate behind the Mamaearth brand. It would now have the financial heft to scale quickly!

Adhuna and Avan will remain involved on the creative side, but the salon business will be handled by the mother company. Adhuna is excited about this new phase of life, hoping to have more time to indulge her passion for horse riding, listening to music, reading, travelling more and maybe learning something new.

Top 3 Takeaways

- It is not what you take off but it is what you leave on that counts.
- Be prepared to work hard.
- Surround yourself with people who are like-minded.

> **Core values:** Be open-minded to new things, new activities. Believe in the power of a team. Never stop learning. You are only as good as the last haircut you did.

'I have worked every day since I was 16 years old and to be in a position where you don't have to work that hard anymore is wonderful. I have less responsibility now. That allows me to do the other things related to the business which I have always enjoyed doing. I've always wanted to learn millinery, so I might just do that now!'

Looking back on her journey, Adhuna reflects that many of her so-called mistakes were actually great learning moments. When they were expanding their business, a couple of times they found the wrong business partners whose ethics they did not agree with or with whom the chemistry was just wrong. Despite struggling to make the partnerships work, they ended up having to call it quits. At one point, the beautiful house they had identified to open the salon in, and on whose renovations they had already spent a lot of money, was sold unexpectedly. The team had to not only find new premises but also a way to compensate for the loss they had incurred on the renovation. Many times, their franchises did not work out or work the way the BBlunt team had visualized. A crucial lesson was to be careful where they placed their trust and, more importantly, to walk away from any situation that involved a moral compromise. Adhuna learnt that not everything would turn out successful. Taking that in stride and moving on was an important part of running a business.

But equally, BBlunt had several people who had joined them as employees and stayed on as friends and family. Adhuna feels the BBlunt team always approached their work with honesty and integrity. They had a simple philosophy that they would explain to their clients, 'Our aim is to make your hair look good 365 days of the year.'

Adhuna feels she owes a lot of her professional success to her relationships and network of friends, who really taught her that creativity and business can go hand in hand. One of the critical things when one wants to turn a passion into a career is to understand how to make it profitable and to marry the hard-headed business numbers side of it to the creative side. What has always been an artist's struggle was converted into an opportunity for Adhuna with the guidance of her mentors, and friends who turned into business partners. When her first mentor set up an independent salon, she learnt the business of running a profitable salon. Through the training programme she was a part of, she understood what goes into delivering consistent quality and the importance of hiring and managing good people. While developing styling products was always an area of interest, the Godrej partnership taught her how to make it scale up to reach the nooks and crannies of the country and how to mass-market a brand. Very importantly, as a business, BBlunt accepted they needed outside help at the right time and brought in a professional CEO to help drive it to the next level.

One of Adhuna's key learnings through her unconventional journey has been to be true to herself. Women are often told to adjust to what is expected of them by society and to follow social norms. Be it in little things like turning cartwheels in a nightclub because she wanted to, or bigger things like deciding to stay on in India even though she didn't have a job, or continuing to pursue her career rather than take a back seat when she had children, she followed her instincts all the way through.

Moreover, for a woman, being self-sacrificing is deified. But she believes that women need to learn to love themselves more, to embrace who they are fully and not allow in those who don't accept them for who they are.

'I am an empath. And I have seen that both my daughters have this trait. I constantly tell them to be aware of this.' While being an empath and dealing with people kindly is important, it is equally important to deal with yourself kindly. Being an empath to yourself can be difficult given ingrained behaviour, but treating yourself as you would your best friend is a great way to ensure you build in the kindness and consideration you deserve from yourself.

Her final sign-off: Use things, love people and be kind!

Hacks to Storm the Norm

Norm: You should be pragmatic in your career choices, not just get carried away by your passion.

It's easy to succumb to the pressure of choosing something 'practical', the tried and tested paths, rather than struggle to create a career in a field that may be more experimental according to your circle of friends and family. But with the changing world today, who is to say that a career in, say, hairstyling won't last longer than a career as a software programmer? You are also going to spend a long time working on your career, so if you find something you're passionate about, that makes it much easier to stay the course.

Hacks:

1. Career ikigai

Make sure that you're good at the passion you want to pursue as a career. Sometimes we may love a particular activity without excelling at it, and that's fine as long as we plan to keep it a hobby and not make a living off of that activity. If you do plan to make it your career, you need to be really good at it. Invest in getting the skills you need in your area of interest, and continue to put in time and effort into upskilling.

2. Do your research

Figure out what professions are available in your passion area and choose one that appeals to you but mitigates the risk. For example, if fashion is your area of passion, you can look at a variety of careers in that space apart from design: merchandising, styling, content creation, journalism, marketing, and so on.

3. Live the dream as an experiment

Explore internships and speak to different professionals in that area so you understand the myriad activities that go into a career in that field. Make sure all of that is something that you can live with, if not enjoy. The passion part is just one piece of your job, but there will be many others that you will need to become successful.

AMEERA
We Don't Have to Be Perfect

Introduction

A renowned entrepreneur and a global thought leader in the healthcare industry, Ms Ameera Shah is the promoter and managing director of Metropolis Healthcare Ltd, a reputed chain of pathology labs with a loyal customer base across India, South Asia and Africa. Metropolis is rated among the top 1 per cent of laboratories globally for its quality systems and protocols. Ms Shah built it over 20 years, from a single unit pathological lab to a multibillion-dollar entity.

Named amongst the 'Fifty Most Powerful Women in Business' by Fortune India (2017, 2018 and 2019) and Business Today (2018, 2019), Ms Shah is the recipient of the prestigious E&Y Entrepreneur of the Year Award in the healthcare category for the year 2021. A global thought leader in the healthcare industry, she has played an instrumental role in changing the pathology industry landscape in the country from being a doctor-led practice to a professional corporate group in an extremely unregulated, competitive and fragmented market. She received a degree in finance from The University of Texas at Austin and is an alumna of the Harvard Business School (OPM Program).

A strong believer in propagating organizational empathy and gender sensitivity, she is also an active financial investor and a business mentor. Shah is extremely passionate about women leadership and empowerment and committed to supporting women entrepreneurs.

Ameera lives in Mumbai with her husband and son. She loves parenting and spending time with her family. During her leisure time, she loves to be outdoors, playing sports like tennis, sailing, and chess.

Why Ameera?

Firstly, daughters born to privileged business families are often seen as having it easy. They can just walk in and take the top job. A common perception is that they don't have to prove themselves in the role. From the outside, it could appear that Ameera walked into the top job at her father's firm and took over with ease when she joined her father's pathology lab, a high-quality one that had built a reputation for specialized tests. However, at the time, her father operated only one lab in Mumbai, as was the norm for pathology labs. There was no 'top job'. Ameera became the driving force that took the company from one lab to a chain with labs across the country, from a value of two crores to a billion-dollar business, negotiating issues like buying it back from a hostile investor.

Secondly, a technical field like pathology respects technical expertise. Despite not being a medical professional, Ameera was able to win the confidence of employees and partners. How did she craft her support systems, including an array of mentors, to help her grow? In addition, Ameera prides herself on being an empathetic, supportive and sensitive leader, while business tends to worship masculine traits like strength and being demanding. Is there a way to balance the two aspects?

Thirdly, despite the law, the concept of live-in relationships has always been a sticky topic and continues to be looked down upon even in educated families in urban India. Can the love between two people be validated only through marriage? Does the decision to not marry yet live together nullify their affection by any standards? Read her story to find out more.

The Best-Laid Plans

The year 2020 was going to be a very unusual one for Ameera. For the first time since she started working in 2001, she was planning to take five weeks off from work. She was expecting a baby in March and looked forward to enjoying some intense bonding time.

But even the best-laid plans are not always in our control. Ameera's son was born on 9 March, came home on 12 March and from 13 March, Ameera was embroiled in calls from the Ministry of Health who were co-opting all major pathology labs in the country to start doing Covid tests. The world was in the grip of the coronavirus pandemic!

Ameera and her husband moved with their day-old baby to their farmhouse on the outskirts of Mumbai with her parents, just ahead of the national lockdown. Despite patchy Internet and mobile connectivity, Ameera's schedule was soon even busier than before: coordinating with government officials, trying to understand protocols that changed from day to day, procuring the tests and safety equipment for her staff and connecting with her team to ensure Metropolis Healthcare, her first baby, was prepped and ready to stand by the nation in its hour of greatest need.

Despite her family members and good staff to help with baby care, Ameera still insisted on chunks of time where she would take charge of the baby herself. Feeding times were sacrosanct, and no disturbances were allowed. She wanted to make sure she had her time free to chat with the new born, and to sing and play music for him. She spent 10 hours a day breastfeeding the baby, while her working day stretched to 12 hours and more. But her biggest regret was that she was physically unable to be with her team at Metropolis, helping them cope with one of the biggest challenges that had yet come their way.

The Contrarian

As a young woman, Ameera could have relaxed and taken it easy. Her parents were both doctors with flourishing practices in Mumbai. But Ameera and her sister were brought up to work hard and to believe that a critical part of their identity came from their profession. A profession was not defined as going out and earning lots of money but as a pursuit of purpose—to have a positive impact on society and make full use of their intellect and their education. They travelled by public transport, went to a school chosen for its diverse students from all walks of life, and there were no expensive foreign holidays. Her parents also made it clear that the girls should be financially independent—it wasn't an option but a necessity. Most of all, her parents brought them up to be adventurous and risk-takers, not protected and cosseted little princesses. 'There was no "Daddy's little girl"', she says proudly.

Ameera reflects that many of her female contemporaries were brought up with traditional ideas of how their lives were to unfold: marriage by a particular age, children by another age and a life devoted to the husband and the in-laws, with the male playing the role of the provider. Even if they worked, their work was more like a hobby or a way of keeping themselves busy than a serious vocation. Their identities were defined by their husbands and children rather than what they did.

Brought up in an egalitarian household, Ameera saw both her parents working very hard. Her mother was a practising gynaecologist who worked 15-hour days and often came home only at midnight. Ameera came to appreciate how many lives her mother had touched and improved through her dedication, and she understood that this was more important than her own natural desire for her mother to spend more time with her. Her father was a pathologist who had started a pathology lab in the nursing home founded by her grandfather.

Another important figure in the lives of the girls was their *bai*, a simple, unlettered woman who has been with the family since Ameera's birth. She was a second mother to Ameera and showed her a simple, unconditional love, as compared to the more intellectual support that came from her mother. Ameera's mother was her role model for the person she wanted to be, while her father's persona was how she wanted others to see her. Ameera grew to admire their devotion to work and their desire to make a difference in the lives of others. Although they were affluent, the family values were geared towards service, dedication and being grounded.

Growing Up Self-Dependent

Ameera enjoyed sports and often played with the boys since very few girls played sports at her school. She regularly trekked in the hills with a group of boys and girls, an experience that taught her invaluable lessons. Right from the age of 12, she liked being a leader and helping others. Among the trekking group of 40–50 people, there would be only 10–12 girls, and they would gravitate towards Ameera when they needed help. 'I liked the idea and feel of being a leader and had a sense of leadership. This helped me manage my own problems better because when I was the leader and motivating them to walk, I could not show my own tiredness to them. I could not reveal how demotivated I was. So it helped me push myself.'

She would go around the group ensuring everyone was doing fine, and even give her own food to them at times. From trekking, she also learnt to adapt to and cope with circumstances, without complaining. 'The thing about going into nature is that it is unpredictable. You can never know what can happen. Whether it will be stormy, rainy or under scorching heat, you have to adapt without complaining.'

Ameera's parents had worked at making their girls confident and independent. Her father taught her how to operate a bank account at 13. The family was a tight-knit nuclear unit, as her father had only one sibling who was unmarried, and her mother's relatives all lived overseas. She grew up with a close group of friends whose parents, too, became extended family to her.

Thus, though Ameera did hear the stereotypical notions of a woman's place in society, it was from people too distant to make an impact on her. 'Don't be like everybody else,' her father always told her. The two parents influenced the girls in very different ways. Her father helped her understand that she did not need to please people in order to be loved and accepted. As a result, Ameera knew that when she looked for a partner eventually, she would find someone who respected her for who she was rather than someone to protect and take care of her.

From the age of 11, Ameera travelled to Europe for the Children's International Summer Village program. It was formed of 80 students from around the world, four from each participating country. Through the summer, the kids learnt to get along with diverse people and understand the ways of life around the world. Ameera loved not only getting to know people and lifestyles from around the globe but also the freedom she got to explore and be on her own.

When she was 14, she, along with three other Indian students, were on their return journey to India. While the kids had loved their time at the village, they were looking forward to going home to their parents. The airport was crowded. There was the typical hullabaloo of people rushing from place to place. Incomprehensible announcements about this flight or that one echoed over the public announcement system. Piles of baggage lay around, traps for unwary travellers to trip over. The kids were busily manoeuvring their baggage carts through the crowd. Suddenly an airport announcement caught their attention: the announcer, who was talking about their flight, said, 'All passengers on the flight are informed that their flight back to India has been cancelled.' The kids came to an abrupt halt and exchanged looks of pure shock, not sure what to do next. Two of the girls burst into noisy tears of panic.

Back in India, the parents of the other children were in a similar state of panic. How would their children make it back home? They were stranded in a country where they didn't speak the language. The parents decided to meet and figure out how to handle the situation. They began exchanging ideas, feeling a complete lack of control over the situation. But these were the pre-mobile phone days. They could not even contact their kids, except through airport announcements. Some of the mothers began sobbing, regretting the day they had decided to let their kids go off to Europe on their own.

Ameera's parents were a marked contrast. They reassured the other parents, 'The Global Village team will help our kids come home. I'm sure they will be fine. Plus, our kids are smart; they'll be able to cope.' They were confident that they had raised Ameera to be able to cope with the situation. Their confidence in their daughter proved to be correct, foreshadowing her future capabilities.

Rather than giving in to the worry that she felt, Ameera realized that she would have to manage the situation. She stepped forward and put her arms around the girls, saying, 'We will get back home soon; don't worry. I'll take care of it.' She briskly strode forward to the airline help desk and asked to speak to the manager. The manager was surprised to find a teenager at the desk, but when Ameera spoke, her calm confidence impressed him. Ameera told him how the group of teenagers was travelling by themselves and convinced him to help them. Between them, the manager and Ameera figured out an alternate route plan to India. Ameera also got the airline to arrange food and a lounge space for the group until their flight. Now that the kids had cheered up, Ameera asked to make a call home to inform the parents about their plan. She ensured that she looked out for the group all the way until they landed back in Mumbai. More than 20 years later, she would look back at this moment and realize that it had been a life lesson in leadership during troubled times.

Career Choices

Though her parents, sister and grandfather were all in the medical profession, Ameera knew this was not something she was cut out for. She would faint at the sight of blood. Moreover, she empathized too much with anyone in pain. Once, a dear friend's father was in the hospital, on his deathbed. Ameera went to be by her friend's side. As they stood outside the hospital and he talked about his fears, she began feeling breathless from her mounting anxiety for her friend and fainted. She knew these sensibilities would not stand her in good stead as a medical practitioner. Ameera studied commerce in junior college and went to The University of Texas at Austin, US, for her bachelor's degree, choosing to specialize in finance.

While her parents paid for the first year of college, she was determined to pay her way through the rest of the course. She found a job on campus that not only made her eligible for a 50 per cent scholarship but also paid her enough to fund her studies. She did a short stint at a start-up before bagging a job at Goldman Sachs in New York, the glittering prize finance students aspired to. But as she began working there, she slowly realized that she was not cut out to work as an anonymous cog in a large, impersonal corporation. At a start-up, she was in a much better position to contribute and to feel the impact of her work. She was also hugely impressed with Muhammad Yunus of Grameen Bank and the ability to create a profitable, sustainable business that made an impact at scale.

She began questioning her choices and wondering if she was in the right place. All the superficial markers of success were in place: a great brand name, a high-paying job, a partner, friends and a full social life. But her heart wasn't in it. She asked herself where she could make the most impact. The answer: India. She uprooted herself and flew back to India, without a plan but with the conviction that she was doing the right thing. Healthcare was a field that naturally beckoned to her because of her family background. She realized that she could create a large-scale impact in healthcare by building an institution.

Building Metropolis

'We grew from 1 lab to 135 labs now. We had one centre. We have 2,500 centres now. We had one city, now we are in 200 cities in India and five countries. We had 40 employees, now we have 4,500. We were valued at $2 million at the time, now we are valued at $1 billion+.'

Ameera decided that there was an opportunity to turn her father's lab practice into a large business. Dr Sushil's Path Lab was a small operation in one location, though it had recently changed its name to Metropolis Labs. Ameera had the vision to build Metropolis Labs as a branded chain of pathology labs, with common protocols all over India. Her dream was that Metropolis Labs would undertake all kinds of tests, use the best equipment, and offer global-quality diagnostics to Indians.

But there were many negative marks against her. She was not a medical practitioner or a trained pathologist, while pathology is a very technical field. The 40 trained technicians looked down on her due to her lack of medical expertise. She was very young—just 21—whereas medicine reveres age and experience. Moreover, she was the daughter of the founder, so it was seen as a hobby she might enjoy till she got married. Many of the pathologists had their own politics and agendas with her father and resented her entry.

Ameera could have tried to shove her ideas down their throats; after all, she was the daughter of the founder. But she realized that only if she earned their respect would she truly be able to create the change she needed.

For the first few years, she and her father worked together. Between them, there were very few ego tussles and more effort at inclusion. Ameera was intent on understanding the consumers' point of view, so she spent time speaking with and observing them as their blood was collected, despite her squeamishness. She undertook various roles—as sales executive, in customer care, in human resources and finance—to completely master the business. She focussed on the business side while her father remained the head of the technical side.

The knowledge she built up of all aspects of the business, and in particular the consumer, helped her win the confidence of the experienced pathologists who worked at Metropolis. Rather than focus on the power struggle, she used her persuasion skills to bring them around to her point of view and appreciate the fresh ideas she brought in.

Four years later, her father was ready to step down and hand over the reins. He knew he didn't have the business sensibility that Ameera did. To scale up the business quickly, Ameera came up with the strategy of buying out the many individual doctor-led path labs across the country, creating a hub and spoke strategy to build business volume and standardize their tests and protocols. Ameera was always clear that she wanted to build an institution that would be global in terms of standards as well as practices.

Building a healthcare brand was a new concept in India back then, where the doctor-patient relationship still lay at the core of medicine. Her vision was to build a business that kept the doctor at the heart of the relationship, but create an overarching brand so that dependence on individual doctors would decrease. The company was firewalled away from the family's personal life. The financial practices of the company were impeccable; there was no dipping into company funds for personal exigencies that one sees in some family-run firms. When they took the decision to go public, it was a small adjustment, not a big hurdle.

'It's like going from single to married, but again, how difficult it is to go from being single to married depends on which way you were single. If you have lived together and you know the family very well already, then the transition is not that painful. Similarly, when we were private, we had independent directors and outside opinions and all of our work was very clean and fair. We already had the spirit of being a public company so the journey was mostly incremental rather than transformational.'

The Hurdles and the Punt

But it wasn't all smooth sailing. In the early years, whenever they had a meeting with investors to raise funds, the investors would insist that her father be present for the meeting, even though Ameera ran the business. It took them several years to feel confident speaking just to her. Moreover, it was a lonely journey.

Metropolis Labs wasn't a family business with a set revenue and lots of experienced family members one could turn to for advice. Ameera had built it from the ground up, and her father was a medical professional, not a businessman. Busy with juggling many things as a first-time entrepreneur, Ameera was unable to keep up ties with the many people she met, a lapse in her personal life that she regrets.

When crucial decisions were to be made, Ameera had no one she could turn to for expert advice. Realizing this shortcoming, she decided to create a pool of mentors for herself—successful businesspeople from varied fields whom she had met over the years. She began reaching out to them whenever she faced a business crossroads and found that they were able to bring in an objective perspective that was invaluable.

One of the biggest challenges she faced was internal conflict with a large shareholder. He had been a private investor since 2001, and travelled to Mumbai regularly. While things went smoothly for a while, by 2005, Ameera realized the shareholder was hostile. There was a tussle for power and a lot of back-room politics that went right up to the board level. A spate of misunderstandings and disagreements on strategy meant that the company could not make progress as fast as its competitors.

By 2015, it was clear that she had to wrest complete control of Metropolis Labs for it to fulfil its destiny. Initially, her thinking was still conservative. 'I was thinking of taking a ₹50 crore loan and increasing my shareholding by 1 or 2 per cent because my vision for myself was too small. This is because the fear of something going wrong was so big that I could not dare to dream big.'

Her partner was one of the sounding boards she tapped. Her father had always told her not to choose someone from a rich family but someone who was self-made. Hemant is an entrepreneur hailing from a middle-class family. When she and Hemant met at Harvard's Owner/President Management Program, they realized that they were kindred spirits in terms of what they wanted to achieve, how they wanted their lives to unfold and, most of all, the sense of purpose they brought to their work. They lived together for a number of years and understood each other very well. Hemant knew she didn't need someone to rescue her, but someone who could help her visualize all the options for herself. 'He is a very encouraging and progressive person. When I told him about taking the loan, he pushed me to think about why I was only considering this and not doing X or Y. As I started opening up my mind, I evaluated all the options and saw that I could actually do other things. But it meant I had to believe in myself and battle all the fears and anxiety that were overwhelming me at that time. I had to go with my gut and be willing to ask for help.'

Ameera evaluated many different alternative options and made detailed plans to finalize her course of action. With the steely determination that is characteristic of her, she decided to take the biggest punt of her career—on herself and her ability—even though some of her mentors thought it was too big of a risk. She took a personal loan of ₹600 crore from a private equity firm and approached the hostile investor. 'I told him, "You invested ₹8 crores in us in 2001 and I have grown it to ₹800 crores in 2015. I will continue to grow the money for you but behave yourself and don't make life more difficult for me. If you do not feel like being in the company, then I will give you an exit, even though, legally, I do not have any obligations to do so."'

He opted to sell his shares, making Ameera the majority holder. Once the company was listed in 2019, she sold off part of her shareholding to pay back the loan. 'I took the loan at an easy interest rate of 20 per cent and I knew that I had to build the company really well to pay the money back. So, I went from having 36 per cent in a company valued ₹2,000 crore in 2015 to a 65 per cent share in a company that was much bigger and much more valuable.'

Fiery and Outspoken

Ameera feels that all too often, women do not bet on themselves enough. They are often held back by the fear of failure. Moreover, far too often, they hesitate to ask for help for fear of being judged as incapable. 'One of the biggest differences between girls and guys is that guys are so optimistic about themselves that they will approach any opportunity they get a hold of, even if they can't do it. They will go through the experience and even if they fail, they will come out as if they succeeded. On the other hand, women don't even put themselves through the experience.'

At the same time, Ameera rues the slotting of women in business as mere wives and daughters, even if they have been instrumental in building and scaling the business. Recently, a well-known magazine reached out to her. They were doing a story on India's richest families and wanted to include Ameera. But with a caveat: they would title the story 'Ameera Shah and family' or 'Dr Shah and family'. Ameera shot back, 'Would you title a story about Mukesh Ambani by his name alone or as "Dhirubhai Ambani and family"?' The journalist replied that the rules are different for men. Ameera declined to be part of the article.

Her confident and blunt nature make Ameera a formidable presence. Ameera's male friends sometimes make condescending comments to her husband, like, 'How do you manage her?' An outspoken feminist, she also finds that many women shy away from discussing women's issues, saying, 'Don't start your *narishakti* now.' In scenarios like this, she feels grateful for the way she was brought up and for her husband, who has the same values.

Untold Traumas

Just because Ameera was a strong person does not mean she breezed through every challenge. In 2016, she faced a difficult situation; one that too many women face around the world: sexual harassment. She had just become part of an industry group of senior people, the only woman in the group. One of the men made a pass at her and made her feel very uncomfortable. Taken aback, she didn't know how to respond at that moment. She discussed the situation with her husband, who asked her what she wanted to do, rather than offering the typical alpha-male response of taking action on her behalf. On reflection, she felt that making an issue of it would draw unnecessary attention to her gender at a time when she was playing in the big league of industry shapers and took a conscious decision to ignore the incident.

Despite her aura of confidence, Ameera believes she has not always dealt with these situations in a way that makes her feel strong. The first such instance occurred when she was bidding farewell to a sports teacher from school. He had been very supportive of her and allowed her to play volleyball with the boys since not many girls played. He gave her advice on how to cope with the world out there and to be careful of boys in college. She gave him a hug, and, suddenly, he planted a kiss on her lips! Utterly shocked, she blamed herself for days and thought that she had given him the wrong signal by hugging him. It was only after a few years had passed that she realized that it was not her fault and went back to file a complaint with the principal.

Unfortunately, the principal chose to ignore the complaint. Many years later, it transpired that the sports teacher was finally dismissed for having misbehaved with several other girls.

When she was 16, she had another close call. Ameera, alone at home, was trying on clothes for a fashion show. Her parents' friend unexpectedly rang the doorbell. Having known him all her life, Ameera unselfconsciously ushered him into the living room and sat down to chat with 'uncle' as she called him. But this didn't feel like the other times he had visited their home. His eyes began roving over her body in a way that made her very uneasy. His comments to her had a flirtatious touch and when he complimented her on how she was looking, Ameera realized that he was being a creep. She felt very conscious of the fact that she was alone with him and unprotected. Somehow she managed to get through his visit, still bound by her upbringing to remain polite until he left. As soon as she closed the door behind him, her knees sagged. It had been a huge stress to retain her composure while feeling threatened for her safety.

Brought up in a family that didn't speak about emotions or troubles, she just could not bring herself to tell her parents about the incident. Every time he came home, she would find excuses not to be in the room or go back to her room as quickly as possible. If he was eating at the dining table with them, she would refuse to pass him the water. Her parents were aghast—why was their well-brought-up and otherwise well-behaved daughter so rude to one of their greatest friends?

Meanwhile, Ameera felt stifled; she wanted to forget the incident and never talk about it, as it made her feel vulnerable and scared. But each time he came home, her anger and anxiety flared up. Finally, she confided in her sister, who was utterly shocked. Her sister, in turn, told their parents, who immediately cut off ties with their friend and ensured he never got close to their home again. But the incident, a betrayal by someone she considered a family elder, left a scar for years.

Ameera rues that, especially when it happens at the workplace, many women don't take up the issue because, having fought so hard for equality, 'we do not want to be treated as the women in the room but as the person.' She acknowledges that when she chose to ignore the incident at the industry meet, she too was doing it with the same rationale.

The Revolutionary Journey

One of the things that surprised Ameera was her realization that she is a deeply emotional person. Ameera's family was, like many Indian families, one that did not tend to talk about their vulnerabilities or their emotions. The value of being stoic was prized. When anything negative happened, the attitude was 'shit happens, move on'. Growing up, she thought that she was a dispassionate, cold person, even though her friends appreciated her nurturing and caring nature. She imbibed that not being able to express oneself was a great strength and rarely shared her moments of doubt with anyone.

However, between 2010 and 2020, as she introspected and worked on her key relationships, she realized that being open and vulnerable is not at odds with confidence and strength. She began to understand that true confidence comes from the ability to be completely authentic and display one's vulnerabilities and insecurities openly. 'If I am sitting and sharing my deepest thoughts and experiences with you today, it comes from the confidence that it does not mark me or say anything about me. Confidence comes from going through all of the hardship and coming out on the other side knowing the pain.'

Since then, she has worked hard to be able to express her feelings to friends and family. Even at the workplace, she prioritizes being there for her team and supporting them. Interestingly, while she is surprised by her own dedication and commitment to work, if there are some aspects of the business that don't excite her, she is not her usual disciplined and detail-oriented self. In those areas, she is happy to leave it to her team.

Like many ambitious people, she is a woman in a hurry, impatient with the status quo. As the leader of the strategic side of the business, she thinks at least five if not 10 years ahead in order to keep the company on the cutting edge. As a result, she sometimes has a tug of war with her employees, who are operating more in the present and ask her to slow down. But she feels this healthy friction only improves whatever the company is trying to achieve. Her critics also feel—and she agrees—that she tends to focus on the one thing that is not working instead of the hundred that have gone right. As a result, it isn't often that Ameera stops to celebrate success.

'I see business as I see life—a revolutionary journey. I would like to focus more on the inputs than the outputs and then see what the outcomes are.'

The meaning of success itself has changed from the time she began. In the beginning, external validation in the form of awards or peer recognition was something she craved. Now that that is abundant, her benchmarks have moved to internal validation—when she feels like she can be completely authentic across her personal life

Her advice to other women facing sexual harassment:

- You were not the cause of this— remember that.
- Don't assume how people will react— you could be pleasantly surprised.
- Talk about it openly—you will heal faster, and it will seem less scary.

and her work. She is not a believer in the phrase 'work-life balance'; she celebrates integration. In an integrated life, all parts of the pie— from work to her family and child, friends and herself—are always present, but the ratio of each portion of the pie keeps changing as life evolves.

'I often say that entrepreneurship is like a mirror, and I feel parenting, too, is like a mirror if you allow it to be. A lot of these things allow us to look within and see really deep facets of ourselves, and sometimes those surprise us positively and sometimes negatively. The important thing is to know that both are okay, and we do not have to be perfect.'

Hacks to Storm the Norm

Norm: Women think taking big bets is a risky business.

Neuroscience research shows that women tend to be more conservative and take fewer risks because we are hardwired to be more sensitive to potential losses. Society also rewards men and women differently for risky behaviour. A combination of the two factors means that women are often less likely to bet on themselves and make bold moves. However, it's worth reminding yourself that risks are almost always necessary for progress.

Here are some hacks that can help you become better at taking on risk.

Hacks

1. Invest in a pool of mentors
Ray Bradbury, the American author, so aptly said, 'Living at risk is jumping off the cliff and building your wings on the way down.' At the same time, how much easier would it be if someone taught you how to build those wings? While it's great to find a mentor at your workplace, sometimes that may not happen. It's a great practice to seek and build a network of mentors within and outside your industry—people who are your role models or whom you look up to for different reasons. They can be great sounding boards, with the objectivity that distance provides and the value of experience.

2. Embrace failure
Create a culture of embracing failure as a learning opportunity instead of punishing yourself. It will encourage the team to take calculated risks, try new things and give them the support they need to recover from setbacks. Letting a team make mistakes can increase the chances of success over time.

3. Set realistic goals
Setting realistic goals can help focus professionals' creativity and encourage them to take risks that are more likely to pay off. Ensure your goals are challenging but achievable and provide regular feedback

and support to help employees stay on track.

If the goals are realistic and have a reasonable time frame for completion, employees will be more likely to spend the necessary time coming up with novel ideas or solutions instead of just completing a task for the sake of it because the deadline is imminent. With the proper time and feedback, teams can concentrate on pursuing untried ideas rather than easy solutions.

APURVA
Lady, You're Not a Man!

Introduction

Apurva is a much-awarded Indian businesswoman, author and entrepreneur. Having worked across the fields of advertising, media and marketing, she currently runs her own venture. Aazol, which she co-founded with her son, is a venture that emerged out of the pandemic to reduce the inequities that we see in the economic landscape today. She believes in the power of diversity to change business outcomes and encourages organizations to invest in it, as well as for women to take charge of their own lives, careers and narratives. She believes that both men and women need to equally hold up the sky and change the world for the better.

She is an alumna of IIM Bengaluru and Stella Maris College, Chennai.

Why Apurva?

Apurva began her career as ambitiously as her husband, who was a classmate from business school. Unlike many such women, however, she was determined to hold on to her ambition even when she became a trailing spouse following her husband's transfers across the country and a young mother. That came with its own trials, including sometimes finding jobs that just did not challenge her enough, even while offering the security of a cushy role and a predictable pay cheque. How she crafted her own breaks out of these situations and worked her way through tough situations, which many people would have taken as a signal to quit, is a story in itself.

In addition, there is the social belief that successful working women do not have successful marriages. This is possibly an outcome that occurs due to various factors, including social conditioning in both men and women and a lack of personal time between two serious careers. How Apurva and her husband managed to negotiate this and ensure both of them flourished is a valuable lesson.

Apurva Purohit

#Teacher #ToughLove #PowerWoman #BossLady

Apurva had just jumped into a very senior position in a media firm after a long stint in advertising, hired by one of her former bosses. It was a quantum leap from her previous position, as Apurva had no experience running media. Still, she decided to go ahead and accept the position, not least because of the confidence her ex-boss displayed in her. But the environment at the new workplace was highly charged. There was intense internal competition and a lot of politics. While Apurva was still figuring out how to make her way, the CEO, her mentor, left. Isolated in that unfriendly atmosphere, Apurva began questioning her ability to get the job done. But as she thought over the life journey that had brought her here, she realized she was made of sterner stuff.

Influences and Inspirations

Apurva's parents were from families that had been displaced during Partition and had to rebuild their lives from scratch. Luckily, they were both well educated, with no family baggage getting in the way of creating a secure future for themselves. When Apurva was born, they were living in Ahmedabad and couldn't think of a name special enough for their first child for a long time until, one day, they came across the name Apurva, which was, funnily enough, the name of a garage service. When they figured out what it meant—unique—they decided that was the ideal name for her, and even to this day, they claim that it is the most apt name for their eldest child.

Apurva grew up in a very supportive family and environment. Her father worked for ONGC. Apurva and her two siblings travelled across the country because of his job, learning to make new friends in each place and quickly adjusting to change. In government colonies, they lived cheek by jowl with people from various regions, religions and castes. The kids of the neighbourhood were in and out of each other's homes, never conscious of each other's state of origin or religion. The only thing they recognized as distinctions were the equally enticing but different smells of the food that each family prepared: *kachori aloo* and *bedmi puri* made by neighbours from Uttar Pradesh (UP); *dal dhokli* cooked by Gujarati neighbours; *sarson ka saag* by Punjabis and *chingri maach* by Bengalis. The kids relished the diversity of flavours and cultures to which they were exposed. It was a very cosmopolitan world—as she calls it, 'India Amalgamated'.

Apurva's mother was very intelligent, competent and driven, a key decision-maker in the household. A bright student, she had studied science and was the only girl in a class full of boys in Punjab. She was pursuing her PhD in psychology when she got married, but was unable to fully channel her potential. Travelling alongside her husband, she became a teacher in schools and colleges and would teach both science and arts subjects. The values she inculcated in the kids included the importance of education, hard work and discipline. At the same time, the equation between their parents became something from which Apurva and her siblings imbibed their values of fairness and equity.

Apurva and her sister grew up without any consciousness of being different from their brother in terms of ambition or ability. Both knew they were as wanted as he was—something that still doesn't apply across all Indian families. The defining principle in their lives was the equality and democracy with which they were raised, across socioeconomic segments, religions and gender. 'We were brought up with the belief that everyone was equal and should have equal access to opportunity.'

When Apurva started studying at Stella Maris College in Chennai, the rule was that everyone had to play a sport. Bookish since childhood except for the mandatory physical education period in school, Apurva hesitantly began playing hockey. To her and her family's surprise, she turned out to be really good at it. In fact, she enjoyed playing hockey thoroughly; it was such a contrast to her studious lifestyle.

Practices were held at ungodly hours to avoid the sticky heat of Chennai weather. Apurva would wake up by 4 a.m., while everyone in the house would still be asleep, and get ready. She would make her way to college through a dark city in which the golden beginnings of dawn were just glimmering against an inky blue sky. Practice sessions were hectic and tiring, as much about fitness as about the techniques of hockey. Warm-ups for practise included jogging around a near-dark field and sit-ups performed in rhythmic unison. She would get exhausted from running up and down the field; often, her legs would be black and blue because a teammate had accidentally thwacked them with her hockey stick. But the sheer camaraderie of being part of a group working towards a common goal, the satisfying feeling of connecting the stick to the ball and seeing it roll into the goal and the thrill of a team victory added up to an incredible feeling of exhilaration.

Apurva became the goalkeeper for her state hockey team. The team qualified to play at the All India Women's National Meet, a huge achievement. They were extremely excited about their selection. Having won most of their matches against other teams with ease until then, they were confident that they would breeze through the state tournament as well.

They lost the first game 7–0.

Then they went on to lose the second: 11–0!

Apurva was shocked. Worse, she took it to heart, convinced that it was her goalkeeping skills that had let down the team and that she would be kicked off the team. In the next practice session, she sagged visibly, unable to concentrate. While her teammates practised enthusiastically, she stood on the sidelines. She had lost her confidence. The coach dropped her from the team for the third match and brought in a substitute player. Apurva felt even worse, but in a part of her mind, she felt the coach was right because she was not a good goalkeeper. Watching the game from the stands, she felt awful, wondering if she had gotten her place on the team under false pretences. In her bones, she knew the team would win with a different goalkeeper.

But something unexpected happened, which made her sit up. The team went on to lose the third match too!

Apurva's mind was in turmoil. Having assumed that it was her fault that the team had lost the first two matches, it was a shock when they lost with a substitute whom she had thought was a stronger player. After the game, the coach called Apurva to talk to her. She asked, 'Do you know why I dropped you? It was not because we lost the previous matches because of your performance. When my team plays, all 11 players must try. But you had already admitted defeat in your mind.'

It was not losing the game but the lack of spirit to get up and move on that had determined her selection for this match. Apurva learnt that it's not just game skills that differentiate a match-winning player from a match-losing one. It's the can-do, never-say-die spirit that gives one the courage to get up and try again after failure. The ability to learn what one can do after a defeat and play again, convinced that one has the ability and chance to win the next game and the next match defines a champion's attitude. The incident taught Apurva a valuable life lesson on overcoming failure—that failures would come along as a part of life, but rather than giving up and assuming that she didn't have the ability to succeed, she had to be strong and have enough self-belief to try again. It was a lesson that would come in handy time and again.

The Role of Difference

Brought up in an egalitarian home and then going to a women's college, Apurva had never faced the ugly side of patriarchy. The first time she encountered sexism was when she went to business school at IIM Bengaluru. With a class made up of many more boys than girls, she found that most of the boys did not think of their female classmates as their equals in intelligence or talent. They were expected to be cheerleaders, just good enough to write the introductions or summaries of the projects that the alpha males worked on.

Slowly, this bias began affecting Apurva. Having been a topper in academics, being considered inconsequential ate away at her. Her grades began dipping. For the rest of the year, she did very poorly in her studies. This added to the misery she had already been feeling. Her self-confidence ebbed.

Then, she had a lucky break. She was selected for a summer internship at a prestigious ad agency. The department head she was assigned to work with treated her with professionalism. He showed her that he had faith in her capabilities by expecting her to deliver work of a very high standard. To her delight, Apurva found that she was not only able to deliver work to those standards, but surpass them. She completed her internship with a pre-placement offer for a job with the agency.

This restored her confidence and self-esteem. She went to campus in her second year as a very different girl from the diffident one who had left for the summer. She was able to start doing well again in her studies. Thinking about the year gone by, she realized that she had let external judgements and expectations define who she was. She had succumbed to imposter syndrome—a feeling that she was not good enough, or not as good as the boys around her. She resolved never to let this happen to her again.

Work-Life Whirlwind

Apurva went on to marry her classmate from business school, Sanjay. He was one year her senior at the institute. They married straight after she completed her degree and started their careers together. It is said that if women have seen a strong husband–wife bond in their parents growing up, they try to recreate that by seeking the same qualities in a life partner. Sanjay had been brought up by a strong mother. Right from the beginning, he invested as much interest in Apurva's career as his own and was an equal partner and parent. He believed her career and ambitions were as important and valuable as his own.

The two of them settled down to a busy life in Mumbai. Advertising was one of the few professions that had a large female workforce and hence avoided rampant sexism. Apurva had a busy and fulfilling schedule between her career and her personal life. The day would start early, by 6 a.m., as the two of them rushed to get ready and catch a local train for their long commutes to work. They would get back home only by 8 p.m. or later, dog-tired, but with the satisfaction of knowing they had put in a great day's work.

Having grown up without much interest in rituals, Apurva wasn't aware of the many religious practices followed by married women. When she was invited to a religious event in the neighbourhood, she went along but did not know what she was expected to do. Hesitant, she asked her neighbour's mother the reason behind one of the rituals. The lady snarled at her, 'But then you got married out of caste after all, how will you know anything?' Apurva was startled. Her life and upbringing had shielded her from casteism in any shape or form and certainly not been a consideration when she got married. Initially, the remark hurt. But after she calmed down, Apurva realized that she didn't want to be one of those women whose lives are bound by social, religious or caste-based expectations. She was much happier to lead her life as an independent individual and preferred to break the norm that the women of the house are obliged to become carriers of religion and culture for the next generation.

A Turn in the Road

A few years later, Sanjay was transferred to Chennai with a prestigious promotion. This meant that Apurva would have to leave her job. She could have chosen to become the trailing spouse without a career of her own, content to follow her husband's trajectory. But she had been brought up to worship at the altar of perseverance and was, by nature, a fighter. She chose to see this as one more obstacle to cross and one more norm to break on her way up the career ladder.

'Now these are some roadblocks that many women have had to deal with, and in several cases, a spouse's transfer has ended up derailing what could have been a stellar career. Women get disillusioned with having to take a secondary seat in marriage where their careers are not seen to be as important as their husbands', and rather than fight for a right to be treated equally, they give up, only to regret it later on in life.'

While Apurva found a job with an ad agency, the role was not as exciting or challenging as the one she had before. She had two choices: she could either choose to lead a leisurely life at her new workplace or she could find ways to channel her energy and drive. Being Apurva, she chose the latter, and started doing extra work.

On a voluntary basis, she would produce a monthly newsletter here, some analysis for another department there, and so on. Word soon spread across the agency's other branches that there was this extra-enthusiastic executive in the Chennai branch who would churn out presentations and analyses for whoever wanted them. All the extra work that no one had the time to do started getting dumped on Apurva. Shortly, she found herself working on a range of new business presentations and proactive pitches across a wide array of client categories with the New Business Director (NBD), who was a dynamic leader who had recently joined the agency's headquarters.

Serendipity? Or Carpe Diem?

A couple of years later, she and her husband moved back to Mumbai, and she re-joined her previous organization. One day, out of the blue, she got a call. It was the NBD she had done pitches for in Chennai. 'I have rarely seen such a work ethic and I want you on my team,' he said. He had joined a new media organization as Group CEO and wanted to hire her based on his past experience with her.

Apurva was surprised and flattered. At the time when she had chosen to take on the work of new business pitches, she had only thought of putting in her best work. She had never thought about it in terms of the impact it would have on her reputation or her later career. Her key learning from this experience was that, consciously or unconsciously, every moment at work had both moulded her as a professional and her reputation. Therefore, it was important to ensure that one did one's best at every moment. *Carpe diem* was something she realized was her life's philosophy, though she had never consciously defined it as that.

'There are points in our lives where, unknown to us, we are going to be under close scrutiny! And the moment that will turn out to be the decisive one and will make (or mar) our fortunes is something we will realize only much later on! Every moment has to matter to us and make a difference, big or small, to the environment and to the people around us. Whether with our colleagues, our bosses, our clients or even the casual meeting we have with the supplier or the office boy, we have to approach every interaction, every task with honesty and with respect. Because while we are doing that, unknown to us, our reputation starts getting created or destroyed!

'All these moments are creating stories about us, and we are leaving behind us impressions that are good or bad, so that 10 years down the line, people will either say, "Oh, she is a great worker", "She is tough but a good people manager", "She knows her job" or "She is a bit of a shirker and needs to be pushed—too many people problems; ethics issues and so on". At that stage, it becomes too late to try and rebuild a reputation, because no one has the ability to go back in time and change the way they behaved.

The truth is that a good reputation cannot be created in a day or rewritten on expensive paper like a CV; or the flaws airbrushed and spruced up, as social media has taught us to do. It has to be assiduously built over millions of moments of being diligent, sincere, hardworking and ethical. And when the big break comes our way, of the CXO position or the willingness of the fund house to invest in our business, what will matter most is what people are saying about us as professionals and the reputation we have built.'

Change Is Here to Stay

Apurva was excited about her new role. As the business head of a media organization, she would now be on the client side of the table, a totally new experience. She looked forward to being able to make an impact, to learn and grow and to be able to create a brand that would stand out.

However, her new boss and mentor left the organization soon after she joined. The atmosphere in the new organization was highly political and toxic. Moreover, Apurva was the new one there, and her colleagues were old hands. The ground was ripe for imposter syndrome to rear its ugly head again! 'I am not trained for this job.' 'This malevolent environment is just not conducive to productivity.' 'How can I be expected to do good work here without any support?' Questions like this plagued her daily, and bit by bit, her confidence in getting the job done was eroding.

One morning, she jolted out of sleep at 4 a.m., heart pounding with the stress she had been undergoing. She made herself a cup of tea and sat on the balcony in the cool darkness, thinking back over her career journey and the challenges that lay ahead. She remembered the many times she had felt like an imposter before and how she had dealt with it. She remembered what her hockey coach had told her when she felt she was unfit to continue as the goalie. Her summer internship experience came back to her—how filled with self-doubt she had been, and how she had ended up surprising herself with the outcome. 'If I could do that at 19, with no work experience, how much better equipped am I today to repeat that success,' she mused. 'I have had years of on-the-job success, I have handled tough clients and demanding bosses with flair and each time I have come out with flying colours. Why should this job or this opportunity be any different? I haven't done this job before but I have learnt how to do the best at any job.' As she sipped the hot brew and drew in a long breath, she could feel herself relaxing.

That was a turning point for Apurva. From then on, her ability to do a good job grew dramatically! This incident helped Apurva to not only consistently chart the right course for herself, but also to find the courage to stand up for herself.

Women and Leadership

She also reflected on the social expectations of leadership, and realized they were all shaped by male leaders. But through her career, she had brought her own style of leadership to the table, and it had worked very well. She vowed that from then on, she would take up the cause of women at the workplace. One of the things she noticed was the gender bias of benevolent patriarchy: in a bid to promote equality or be good to female employees, bosses often end up either not giving them challenging assignments or being less exacting in terms of the output expected from them. This turns out badly for women in two ways: 'bonsaiing them' as Apurva puts it, and leaving them unprepared for leadership roles or growth in their career by artificially stymieing their learning. On the other hand, there is veiled resentment from male employees for the soft treatment women get, making it harder for them to command the respect of their colleagues.

Apurva made it a point to ensure that men and women got the same jobs and opportunities, thus levelling the playing field. When she noticed that at Radio City, female RJs were not assigned the late-night slots for their safety while commuting, she sprang into action. Rather than reduce the opportunities for female RJs, she ensured they had access to office transport and, thus, access to anchor marquee shows as well.

The second thing she did was to ensure that there were enough, and, more importantly, visible female role models at the senior level. This meant not only pushing women to apply for and be ready to take CXO roles, but equally ensuring that once they had reached that position, they were seen and heard. Many senior women shy away from being positioned as diversity champions lest their professional achievements get construed as 'diversity promotions'. It's not uncommon for women to shy away from addressing issues related to gender when they achieve top leadership roles so that they are not accused of 'favouritism' or 'feminism' which is seen in a poor light in corporate corridors. Apurva had to convince women leaders not to get trapped in this belief. More importantly, she had to ensure that all stakeholders understood that these women were competent and had reached that level solely on merit. Once both the women leaders and the stakeholders were reassured that it was merit and not gender that was behind their promotion, the senior women became comfortable with being perceived as role models.

'I remember one young girl walking up to me and telling me that when she saw so many women leaders at Radio City she felt encouraged and believed that it was an organization where any woman could reach the top, unlike her earlier organization where there was not a single woman at senior leadership levels. While her previous CEO had also advocated gender diversity, she had always felt that it was more talk than walk because of no visible demonstration to the contrary.'

The traits that define leadership, as commonly understood, are largely masculine, since most spheres have male leaders around the world. Be it in government, business or sports, we see more men at the leadership level for a variety of reasons, and thus, male behaviour becomes synonymous with leadership behaviour. Apurva took a conscious call to buck this norm.

As a leader, she wanted to be authentic. To her, that meant acknowledging the differences between men and women rather than blindly emulating male leaders. 'Often, female leaders try to emulate male leaders around them because they see the default gender of good leadership as essentially male; but the fact is that women make for far better leaders because they apply lessons learnt from the perspective of ground zero, from a practical mindset, and from the quotidian-ness of everyday living.' Breaking the norm, Apurva learnt to neither be apologetic about her gender nor use it to gain an advantage at the workplace.

For instance, Monday morning reviews tended to be very stressful. Led by a competitive and hyper-aggressive work environment, they turned out to be sessions where senior leaders of different departments often took turns sniping at each other. This was a far cry from the empathetic and cooperative culture Apurva wanted to build. She decided to turn them into cake-meetings—meetings where she would bring in a cake freshly baked over the weekend. The first half of the meeting would be spent discussing what everyone had been up to over the weekend.

Initially, this met with pushback from the male leaders who derided the idea, saying they did not want to become part of a 'kitty party'. But over a period of time, everyone started enjoying the informal interaction. As they started getting to know each other better, the hostility died down, and collaboration improved dramatically.

'It may have been perceived as a female clichéd behaviour from the outside, but at its depth, it was a leadership behaviour with the goal of aligning HODs together to get the best out of them. Being comfortable in your own skin takes time, and when you are the only woman in the room, it is very difficult to not start behaving like all the males, but I keep telling myself that the only way to be a good leader is to be as authentic as possible. If I am female and that comes with its own set of differences, so be it. I would rather be authentic and female rather than inauthentic.'

Apurva also asserts that women often don't exercise the muscle of choice because they hand over their reins to circumstances, parents, husbands, bosses and children. Unfortunately, this behaviour is prevalent in society, and very few women have had the courage to break the norm. Unless women strengthen that muscle by repeatedly using it to make their own choices, they will never be able to take control of their lives. Luckily, she had been brought up by parents who not only backed her ambition but also gave her the confidence to make her own choices.

Now in her mid-fifties, Apurva believes it is time to say, 'I have enough for my wants and needs and have satisfied all ego-fuelled desires, and it is time to give back with gratitude.' She wants to work on reducing inequalities, social or economic, and giving more opportunities to the less fortunate. She is also interested in trying to reduce environmental degradation by making personal lifestyle changes and using her skills and resources to create an impact at the bottom of the pyramid. She has set up a company with her son to work with rural self-help groups and women microentrepreneurs to source traditional and forgotten food products and give urban consumers healthier local food choices.

Her advice to young women starting off (or her message to her younger self) would be:

1. Never think of your career and family as either/or. You need to and must have both in order to fulfil your true potential.
2. Financial independence is the truest form of independence.
3. The person you marry is the single most important career choice you will make.
4. You are not here to become a paler version of the men around you. You are here to be unabashedly you! Therein lies your biggest strength and superpower, and your ability to bring change in the world around you. So, celebrate your uniqueness.
5. Women are far better leaders because they have clarity of thinking, practical good sense, implementation skills, the ability to take tough decisions and the empathy to create bonds with their teams.

Hacks to Storm the Norm

Norm: It's alright for women to quit when it gets too hard.

Hacks:

With the best of intentions, when women are going through tough times at work, people around them will say, 'Why do you need to work so hard? It's okay to quit,' not realizing that they are essentially telling her that her career doesn't really matter. But we know how much our career—into which we have invested so much time, effort and passion—means to us. Even at the toughest times, we know we might regret throwing in the towel later. This is not to say that if you're truly in a toxic environment and think you will feel happier for it, you shouldn't walk away. But before you consider that final move, here are some things you can do that can help.

1. Build your own support system

Get yourself a good support system of friends and family who will be there for you to vent, cry and then help you get back on your feet. Consider hiring a leadership coach who can help you build resilience. Build your individual equations with top management and find allies.

2. What happens in Vegas

Sometimes berating ourselves for a mistake makes it hard for us to keep going. While it's important to take responsibility, toxic self-blame cycles serve no one. It's alright to say, 'I've made a mistake', learn from that and move on, rather than rehash the past, indulge in what-ifs and wishful thinking or worry about it into the future.

3. The rule of 5-5

Whenever you face an issue, take a moment to think about whether or not it will matter in five years. If it won't, don't spend more than five minutes stressing out about it. Move on.

CHIKI
The Pragmatic Feminist

Introduction

Rudrani 'Chiki' Sarkar, 43, is the founder of Juggernaut books. After her undergraduate degree, Chiki began her career with Bloomsbury Publishing UK as an editorial assistant. After seven years there, she moved to India as the editor-in-chief of Random House, before taking on the role of publisher at Penguin India. She then led the merged entity Penguin Random House India before starting Juggernaut Books, then an app-based publisher. Instrumental in publishing many of the subcontinent's finest writers, Chiki also launched the careers of acclaimed writers such as Rujuta Diwekar, Twinkle Khanna and Ankur Warikoo; Nobel Prize winners Abhijit Banerjee and Esther Duflo and Booker Prize winner Shehan Karunatilaka. She was named one of the World Economic Forum's Young Global Leaders in 2015.

She lives in Delhi with her family.

Why Chiki?

Priyadarshini Narendra grew up fascinated by reading and books, and often wondered what a career built around reading books would look like. It was many years later that she discovered the world of publishing and the fascinating fact that it was an industry that was refreshingly gender-imbalanced in favour of women. However, the number of women CEOs in the industry is still too small.

Chiki was the editorial head of several leading publishing firms before setting out to build her own firm, which broke new ground in terms of the people they chose to publish, how they chose to publish and how they marketed and sold their books. We wanted to understand what gave her the courage to take the plunge into entrepreneurship. How did she manage the tough negotiations that are an integral part of publishing? What gave her the confidence to break new ground within how books were published and marketed, rather than perfect what was already working? Most of all, we wanted to know what women could learn from her example to apply to other fields.

The Great Leap Forward

When Chiki moved back to New Delhi, India, as inaugural editor-in-chief at Random House, it was a seminal move. At just 28, she was among the youngest ever in that role. Having begun her career just seven years earlier as an editorial assistant, this was possibly the fastest progress up the ladder anyone had made.

Yet, she says of that time candidly, 'I cried every day for a year. I found the work overwhelming. I didn't have a support system in Delhi. I didn't know jacket designers, copyeditors, how things worked, I didn't know writers. Not only did I not have a professional network, I didn't have any friends. I was incredibly lonely.'

Silver Spoon and Golden Pages

Until then, Chiki had led a charmed life by most standards. Daughter of Aveek Sarkar, chief editor of the Anandabazar Patrika group of publications—home of the venerable Anandabazar Patrika newspaper—she was born into enormous privilege and affluence. Her mother was a career woman who did a variety of things, including founding an art gallery that she still runs. Her family was very prominent in Kolkata and beyond; they were intellectual, wealthy, respected; and they travelled abroad on holiday—an almost unheard-of luxury for those times.

At the same time, it was an unusual-of upbringing. Her parents were very busy with their own careers and rarely at home, leaving Chiki and her sister by themselves most of the time.

'At the time, we used it to our advantage. We skipped class, we told our tuition teacher that mom told us not to go but how would mom know? What defined my childhood was being left alone to do my shit and it suited me perfectly,' Chiki says with a laugh. One of the things she remembers fondly is that every time her parents travelled abroad, they would make it a point to research what books were popular among children of Chiki's and her sister's age and bring back whole suitcases full of them.

> ### CHIKI'S SUCCESS HACKS
>
> - Do not be defensive. If someone says you've done something wrong, embrace it and make sure you never make that mistake again.
> - Do your work. I don't think nine-five is enough at least three times a week.
> - I follow Barack Obama's tip in which he decides what he has to do the next day the night before. And that allows him to sleep calmly and wake up very focussed.

With a house full of books, it was only natural for Chiki and her sister to become voracious readers. Chiki's selection of books was eclectic and uncensored.

'For a bookie nerd, you rebel through reading trashy adult books. You want to be that person that has lots of sex and drinks, wears high heels and drives Cadillacs, but you're not. I was reading Mills and Boons, old editions of *Life* magazine and gossipy biographies of Elvis Presley and Grace Kelly, and then I was also reading T.S. Eliot or the Romantic poets and Camus.'

Despite being allowed to *run wild* by her parents, Chiki grew up to have a very strong work ethic, built further by observing her parents, and an innate sense of discipline and ambition. These traits would go on to shape her career, giving her the grit to withstand a year of unhappiness, as well as the vicissitudes of turning entrepreneur and the ability to envision a new course for herself.

'What I didn't realize, at the time, was that I had inner self-discipline. For example, when I was 11 or 12, I said to myself that I want to read all of the nineteenth century classics, and I read them pretty conscientiously. I read all the Jane Austens but did I understand them at 13? No, I don't think so.'

Growing up around career women with independence and a strong voice, Chiki was brought up to think of a career, and with her passion for reading, it was not unexpected that it would revolve around the fields of words and writing. Entering the world of newspaper publishing may have seemed a natural progression, but she was driven to chart an independent course.

At 16, Chiki left Kolkata to go to school and then went on to college. While still a student at Oxford, Chiki ran into the incredibly successful chief editor of Bloomsbury Publishing, Alexandra Pringle. In 1999, five days after her completing her undergraduate degree, Chiki joined Bloomsbury. Bloomsbury was a small publishing house, but in 1999, they published their third *Harry Potter* book, *Harry Potter and the Prisoner of Azkaban,* and suddenly both the series and Bloomsbury were phenomena!

She enjoyed life in London tremendously. 'London was the home of my heart…I could have continued living there for years,' she says. Alexandra took Chiki under her wing, almost like a second mother, and taught her the ropes. In a business that depends on relationship building, Chiki forged strong and lasting connections with many authors. She learnt to keep a toothbrush and paste in the office so she could come in from a night of fun and get right back to work. Her knack for understanding the zeitgeist, having a finger on the pulse of readers and separating the wheat from the chaff in the 'slush pile' or piles of manuscripts from unknown authors had her quickly scaling the career ladder. An appetite for taking risks, a sharp and innovative mind, editorial instincts that could restructure a book to be much more readable and an unbeatable drive made her a name to be reckoned with.

The Healthy Headache

After several years in London, Chiki felt she was starting to stagnate, both in terms of her career and her personal life. India was an exciting growth story at the time. She decided to uproot herself and move to Delhi, a city where she knew no one, with a leadership role at Random House. It was a huge leap up the ladder, and Chiki was excited about it.

When she landed in Delhi to pick up the reins, however, she realized that it was going to be even more challenging than she expected. There was scepticism about her selection for the role. Many people questioned if she was suited for the job, given that she had no leadership experience. Some even wondered if she had got the role because of her father or family connections. Several older male writers refused to take her seriously, though she believes it was a reflection on her age rather than her gender. Candidly, Chiki admits that she understands where people were coming from, given her age and experience at the time. But rather than dwell on it, she preferred to focus on her work and let it speak for her.

In Delhi, she was new to the local tricks of the trade. In the UK, she was used to receiving manuscripts from literary agents. India didn't have any at the time, so publishers needed to be entrepreneurial and commission books on their own, coming up with a constant stream of ideas. She didn't know book designers or cover artists. On the personal front, she didn't have any friends she could pick up old relationships with, so it was an isolated, lonely life. What kept her going, despite her misery, was knowing she was doing the right thing for herself. The discontent stemmed from finding things hard rather than a feeling of despair. She has a unique take on how to cope: 'Unhappiness is like having a headache, and unless it's a headache that puts you into bed with a pill, you're going through the day with a headache, no? That's how I feel about unhappiness. It doesn't stop me.'

Extremely energetic and itching to do more, even during our Zoom interactions, Chiki multitasks furiously. When she joined Random House India, it was new and did not have a formidable stable of talents, unlike competitors like Penguin or Harper-Collins. It would have been an uphill battle to persuade established authors to shift their loyalties. Chiki made a strategic choice to focus on gaining and promoting new talent. Authors like Namita Devidayal, Mohammed

Hanif, Aman Sethi, Basharat Peer and Shehan Karunatilaka owe their beginnings to Random House.

She also got in touch with the dean of IIM Ahmedabad, saying she wanted to do management books. To her delight, he agreed, and they launched the popular IIMA business books series. Her ability to spot opportunities in the market led to Rujuta Diwekar's first book, for example, paving the way for Diwekar's wellness guru status. Her *Don't Lose your Mind, Lose Your Weight* remains India's top-selling diet book of all time. Chiki focussed not only on identifying and hand-holding new voices, but also their sales and marketing. With a creative mind churning out 10 ideas a minute, she ensured her authors got commendable publicity and therefore sold much more than the 2–3,000 books that were the norm. In addition, her ability to quickly analyse failures, glean learnings from them and move on helped her sharpen her expertise.

From Random House, Chiki was headhunted for the role of publisher at Penguin India—thrice the size of Random House India, and arguably the most important job in publishing in India. Her biggest challenge with the move was learning to negotiate the bureaucracy of a large company and managing a team that she had inherited. Driven and bursting with ideas and chutzpah, Chiki was a hard taskmaster who could be both intimidating and inspiring to her team.

Chiki then went on to head the merged entity behemoth that was Penguin Random House India, the largest trade publisher in the world. Among the books she helmed during her stint at Penguin were Sanjaya Baru's mega hit *The Accidental Prime Minister*, Twinkle Khanna's *Mrs Funnybones*, which launched her writing career, and Pulitzer Prize winner Katherine Boo's *Behind the Beautiful Forevers*.

Shattering the Ceiling with the Juggernaut

Despite her powerful position in the publishing industry in India, Chiki began to feel dissatisfied with the level of agency and say she had in decision-making. Indian publishing is a relatively small portion of the global publishing market. Indian sales or profits make very little difference to the total balance sheet. As a result, Indian publishers play hardly any role in policy-making or setting the future course of the business. Moreover, as with any other large multinational, decision-making was much slower as it trickled down various departments.

'If it was a sales question, then sales would look after it. If it was a digital question then there was some digital person. It was very siloed. In the end that is what the publisher does. But I was asking bigger questions of myself. There was a lack of coalescence which I personally found very difficult.'

Never one to miss an opportunity to grow, even if it meant a leap into the unknown, Chiki quit Penguin Random House India in 2015 to set up a mobile-first publishing house, Juggernaut. She put together a team of editors she had worked with previously. What excited her the most was experimenting with ideas, crafting a new space for the book from the printed word to the mobile app, and the freedom she would have to make decisions on everything, not just the selection of the book itself. 'I like doing things that are different, I get very excited by the new. I never think whether it will work or not work. Although I run a much smaller business in revenue, I feel the jump in empowerment.'

She charted a conscious strategy to rope in a number of celebrity authors for the company. She was always interested in finding new ways of marketing and promoting her books, and at Juggernaut it was easy and quick to go from idea to action. She talks about how Juggernaut went from wondering whether they should sell Karan Johar's memoir through his Instagram page to executing it in a heartbeat. Working on Kareena Kapoor's *Pregnancy Bible*, they reached out to Amazon, which is now reprogramming its baby page according to Kareena's shopping list—something that Chiki may not have been able to pull off in her earlier avatar.

'I'm really interested in not just making the book, but all these other things that you do alongside the book. For example, I realized that I was worried about the Kareena Kapoor book because pregnancy is a health issue. Readers will want good health advice, right? Now Kareena is in *Vogue* magazine; she stands for glamour, beauty, celebrity. I thought about if people would pick up Kareena's *Pregnancy Bible*. Will they think to themselves, "Accha, you know what, I'll read the article in some magazine, but I don't want to buy this book. Why should I just do what she says?" So, I contacted India's association of gynaecologists and obstetricians (FOGSI) and asked them to vet the medical information in the book and endorse it if they approved of it. They agreed, and now we are the only pregnancy book in the Indian market that is endorsed by FOGSI. I don't know who would take that call if I were in Penguin—is that editorial work or a marketing call?'

Juggernaut was a prime example of Chiki's talent for innovation and spotting market gaps. The mobile revolution, particularly smartphones, was still nascent, but she saw an emerging opportunity. The sales numbers for the Kindle were still very small in India, and Chiki realized that the omnipresent device would be the mobile phone. Juggernaut launched with a mobile app when publishers were still thinking mainly print with a sidebar for Kindle. The mobile format allowed Juggernaut to experiment with a variety of formats that brought in more readers into its fold—single short stories, serialization of novels and a host of novellas. In addition, she opened up the platform to other publishers, rather than reserving it for Juggernaut books only. This enabled the app to offer a much larger repertoire of reading material, thus catering not just to the literary and habitual reader but the emerging and occasional reader as well.

One of the things that helped Juggernaut sell more was Chiki's gift for innovation when it came to marketing—she thought of things no one else had done until then and was quick to execute them. This led to an enormous advantage when it came to making books fly off the shelves. She also brought to Juggernaut her formidable gift, honed over the years, for producing content tuned to the zeitgeist. For example, she recently commissioned a book about the concept of *Sewa* and why the Sikhs are always at the forefront of relief work in every calamity, apt in the wake of the Covid relief work undertaken by the Sikh community.

Becoming a CEO brought new challenges and new skills to the fore. As a small company, they were cash-strapped. The relentless need to make profits in order to stay afloat and be able to pay all the employees has kept her up at nights. As a result, she has built her profit-making muscles and is now as interested in how to sell books as she is in the books themselves.

For example, Juggernaut took a strategic call to have a book list that is 95 per cent non-fiction (since it sells more than fiction in India), producing bestsellers like *Do Epic Shit* which sold almost 200,000 copies and critical hits like *Early Indians*. Even their fiction list doesn't consider books that are likely to sell less than 5,000 copies, which is significantly more than the industry benchmark. While the love of the written word may make a particular book attractive, Chiki won't bid for it unless she is convinced about its ability to sell, and judiciously looks at the amount bid versus the expected sales. Recently, she turned down a book she loved reading and would have enjoyed publishing, because the author was expecting an advance that would have made it unviable in terms of profit.

Feminist or Pragmatist

She reflects on the conflicts that come with being CEO on the one hand, and being a genuine egalitarian who wants more women to succeed at the workplace on the other. She feels that sometimes the government's well-meaning efforts actually make it harder for small businesses to employ women. For example, the Indian government mandates six months of paid maternity leave. For a small business, that adds up to a year's worth of paying two salaries for the same job, something most of them can ill afford. 'Salary to the person taking the leave and the salary to the temporary hire. You essentially increase someone's salary payload. Even in my small company, my editor took a paternity leave when he and his partner had their children. There was no question. But it puts a tremendous pressure on a small business. It's really, really difficult.' In Europe, companies are subsidized for giving maternity leave to their employees, and she feels something similar could be a valuable catalyst to enable small companies to bet on women. In publishing, where each book has a long gestation period, she wonders how even large companies are able to cope. 'I've had conversations with my ex-boss who is an old-school feminist. She works for a big company, and they can afford long maternity leaves. But if a woman takes a whole year off, which is now the law in Europe, in the publishing world that's a lifetime.' Each editor has a particular vision for a book. If that editor goes away on leave for a year, the next editor may not have the same vision, which will end up impacting the quality and sales of that book. Long leaves can destabilize a three-year process, not just at the level of revenue, but also at the level of authors and production persons. At the same time, she isn't sure what would make things easier, apart from the government providing facilities like creches and day care facilities for parents.

Chiki strongly refutes the idea of a glass ceiling in the publishing industry. Publishing houses look for people from a humanities or arts background, and the field pays less than most corporate jobs. They tend to employ more women, and there are several talented and powerful women leaders on the editorial side, which is where the glamour and glory lie. She feels that the real question to ask is why there hasn't been a single woman CEO of an Indian publishing house. 'Maybe at the very top there is still a glass ceiling, not because the women in publishing are settling, but because, at the deepest level, we don't have the confidence to say, "I am going to learn another skill set and get the topmost job."'

Mirror, Mirror

She credits her husband with being a feminist who has never even questioned equality. He and Chiki split the work of running a home and managing a family, consciously and unconsciously, down the middle. 'He is a stellar person and I take his support for granted; it's a part of the furniture of this house and that quality has allowed me to do everything.' Born in the US, he grew up used to seeing an equitable division of managing a home and family alongside work.

However, despite that and the privilege she recognizes of being able to afford any amount of good help, running Juggernaut hasn't come without its share of heartaches on the personal side. She wonders if she has taken a step back in some way because she had children.

She remembers the first day she was leaving her two-month-old son at home and heading back to the office. As she closed the door behind her, Chiki felt tears pricking her eyes. She got into the car and wept silently all the way to the office.

'But as I neared the office, I gave myself a stern talking-to. I am very narcissistic. I love my reflection. I really like myself; you can't make me dislike myself. My husband is always teasing me that whenever there is a mirror, Chiki's looking in it. But strangely enough, I also use the mirror to calm myself. I'll have 30 minutes of feeling very panicky, with my heart racing. Then I'll look into the mirror and talk to myself.'

She pulled out her compact to see if her tear stains were visible on her face. And then gave herself a pep talk.

'Chiki, your son will be fine. You have great help looking after him while you're at work.

> **How can workplaces make it easier for women to rise?**
>
> • Ensuring more flexibility and WFH options.
> • Creche culture, so the working day has a finite end.
> • Government subsidies for maternity leave, like in Europe.

Meanwhile, you are the founder of this company. It's really tiny, and we're cash-strapped. This company is like your child too, it needs you to step up. And you have employees who are dependent on you. So, get your shit together.'

By the time she entered office, the tears had disappeared. And as the day wore on, she was so busy with the myriad decisions that had to be made that she forgot about her guilt.

Being good at compartmentalizing helps. At the same time, she admits that she doesn't have the world-beating ambition that some men seem to have. She remembers meeting the CEO of an Indian unicorn on a bank holiday, who had planned to be in meetings throughout the day and sheepishly told Chiki, 'My wife and kids hate me.'

'Meanwhile, I was thinking, "I have to be back home by 6:30, put my son to bed and clean the bathroom."'

'Motherhood sometimes sucks out my energy,' she admits. But she feels that maintaining a work-life balance is equally hard on anyone, male or female. She sees her husband, a very hands-on parent, struggling to carve out equal time for all his roles as much as she does. On working days, she often pulls a second shift of work in the evening, after putting her son to bed.

As a business leader, she believed she had to present a stoic, positive front to the team and the world outside. She learnt to put away her feelings because she thought teams needed to see a leader who was always calm and cheerful. So much so that she had difficulty in admitting that she felt stressed or low even to her closest friends and husband. She has only recently started sharing her feelings more honestly, at least in her own space. But characteristically upbeat, she cites Nora Ephron's speech, 'Yes, it's a mess, but aren't you lucky you have it? You're a generation where you can work, you can earn your money, you can find your voice and yes, you have a child and a

---

What I've learnt as CEO: Being tougher about hiring, about what employees bring to the team, about whether we've done certain things or not.

Being much more sales-centred. Being brutal about saying we want this novel, it's a great novel, but if we have to pay 10 lakhs, we don't think it's worth it.

That people are open to being propositioned, whether it is in investing in the company or an idea for a book. Ask people anything, knock on the doors and don't feel embarrassed or self-conscious. I asked Ratan Tata to take part in a book-reading once. It was for a good cause. He turned it down, but I didn't feel foolish at having tried.

husband.' Relishing what she refers to as a 'glorious *khichdi*', she has never thought of quitting.

Looking back, Chiki sees her life as a largely positive, straightforward progression with a few bad patches. 'My memory of my past is that things have been more good than bad. I hate being a victim of circumstance. I think I'm basically a very optimistic, positive person. I don't play victim. I tell people that once you're past 30, you have to own everything that happens in your life; you can't blame it on the past.'

Hacks to Storm the Norm

Norm: Women are too risk-averse and demonstrate a greater fear of failure.

Hacks:

Research shows that boys and girls grow up with the same amount of propensity to take risks as youngsters. However, as they grow up, society rewards their risk-taking behaviour differently. Girls are taught to view risk-taking as dangerous and choose less risky options, while boys are praised for their derring-do, and, thus, have a higher propensity to make riskier choices. Whether you're a man or woman, it's important to take a certain number of risks and, at the same time, ensure that those risks are worth taking, regardless of success or failure. Like any other muscle, the risk-taking muscle needs regular exercise to keep it strong.

1. Change your frame of reference
An important way to think about risks is to reframe them. What do we typically mean by risk? When the possible negative outcomes outweigh the positive ones. So, when you're looking at the possible consequences of a decision, first write down the worst-case scenario if you go ahead—the most terrible things that can happen. Then write down the best case—the finding-a-diamond-in-a-puddle type of life-changing things that can happen. Rank the items in each list on a

scale of 1–10 based on how life-changing they might be. When you compare the two, you'll see that many of the things you thought of as high-risk might have the possibility of being life-changing in a terrific way.

2. The pursuit of perfection kills action
Don't bother being perfect. At the workplace, 80 per cent good-and-executed-in-time beats the 100 per cent flawless solution that takes years to put together. The search for perfection, yet another ingrained behaviour among women, often defeats the impetus to take action. It will mean you'll experience failures, but the lessons from those failures are often what will lead you to success.

3. Make it less BHAG
Sometimes the BHAG—Big Hairy Audacious Goal—might feel too big and scary to drive you to action. If that's what has you frozen in place, try breaking it down to a series of smaller goals and, more importantly, a series of smaller steps that will get you on your way. Put together an action plan just for two weeks. For example, if you want to run a marathon for the very first time, set yourself a simpler goal, like running for five minutes every day, and check back in after two weeks. You'll find that you've come a long way from where you started just a few weeks before.

DIPALI
Embracing Change, Finding Purpose

Introduction

Dipali Goenka, CEO and MD, Welspun India, grew up in an affluent family in Jaipur. Married at the young age of 18, she is now a leading name among Indian entrepreneurs. Known for playing a major role in steering Welspun India towards becoming one of the largest home textile companies in the world, she also champions the causes of sustainability, inclusive development and gender parity at the workplace. Brand ambassador of WEConnect International, Dipali was instrumental in increasing the percentage of women employees at Welspun from 7 per cent to 24 per cent.

As a woman in the largely male-dominated field of textile manufacturing, there has been a threefold increase in the number of patents received by the company during her tenure of more than 20 years. She is accredited with introducing the latest blockchain technology for textiles. She was ranked at number 16 on the *Forbes* list of Most Powerful Women in Asia, and at number 4 in India, in 2016; among the Most Powerful Women in Business by *Business Today* in 2021; and among the Most Influential Women in India by *Business World* in 2022.

Dipali Goenka has completed the Owner/President Management Program (OPM) from Harvard University. A mother to two daughters, Dipali is also a fitness enthusiast and a trained Kathak dancer.

Why Dipali?

Sometimes, when the world sees the wife of an entrepreneur or business owner getting involved at the workplace, all it perceives is a woman frivolously 'dabbling' in something she doesn't have any expertise in as something to pass the time. How much harder is it for someone who is born with a silver spoon in her mouth? What can someone like that know about the struggles of a real entrepreneur who has had to succeed from scratch? And how can someone who entered the workplace so late in life be serious about her career?

Dipali's case is interesting because she hails from one of Jaipur's most affluent families. Not only has she experienced the struggle from the inside, but has also crafted her career after starting her first job when her kids were in school! Despite a lack of experience, her burning desire to contribute and her passion for learning ensured that she soared right to the top.

First Day on the Job

Dipali felt a pang as she walked into the old-fashioned, dilapidated-looking office building in Andheri. She felt as if she had already run a marathon, though her work day had just begun. She had been up since 5 a.m., ensuring that breakfast and lunch were ready for her daughters, her husband and herself, and that the house was in apple-pie order. After dropping her daughters off at school, she raced across town to be the first one in the office.

At 29, it was her first day at work—not just at this job, but at her first job ever. It was a huge undertaking for her because she hadn't been brought up to think of a career. She was anxious about joining her husband's firm, hoping she wouldn't make too many mistakes and would add value. Even more important, she wanted to be known for the work she did rather than for being the chairman's wife.

At home, when they had their first tentative conversation about her joining the firm, both were slightly hesitant. He worried whether the home and the kids would continue to be looked after with the same zeal. She worried about how she would cope with having to manage everything. Moreover, she hadn't worked before and worried whether she would be able to contribute or be useful. She worried that her inexperience and lack of knowledge might make her look foolish and make her husband look bad. She was very clear; she didn't want special treatment just because she was his wife. She said, 'At work, I want to be just another employee. No less, but certainly no more. I don't want anyone to make any special concessions or give me the benefit of the doubt just because I am your wife and I don't have any previous work experience.' BK Goenka, her husband, said, 'Don't worry about that. I am more likely to hold you to higher standards than any other employee because you have seen us build this up from the first brick onwards. You will be expected to know better and do better.'

As she walked into the near empty office, she wondered what the other employees would make of her. Would they be wary, expecting her to be the boss's eyes and ears in the office? Would they try and flatter her, thinking that that would put them in the boss's good books? She worried that other employees would be suspicious of her. But she knew that this was something she had to do and that there was no time like the present.

Coming from a conservative Marwari family and being married into a similar one, she had faced a lot of pressure to try to have a son after giving birth to two daughters. The community is fairly patriarchal, and the ingrained belief is that only a son can inherit the family business. Dipali was keen to bust this norm and prove that women are just as good as men. She wanted to ensure that her daughters grew up with a female role model who proved just that, so they wouldn't have to face the same pressure. She knew that she had to start working and, what's more, be acknowledged as a huge success at the workplace. She knew what a journey she had traversed to reach this point.

The Girl from a Raj Parivar

Born into one of the most well-known and affluent families in Jaipur, Dipali and her siblings grew up in the lap of luxury. The family owned several movie theatres across Jaipur, Delhi and Mumbai, as well as other businesses, and lived in a beautiful home surrounded by a large garden in a posh part of town. Dipali's mother, who holds a double MA in mathematics, was a homemaker involved in charity work. Trained to have a sense of noblesse oblige, her parents believed in philanthropy and spent both time and effort in helping out various people.

The kids were brought up in a cocoon of pampering, were never allowed to step out of the home except in the family car and were always accompanied by one or two attendants. As a child who loved food, Dipali was chubby. Worried for her, her mother kept trying to nudge her toward healthier habits, feeding her only apple slices for breakfast at one point and making her run around the garden. Dipali and her sister studied at Maharani Gayatri Devi Girls' School—one of Jaipur's most prestigious schools. The school was well connected, and so the students got a lot of exposure to famous personalities. In 1980, Prince Charles visited the school as part of his India tour. He played polo with the Jaipur royals, and Dipali eagerly watched the match with her family.

A good student, Dipali also learnt kathak and Hindustani classical singing outside of school. One of the people who made a lasting impression on Dipali was her geography teacher who took the students to Jaisalmer to learn all about sand dunes. She made learning fun—an attitude Dipali later adopted for her workplace. With an interest in education, Dipali wanted to teach when she grew up.

And then one day, out of the blue, their perfect life changed. Their father became seriously ill and was no longer able to step out of the house or attend to work. After the initial shock, their mother seamlessly took over the reins at the workplace. She began handling everything, from tracking the revenues of the film distribution business to going to the factory and negotiating with workers. What's more, she did it all in her trademark sarees, with her head covered. Dipali learnt two powerful lessons that would shape how she made her own decisions in life—one, that a woman can cope with anything she needs to, and two, that she can do it in heels, chiffons and Chanel perfume.

'In Rajasthan, your head is covered as you are a woman and lead a group of men in a boardroom. You maintain that dignity towards your culture and yet display leadership and equality.'

Attractive, stylish and soft-spoken, yet utterly clear about how she wants to drive her business, Dipali seems to have taken these lessons to heart.

Too Early but Not a Hurdle

By the time Dipali turned 18, her father's health was on the decline. His dream was to see his children settled. As the eldest, Dipali's turn came first. Her father wanted to see Dipali suitably married. Her mother was very concerned about how much time he had left and wanted to fulfil his dream. She put the word out that they were looking for a suitable match for their daughter.

Someone introduced them to BK Goenka, a young man who started his business at 18. He owned a theatre and a restaurant in Jaipur. Dipali's mother and father were very taken by him. Though he wasn't in the same league financially, and his business was at a fledgling level, they could see his potential. They were impressed by his ambition and drive, and felt that he would be a great match for their daughter.

One afternoon, Dipali walked into the cool, marble-floored hall of their home, after a long, tiring day at school. A student in Class 12, she had a lot of studying ahead of her. She was looking forward to a quick snack before sitting down at her study desk. The maid came to her with an urgent message. Her parents wanted to see her right away. Surprised, she put down her school bags and quickly brushed her unruly hair before going into the flower-filled sitting room. 'We have some news for you,' her mother said, before she had even had time to sit down. 'You are getting married next month. We have found you a suitable match.'

Dipali was stunned. She had not even begun to think about marriage. She had been formulating hazy plans about going to college, like the rest of her friends, and studying further. She had been looking forward to working, maybe as a professor. She was silent, absorbing her mother's words. Part of her mind protested. Marriage seemed like a sudden jolt into adulthood, one that she wasn't ready for.

And yet, with the way she had been brought up, her parents' word was law. There was no question of protesting. 'At that age, I never knew I could question anything and accepted that if she was telling me to get married, I would get married.' She caught the way her mother glanced anxiously at her father, who was drooping on the sofa, barely able to sit up. She could feel that there was more to her mother's words than she was letting on. She agreed.

The school principal was very concerned about the sudden marriage. 'I will come and speak to your parents,' she said. Dipali looked at her, half hopeful, half resigned. She knew that once her parents had made a decision, they were very unlikely to change their minds. True to her word, the principal called on Dipali's mother.

'I'm worried about the decision you have taken regarding Dipali,' she said. 'Dipali shows a lot of promise and could really achieve something. Don't you think she is too young to be married off?'

Dipali's mother looked at her steadily and said, 'Whatever promise she has can be achieved even after her marriage. Look at me. I was a double MA in maths, but after marriage I was a housewife for several years until a family emergency made me take over my husband's responsibilities. And I have managed it successfully, without any training. I am sure that Dipali can achieve her potential even after marriage. But right now, for my husband's sake, she has to get married.'

Embracing Change

Soon after her marriage, Dipali's sister died of renal failure. Then, her father succumbed to his illness—another huge tragedy for the family.

One of the things that Dipali remembers is how many people came up to the family at her father's funeral and remembered him for the help he had given them. This cemented Dipali's desire to be involved in philanthropy, something that she would take up later in full measure.

Dipali moved to Mumbai with her husband after marriage. She realized that BK Goenka's family and hers were quite different culturally, although they both belonged to the Marwari community. He was from Haryana and a first-generation entrepreneur, while Dipali's family were Rajputs and 'to the manor born'. '*Tumhare yahan toh chor ko bhi chorsa bolte hai*,' her husband joked. She appreciated his drive, his ability to get things done quickly and his strength in taking risks. She came from a more leisurely background, where every decision was carefully thought through and debated, perhaps for months. She was also much softer spoken, while he could be quite brusque when it came to getting things done.

But the two of them were very young—he was just 21 when they got married—and they found a sense of partnership together. Dipali was in charge of the home, while he worked on getting his business up and running. At that stage, with everything BK was trying to do, Dipali saw it as her job to keep the home front humming smoothly. While her schoolmates were still attending college, Dipali was learning to manage a household. As she says, her university is life itself.

The couple lived by themselves, which was another big change for Dipali, who came from a joint family that had 15 people at every meal. She didn't know how to cook, so she learnt everything from scratch. After years of being waited on hand and foot by an army of servants and cooks, Dipali had to manage things on a limited budget. It was hard going at first. She felt out of her depth at the many things she was expected to know and manage on her own. She missed her friends, her family and the comfort of her maternal home. She felt lonely and at a loss sometimes. But Dipali knew that if she ever picked up the phone and complained to her mother, she would not listen. She would just tell her to adjust and leave her to find her own way. She had to fight her own battles and learn to keep going even through the tough times.

In 1991, BK Goenka started a textile plant. A year later, he made a trip to Europe to buy equipment. Dipali was immensely excited and wanted to go along—they hadn't been abroad together.

'Now you can see how close to our hearts Welspun is. I have seen BK through his struggles to build it. Those were very different times. We didn't see money until 2003—after almost 15 years. The first trip to the UK and the USA were business trips. My husband told me that he couldn't afford to buy me anything and that I had to satisfy myself with window shopping only. People won't believe it now, but we have spent such days.'

Growing Up and Looking For Meaning

Within a couple of years of marriage, Dipali had two young daughters to look after. Her mother-in-law passed away soon after she had her first daughter. After the birth of her second daughter, she decided to get into fitness in a big way—a habit that has stayed with her. A few years later, with an earnest wish to become a college graduate, she started a degree in psychology. Her days began as early as 4:30 a.m., so that she could fit in exercise, cook for the day, see the kids off to school and attend to household chores before she could sit down with her books. It was a taxing time since she had a household and children to manage, alongside her studies. But determined to do well, she stuck to her rigorous schedule and came out with flying colours.

In many ways, she grew up with her daughters. She loved spending time with her girls. Praying together became a big part of her life after her marriage, as BK believed in pujas and regular worship. But it wasn't enough. She had a larger sense of purpose and a drive that needed expression. Dipali wasn't a very social person and didn't like the idea of attending parties with the same people day after day. She was keen to use her mind. She wanted to push herself and do more, and be more than a housewife.

While she was eager to know what was going on with her maternal family and their business, she was not given the opportunity to be involved. In the community, once she was married, she couldn't be involved in much to do with her birth family. 'It's all my brother. This again comes from the tradition that once you are married you can't be part of anything this [her mothers'] side.'

As time went by, she faced immense pressure from her in-laws to have another child. After all, she had only had two daughters. 'Where is the son who will inherit the business?' she was asked.

'I had two daughters, and, in Marwari society, they always want a boy.'

She looked around for an opportunity to do something meaningful, especially goaded by her desire to provide her daughters with an example of what women could do and what they could achieve. That was when she discussed her desire to work with BK, and he agreed to let her come to the office. However, there was a strict demarcation of roles—she still had to look after the household and their daughters. Moreover, he gave her a mandate, insisting, 'If you want to come and work, you are not my wife here. Work like an employee.'

Stepping Up

Dipali knew that she had to prove herself not only to the other employees who thought she had it easy, but also to her husband. There was no spare office space at the Welspun office so Dipali worked from the factory in Andheri. There was no suitable room for an office space, so she took what she could get, working in a corner of the ramshackle godown (a warehouse) or sitting in a room that had seepage on the walls.

Dipali anticipated adverse reactions from the other employees but was prepared to deal with it. She didn't expect to win over everyone on day one and had the wisdom to understand that it would take time and interaction to overcome this hurdle. She ensured that she spent dedicated time on the shop floor every week. This hands-on approach not only allowed her to cultivate essential skills like time management and decision-making, but also reinforced the value of collaborative efforts within the organization.

Later, as she moved up the ladder, she consistently maintained an open-door policy, encouraging a culture that valued dialogue and feedback. Always open to the thoughts and ideas of the team, she was good at accepting feedback. She took a tailored approach when dealing with team reactions, recognizing everyone's uniqueness. This approach not only dispelled any preconceived notions but also created an environment of curiosity and openness.

Her daughters took her turning into a career woman very differently. The older one was proud of her and thought it was very cool. The younger one felt she was being neglected and didn't get enough time with her mother. But Dipali knew that what she was doing was paving a path for them as much as for herself.

Her days were hectic, since she was essentially working two jobs— managing the home and the children alongside full-time employment. Sometimes it seemed like she was always rushing from one thing to the other. She was the first employee in office every morning, reaching before 8 a.m., so she could put in a full day's work before rushing home by 5 p.m. to help the kids with their homework. The thought of letting go of one set of expectations to take on another never occurred to her; she wanted to excel at both.

'I could never go to the PTAs. The school started around 7:45 a.m. I used to leave home at 6:45 a.m.'

While she was busy working, her father-in-law, who was staying with them, was diagnosed with cancer. Dipali was horrified and wanted to spend all her time tending to him. But he was very proud of his daughter-in-law and encouraged her to work. Even when he was hospitalized, he insisted that Dipali should go to work rather than sit by his side.

She began by understanding how to use the computer—she had never used one before. She took on any job she could get her hands on, including working with the new design studio they were setting up. During our calls, she enthusiastically talked about her desire to grow. She was hungry to learn quickly, and absorb everything she needed to know. Then, she spent a lot of time visiting distributors and observing consumers on the shop floors in different cities to understand what they were looking for. She observed something that had not struck the men around her who had been in the industry for decades. She noticed that the majority of shoppers were women. They were the ones who made choices about the material, colours and designs they wanted in their homes. Yet, the entire industry was male-driven—from manufacturing to merchandising to marketing. It appalled her that men were calling the shots in an essentially female-driven industry, and she vowed to change it.

She came up with the idea of launching Spaces, a premium brand of home linen. She saw that customers were starting to invest more in the aesthetics of their home and were willing to invest in items like bedsheets and comforters. It wasn't easy to head a new brand and launch it from scratch while continuing to run her home seamlessly. In a chairman's meeting, BK rebuked her publicly, 'If you think this is a hobby, you don't have to be here.'

With both of them involved in Welspun, the office conversation often carried over into the home.

'It has been really tough for me and it has been from my end more. I have tried to keep the balance. I think our obsession with Welspun doesn't end, and so I keep it in a box while he is still trying to do so. Even on our anniversary, he would ask—what are your numbers, what are the sales trends?' she says ruefully. Dipali started to find it overwhelming, because she wanted the home environment to be a place where she could relax, but now it felt like she was always on call. It started affecting their personal relationship, as she felt that she was always speaking to her boss, be it at home or in the office. She finally had a talk with BK, explaining that being continuously engaged with office work was not productive for them, neither as business owners nor as a couple. They needed to be able to relate and spend time as a family. She got her way and they both agreed to leave office talk at the office.

Her husband's cousin, RRM, was her mentor at the company. At the end of the year, he sat down with her for a performance review—the first time she had been through the process. He gave her feedback that she felt was harsh. Dipali was very upset. She took it as a personal failure and felt that she had let everyone down. For days, she struggled to be her natural, buoyant self as the words spoken during her performance appraisal kept echoing in her ears. Then, one day, when she was at work, she caught herself doing what RRM had highlighted in her review—taking on too much and not being able to prioritize tasks. She realized that the feedback was actually logical and given in the spirit of helping her to do her best work.

'Earlier, I used to feel very let down and bad. But I am not God. It is okay. If you run a business, failures are part of the business. I don't mind harsh feedback anymore. RRM always feels I can do better and that's tough, but his feedback is very logical, motivating and constructive.'

While Dipali initially started working because she felt that she had to prove a point to others, she started enjoying the work and seeing the results of her ideas and the impact she was making. She saw that she had a knack for spotting gaps in the market and executing ideas that tapped the opportunity. Her self-belief began to grow. She realized that she was the most excited or thrilled when she herself felt that she had done a great job, without waiting for anyone else's praise. Over time, she learnt that while feedback was meant to help her improve, the one whose respect she was really fighting for was her own.

Rolling Up Her Sleeves

By and by, Dipali wanted to work at the main company, Welspun, which was the lifeblood of the group. Spaces was a smaller offshoot, and she was eager to plunge into the manufacturing heart of the company. It was at this point that she decided to pursue the OPM Program at Harvard University. There, she was surprised to notice that out of 120 course-mates, only 10 were women. Gender imbalance didn't just exist in India, it was the same across the world, she noted.

In 2008, she moved to Welspun. It was made very clear to her that even though she was keen on joining Welspun—her family-owned business—absolutely nothing other than her entry into the company would be handed to her on a platter. It was time to start from the ground floor all over again. At the same time, she faced a lot of flak from the outside world about her decisions at Welspun. 'When I went into Welspun, it was tough. People started asking whether Welspun was serious about the business because I didn't know anything. I had just come on board and some internal people were wondering whether Welspun was serious about textiles as they were flourishing in the pipe business. There was talk about closing the textile business. Somebody called up RRM, asking, "Why are you doing this? Why did you get BK's wife who doesn't know anything?"'

Undaunted, she put her endless desire to learn to good use and quickly learnt the ropes. She believed in the dictum that you have to ask questions if you want to get anywhere. 'If you ask a foolish question, you are a fool once, but if you don't ask that question you are a fool always.' Slowly but surely, she became the face of the brand, the one that customers turned to and the one who spoke to the media. 'I received feedback and developed myself. I went 10 steps beyond and that was the only way it could be done. Customer centricity was everything for me. Even if the customer called me at midnight, I would call back just as quickly. And all customers recognized me for this.'

In 2016 came one of the biggest crises the group had faced. On a hot, muggy August day, Dipali walked into the gleaming glass and steel office in downtown Mumbai, a far cry from the ramshackle factory in which the company had begun, back from a business trip to New York. She was looking forward to an easy couple of days. There was a letter from Target—a leading US departmental store—on her pristine office desk. Surprised, she opened it to find a bombshell. The bed linen they had supplied wasn't the 95 per cent Egyptian cotton it was supposed to be. Target was threatening to cut off their decades-long relationship with Welspun and go public with the problem. Not only that, Target was offering a refund to all its customers. She quickly opened her email to find a similar message from Walmart, another major buyer.

Dipali was horrified. She wondered how this could have happened on her watch. She spent frantic hours conferring with her team. By the end of the day, she had a plan of action ready. She flew back to the US on a whirlwind trip, criss-crossing the country. Working 18-hour days, she met each and every one of her buyers. She promised each of them a complete refund as well as an investigation into the matter so that it didn't happen again. Meanwhile, the stock had fallen by 47 per cent in four days. The family's net worth had tanked by $600 million!

By the end of her week-long visit, the buyers had been pacified and had all agreed to continue their contracts. Once she was back, the company employed the global accounting firm Ernst & Young to review their sourcing strategy and identify the problem. In a bold move, they owned up to a mistake in their purchasing strategy (which was standard industry practice) and announced that they would tighten their purchasing norms.

'The world came crashing down. It was great learning for me. I learnt as a leader. For me, putting the whole company at risk scared me. I told the customers everything and I promised I would go back in a month, and I did go back in a month.' Every month, Dipali flew from Mumbai to the US, meeting all her customers and telling them what progress had been made to fix the problem. This gave them confidence that Welspun would stand by its commitment and eventually lead to immense loyalty.

After the immediate solution was implemented, the company turned to blockchain technology to ensure this would never recur. The final products Welspun sells comes at the end of a long supply chain with several producers involved at different stages.

Welspun developed a specialized platform using blockchain technology that helped everyone, from retailers to farmers to manufacturers to suppliers, traders, certifying bodies and end consumers—to track raw materials throughout the supply chain, from their origin to the end product. A customer or an end consumer can trace whether the materials used by Welspun are created by producers who follow ESG metrics such as water usage, fair pay, power consumption and gender equality, among others. All the manufacturing processes are captured in real-time using a scanning system, to enhance efficiency and accountability.

Blockchain systems make the information in the system resistant to tampering or alteration, ensuring its integrity and immutability. This creates trust and transparency and is a signal that Welspun bets on its authenticity and stands by its commitment to ESG principles. Acknowledging and then fixing the mistake made Dipali's relationship with her customers stronger than before.

Empowering Women, Empowering the World

Dipali has given her daughters a slightly different upbringing compared to the way she was brought up. There is a focus on individuality rather than family orientation. Unlike her own mother, her daughters know that while she encourages them to work things out on their own, she is always there for them to fall back upon. She wants to ensure that her daughters never feel isolated when they have a problem. When her daughters got married, Dipali told both her sons-in-law and her daughters to create a sense of partnership in what men and women do together.

Another challenge she advocates for women to surpass is that of maternal guilt. Dipali believes that women need to start working at their jobs and living their lives so as to be sources of inspiration to their children. She feels this is a must for daughters who will one day grow up to join work undaunted, and for sons who will eventually be pillars of strength and support to the women around them.

Dipali feels that businesses can be agents of change, and that inclusive growth should be embraced by all. When Dipali joined Welspun, only 7 per cent of their workforce were women. Today, the company has achieved a remarkable milestone of having 24 per cent women employees, which is uncommon in the male-dominated manufacturing industry.

While she acknowledges the privilege she has been afforded, she is of the firm opinion that believing in and respecting yourself is of prime importance. In the spirit of this belief, the Welspun group announced its 'Women of Welspun' (WoW) initiative to provide an environment of growth and opportunity for its female employees. Launched in

2021, this initiative aims at driving a culture of equal opportunity across designations in the organization and reducing the gender gap. The WoW community support network serves as a platform for the women in the Welspun workforce to share their experiences, inspire each other and receive mentorship from senior members of the team, thereby helping shape the next generation of women leaders.

Welspun undertakes an upskilling program, WoW Conscious Women Program, for women employees in assistant manager to senior general manager grade roles and actively recruits more women from business schools, with a career plan to groom them for middle management roles. In addition, as part of its Corporate Social Responsibility initiatives, Welspun sponsors women athletes from disadvantaged backgrounds to find the right training.

'We have come a long way since then, but the goal for me, as I continue taking this program forward, will remain the same—higher representation of women in the organization, an environment that supports their growth in reaching their desired roles and ensuring the holistic well-being of every woman,' Dipali says.

Dipali believes that we should leave the world better than how we found it and has already taken many measures to make Welspun a more sustainable venture, from looking into hydroponic farming of cotton to planning to obtain 100 per cent organic cotton by 2030. Today, she increasingly focusses on her philanthropic activities as well.

She invests time in the running of various Welspun initiatives, some of which empower rural women by establishing sustainable farming and non-farm-based livelihood opportunities, or enhancing preventive and curative health for adolescent girls, women and the broader community. Fostering agricultural sustainability, digitizing schools, empowering the next generation of learners and their teachers, nurturing green initiatives in local communities and road-safety initiatives are some of the causes she espouses with a focus on creating real impact at the grassroots level.

'Being called the "CEO with a soul" is my greatest award, and I hope it inspires others to prioritize not just employee well-being, but the betterment of communities. I genuinely believe in the transformative power of our actions to bring about a positive change in society. I am of the belief that it is not just a duty, but rather a way of life, creating a positive ripple effect across diverse aspects of society.'

Hacks to Storm the Norm

Norm: Those born with a silver spoon can never understand the values of struggle and hard work.

They are perceived as being free from life's toughest challenges and 'having it all'. But being raised in affluence brings a unique set of pressures and hidden mine traps. The silver-spoon generation is under immense pressure and constant scrutiny, which leads to them being more deserving of respect, as they have bigger shoes to fill, more people waiting for them to fail and more expectations from them. And when such people come and join family businesses in privileged positions, sceptics perceive them as individuals who have failed at all their attempts at outside projects. They enter the business to take the throne and give orders without understanding the fundamentals of the business.

Hacks:

1. Shed the tyranny of legacy and shape your own destiny
Many of us have found ourselves in situations where we believe it's necessary to dance around the existing expectations and norms to be on the side of legacy. While there is comfort in retaining the status quo, it may be possible for conflict-avoidant behaviour to spill over into other aspects of a person's life and lead to a lack of self-confidence as well as challenges with self-esteem. It is therefore important to be assertive, start slow and set realistic expectations.

2. Set realistic expectations and start slow and low
In business families, there is the pressure to perform well. In the family company, there are the family members who are judging your capabilities and competency and are quick to write you off at your first mistake, while the non-family member may have been given a

second chance. Therefore, it is important to not start with a position of responsibility but earn your way up the ladder. Develop an assertive communication style that will likely lead to positive changes in your life, but the process of learning and implementing it will likely take time. It can be important to be patient and allow yourself to start small.

3. Be wise and smart

We have found that the next generation are street smart, even if not necessarily academically smart, and this takes some getting used to. While their academic performance may not be ranked amongst the highest, they usually make up in their holistic approach and common-sense approach which is typical of entrepreneurs. We often find them able to calculate mentally what would make others reach out for calculators or spreadsheets. This could be due to their exposure to business concepts from a very young age.

EKTA
Never Give Up

Introduction

Ekta Bhyan was born and brought up in Hisar, Haryana. She became quadriplegic after a road accident when she was 18. Since then, she has gone on to become a para athlete, representing India in the women's club and discus throw events. She won medals in the IPC Grand Prix in 2016, 2017 and 2018, a gold medal at the 2018 Asian Para Games and competed in the Tokyo 2020 Paralympics.

Having won the 2016, 2017 and 2018 National Para Athletics Championships, Ekta received the National Award for Empowerment of Persons with Disabilities in 2018 and the State Award of Haryana, 2019. She works with the Haryana state government as an employment officer.

Why Ekta?

Girls in India grow up under various social biases surrounding the way they are supposed to be. An old saying (that is hopefully going out of use) is that daughters are a burden on the family until they are married off. In addition, we tend to consider people with physical or mental handicaps as burdens, doomed to be dependent on their families and unable to fend for themselves in any meaningful way. They and their families become objects of pity.

Ekta Bhyan, a quadriplegic, confounded both sets of norms, not only qualifying for a career in the civil services, but also becoming an internationally-renowned athlete who was tipped to be a winner at the Tokyo Paralympics. How did a girl born and brought up in a small town in Haryana, a state with a gender ratio of just 879 women for every 1,000 men, aspire to such heights, that too with severe paralysis? How did this 'underdog'—as society regarded her—slay the Goliath of social, physical and self-imposed limitations?

Ekta Bhyan

It is every athlete's dream to be chosen to represent their country. Once that happens, the athlete waits eagerly for the chance to hold the national flag on the podium and hear the national anthem playing. It's a moment to cherish and one that very few get to experience. For someone who was never sporty growing up, paralysed from the neck down and written off by many as a burden to her family, it was an unbelievable moment.

Ekta Bhyan began life in a joint family in Hisar, living with her parents, two siblings, grandparents and several aunts and uncles. Her grandfather had moved to the city from his village in search of a better life for his children. Her father, the eldest son, worked in the Haryana Government's horticulture service. As was common in many joint families, he bore the responsibility of ensuring all his siblings were well-educated. He had similar aspirations for his own children, regardless of gender—he wanted his daughters and son to study further and have careers of their own. Her mother, who is a matric pass, is a homemaker. She was keen that her son should have a good career but also wished the same for her daughters. This is a significant trend that goes against patriarchal norms. Girls are neither encouraged to pursue higher education nor are they expected to aspire to a professional career. This broad-minded upbringing by her parents went on to shape Ekta's vision of her future.

The joint family often played host to relatives visiting from far-off towns and villages to access better medical care in Hisar. Accompanying them to and from medical centres, Ekta saw that those doctors not only had flourishing careers but also received tremendous respect and love from society. She observed their capacity to change people's lives. The extended family and their friends had great expectations from

Ekta. Intelligent and hardworking, she loved biology as a subject at school. She and her friends often discussed their career ambitions with each other. Encouraged by her grandparents, she dreamt of becoming a doctor from a young age.

When Life Has Other Plans

However, an accident of fate changed her dreams. When she was 18, Ekta enrolled in a coaching class for medical entrance exams. Gaily waving goodbye to her mother, she had set off in a car with six classmates for her first session. It was a long journey to Delhi. While the driver manoeuvered the car through crowded streets choked with trucks parked everywhere, the girls read their notes. The car tyre developed a puncture, and they came to a halt by the side of the road at the busy Kundli border between Delhi and Sonipat. The driver busied himself trying to fix the spare in place. The girls were impatient, looking anxiously at their watches; they didn't want to be late to their first class. And then, the world went black. An overloaded vegetable truck that was approaching from behind lost its balance and fell onto the parked car and its occupants!

Ekta was semiconscious. She was first taken to a clinic in the neighbourhood and then by ambulance to a hospital in Delhi. She didn't know the extent of her injuries but since she wasn't in too much pain, she assumed it was something like a fracture that could be easily healed over time. She retained her wits and was able to share her home landline number with the people around her.

It took her family almost three-four hours to reach the hospital. Her father hovered into her field of vision. She said hello, her voice a hoarse croak that was barely audible. Her father's eyes were moist. Had he been crying? She told him about the accident and asked about her injuries. He said the doctors were still working on it. Ekta's eyes widened. She didn't understand what this meant. 'Papa…my friends?' she asked hesitantly. He told her that they are also getting treated. It was only many days later that she would learn that five of them died on the spot. Ekta was lucky to have survived.

The government hospital to which she had been taken refused to operate upon her. They didn't have the facilities or know-how to treat her. She had suffered very serious and severe injuries to her spine. She couldn't move her arms and legs at all. Ekta struggled to make sense of this. In her mind, she could see her body responding to what she wanted it to do. But in reality, she couldn't make her arms or legs move even the slightest bit. She felt enraged and helpless at what had happened and often lay awake at night, flashing back with horror to the accident, wondering when she was going to be able to get back to life as usual.

Her father and his friends ran around with her records to hospitals in different cities, looking for doctors who would agree to treat her. Finally, her father approached the Indian Spinal Injuries Centre in Delhi, a hospital set up by Major Hari Pal Singh Ahluwalia, who himself had suffered a similar injury. Ekta was admitted there. Since it was a private hospital, the medical expenses meant that her father had to take a loan.

Time Slipping Away

Ekta was worried about the cost but hopeful, looking forward to resuming normal life. She assumed that with better care it wouldn't be too long before she was back at home, preparing for her exams.

At this point, she was unable to move below her neck. She needed someone to help her bathe, to brush her teeth, lift a spoon to her mouth and turn over in bed. She had no control over her bladder and bowels, which was humiliating. When they sat her up in bed, unless she was firmly propped into place, her body would slump over helplessly. To her, it felt like watching someone else's body.

It was equally difficult for her parents and family to not just watch her struggle but to help her perform each activity. It took a psychological and physical toll on them, since they needed to support her passive body to sit or help her lie down again. They had to be careful to do it with the right posture to prevent injuries to themselves. They needed to find extra time during their day to attend to each and every need of hers since she was unable to do anything for herself.

Her focus was on trying to get better and back on her feet as quickly as possible. She went through a series of spinal surgeries and the nurses, doctors and physiotherapists put her through a range of treatments. She had to be active for physio exercises and learn to sit, eat and perform various other tasks all over again.

Days turned into weeks, weeks into months. Nine months later, Ekta hadn't even begun walking. Ekta fretted about losing time.

'Mama, when will I get out of the hospital?' she moaned. 'I have so much preparation to do for my entrance exams. So much time has got wasted. *Itna time waste ho raha hai yahan.*'

One day, the doctors approached her parents and suggested that it was time Ekta went back home. She was shocked.

'Why should I go home before my treatment is complete?' she questioned. The team of doctors who had been treating her advised that, given the high cost of hospital stay, it would be better for her parents to take her home and get a local physiotherapist to work with her. She knew what to do and could keep improving at home. They had done as much as they could. Ekta still did not understand that she would not be able to move her limbs anymore; part of her mind refused to accept this. She was living in denial, assuming that if she kept exercising and getting the care she needed, she would be able to resume her previous life.

At home, things were very different compared to how they were earlier. From being the cynosure of all eyes, she had become an object of pity. Visitors ignored her even when she was in the room and spoke to her parents, asking how she was and whether there was any improvement. When she visited relatives, they asked her mother what Ekta would like to eat or drink, as if she was incapable of speaking for herself. The people at the salon would ask her mother what style of haircut to give her.

The equipment required for her, including the wheelchair, was very expensive and burdened the family finances. Her father ran through all his savings and was forced to borrow money from relatives to provide the basic facilities Ekta needed. In addition, most public spaces were not built for the mobility-challenged; going anywhere posed such a huge challenge that she preferred to stay at home, where she could avoid the curious or pitying gazes of passers-by. From being someone who thought she was going to be an achiever to becoming someone stuck inside the four walls of her home was a huge change. Ekta struggled with her emotions, going from rage to depression. 'Why me?' she wondered. She often rewound the moment of the accident and re-imagined the situation differently; that the truck never fell over or that the car didn't develop a puncture and completed the journey smoothly. It was difficult not to lapse into self-pity. But her parents remained very positive in front of her, regardless of how they were feeling. They encouraged her to be optimistic and tried to keep her cheerful. When she felt low, she talked to her parents and her friends about her mood and they helped her shift to a more positive frame of mind. In a way it helped that the doctors had not told Ekta she would never walk again, giving her a shred of hope.

Dreaming On

Ekta refused to let go of the hope that someday she would surprise everyone by making a full recovery. In her mind, she played a scene where she sprang up with a flourish from the wheelchair that kept her tied down. But she realized that regaining a range of motion could take a long time. Becoming a doctor was no longer an option. It would put too much physical strain on her body, and she would not be able to cope.

She wondered what kind of future she could aspire to. Her parents were optimistic by nature and didn't let her give in to self-pity at any stage.

'*Toh kya hua agar doctor nahin ban paayi?* You are bright. You can study something else instead,' her mother urged. They encouraged her to complete her bachelor's degree. Many people, including some family members, ridiculed the idea insensitively. What was the need to study further when she could not do anything with her education, they asked.

'People said, "*ek toh ladki upar se handicapped.*" Or "*Padhai kar bhi legi toh kya kar payegi.*" (Not only is she a girl but she is handicapped as well! What will she achieve even if she completes her education?) When I resumed my studies, it was considered a waste of time as the perception was that I wouldn't get a job. People used to say, "*Padhai se time pass ho jayega.*" (She can study to pass the time.)'

Ekta and her parents ignored them. She decided to take up English literature. Having an agenda for the next few years helped her to not focus exclusively on her disabilities and gave her something positive to look forward to.

'I decided to do a basic degree (bachelor's) first, without making career plans for the future. But gradually, I developed an interest and found solace in books. I was sure that I had to be financially independent and studies were the only medium to attain this.'

At an age when girls are conscious of their looks, it was a difficult adjustment for Ekta to be the girl in the wheelchair. From being an active young girl, she now needed a caretaker all the time. Just setting foot outside the home took a lot of courage, as she had not gone out for over a year. Luckily, her college principal and teachers were highly supportive. Her parents accompanied her to college as she needed two people to help her from the car to the wheelchair and vice versa. Her father dropped her off to college before going to the office and took a short break to help get her back home again. An understanding boss helped facilitate his unorthodox breaks. Her mother adjusted the household chores so she could make time for this additional activity. Her parents ended up having to run a balancing act between Ekta's needs and those of her siblings, and was at times, it was a struggle to give each of them equal attention. Her siblings were steadfast rocks through all of this, maturely understanding her situation and ensuring they stood firmly by her side, whether she needed physical help or emotional support. In addition, the extended family were all based in Hisar and the whole family came together whenever Ekta needed help.

Her classmates reacted to her in different ways. Some were curious about why she was in a wheelchair and asked her many questions. Some were dismissive or uncomfortable and ignored her presence. One day, bustling down the college corridor, a girl tripped over Ekta's wheelchair but failed to recognize Ekta as her high school classmate. Many others were friendly and helpful. Since Ekta couldn't do anything independently, they shared their class notes with her, helped her eat and learnt to wheel her along to the library safely without bumping her. She hung out with them on the lawns, and they all mimicked their teachers, giggling helplessly. One of them became her best friend.

Ekta worked harder than most others in many ways. She had to learn a new way to study and retain information. Most people use a combination of reading, making their own notes, attempting practice papers, making mental maps, etc., to retain all the information they have studied. But many of these activities were no longer possible for Ekta. She grew tired if she sat for too long. She was unable to hold up a book and read it or underline her notes, so someone else had to hold up the book and underline the passages for her. She couldn't visit the library or study from reference books that were kept there on her own. When she got access to a reference book, she couldn't turn the pages by herself. She was unable to write, so taking practice tests was a herculean task. It took a huge amount of determination and tenacity to keep at it.

But at the end of the first year, Ekta found that she had topped some subjects in college and her scores put her among the toppers in her class. That helped her regain some of her confidence. She was no longer just the girl in the wheelchair, but the girl who was among the toppers despite being the girl in the wheelchair. She had always loved studying and academics, and academics had not let her down. Her teachers were very impressed. They had always encouraged her but when they found that she was such a good student, they became even more supportive. Her classmates also appreciated her courage, her hard work and, most of all, her intelligence.

A Ray of Hope

Ekta enjoyed her years in college and felt a sense of purpose return to her. As time passed, she realized she hadn't recovered any movement. Slowly, she understood and came to terms with the fact that her immobility was going to be a lifelong condition. But she still wanted to make something of herself and find a purpose in life. Moreover, she did not want to be a burden on her parents and aspired to be financially independent—a learning she has imbibed from her mother since childhood.

She began going through government job ads in newspapers and applying for whichever ones seemed suitable. She entered many competitive exams for government jobs, but failed to qualify—sometimes by as little as one or two marks. Simultaneously, she pursued a graduate degree in psychology. At last, one day, her efforts were rewarded—she qualified to become an auditor in the Food and Supplies department of the government. She was thrilled that at last she could be financially independent. Her parents and the rest of her family felt proud at how far she had come.

Her new office was on the fourth floor of a government building. Her father dropped and picked her up from the workplace. On the first day, as her father wheeled her into the lift and pushed the button for the fourth floor, other people in the lift spoke over her head to her father, asking who she was and why such a young girl was in a wheelchair. They were taken aback by his answer that she had come to join her new job. Initially, her colleagues were befuddled by the prospect of working with someone who was paraplegic. They were not sure if she would be able to handle the requirements of the job. They approached her a little nervously, treating her with kid gloves. Some asked her hesitantly about her disability. But Ekta put them at ease, chatting and joking with them and asking penetrating questions about her work. Over time, they got used to the wheelchair. They learnt how to adjust to her disabilities without overcompensating or treating her as less capable.

Soon, Ekta came to understand the details of her job and started enjoying the work and earning her own money. Yet a voice inside kept whispering to her that she was meant to do more, to achieve more. She decided to apply for the Haryana civil Civil Services Exam. Again, there was no shortage of disbelievers who felt that she had already done far more than could be expected of someone with such severe disabilities, and that there was no need to keep going after more. But her family and close friends believed that she had every right to try and achieve her dreams. So while she continued to work as an auditor, she prepared for the Civil Services Exam. Even her colleagues helped her prepare, filling out forms, quizzing her or writing down answers that she dictated to practice test papers. They became her cheerleaders and encouraged her to do her best.

Incredibly, she passed the preliminary exams in her very first attempt. That gave her additional motivation and confidence that she could do it. Hard work had never scared her. She pushed herself even harder, determined to succeed. Finally, in 2013, she got through the Haryana Civil Services entrance process. It was a great day—the entire family celebrated her win. No one else in the family or friends' circle had even aspired to such a job, let alone qualified. Ekta became an inspiration for everyone she knew.

She joined work as an Assistant Employment Officer with the Haryana government in Hisar. Her story was written about in the local newspapers as well, and this would play a key part in what happened next. Amit Kumar Saroha, a quadriplegic Arjuna Award winner from Haryana, read about her. He contacted her to ask if she would be interested in taking up parasports. Ekta was curious—she had always been more studious than sporty growing up. She didn't have any idea that one could play parasports, especially with such severe disabilities.

Training Time

They began her training with simple exercises designed to strengthen her muscles. The first few days, she found it difficult. With her extreme paralysis, she had not done any physical activity in years. But as she started exercising attentively, she felt a new kind of satisfaction in her growing physical capability. This was something she had not experienced before. Moreover, being out in the open air with the fresh breeze gave her a different feeling of freedom.

There were no parasports facilities at Hisar. Not only that but there was no gym on the ground floor, nor a lift to help Ekta get to the first or second floor location. Every day, Ekta worked on her fitness at home, after her workday ended. On Fridays, she travelled for an hour and a half to Sonipat for her sports training. Her parents travelled with her every week, and the family stayed at her maternal uncle's home until Monday morning.

Coach Saroha introduced her to the club throw, the only parasport she could pursue. The first time she picked up a club, she didn't even know how to hold it. But she was a quick learner and soon began competing at discus and club throw events. Participating in a club throw was not easy for someone who was quadriplegic. She couldn't hold the clubs as she had zero finger movement or grip, and it was the same with wrists and triceps. She needed a special glue to be put into her hand, which helped the club stick to it, and then had to jerk her body so the club was released, without falling out of her wheelchair.

Ekta says, 'We work on a technique. It is the speed and angle at which we have to give a jerk so that it is released at the right time and right angle.' It took a huge mental and physical effort. She had special gloves from the United Kingdom to grip the pole with her left hand while throwing the club. In addition, four belts were used to secure her to the wheelchair, so she could maintain her balance while throwing, since she didn't have abdominal strength.

Laughing, she says, 'Sometimes I ended up hitting my own head with the club, if it is not released on time. Sometimes I hit the person who is assisting me. While I am doing my practice sessions, I make sure my team is far away from me so they don't get hurt.' She narrates an incident in which someone had kept their mobile phone far from her on the field. In a stroke of bad luck, the club landed precisely on the mobile phone and smashed it to pieces!

A Whole New World

In 2016, she participated in her first national parasports event. She was very nervous about it since she had begun learning the club throw just that year. But her coach insisted that she participate, giving her confidence. 'What's the worst that can happen—you won't win? That's okay, it's your first competition, what is important is that you do your best.' Just before the event, Ekta visualized herself stepping into the arena and doing the very best that she could. To her great surprise and delight, she won the gold medal!

Her coach told her she had qualified for the Athletics Grand Prix to be held in Germany. This was the first time Ekta would be travelling abroad. Both her parents would have to travel with her, in order to make it possible for her to deal with everything on a day-to-day basis. Ekta would have to pay for three tickets, not just one. She thanked her good luck that she had a job with the civil service.

As an athlete, Ekta had to buy special equipment to help her stay fit to participate. The nutritional needs of an international athlete meant special food. Apart from that, her wheelchair was also quite pricey. Ekta felt lucky that she could afford to pay for all of this, since she had a job. But it also made her conscious of how much there was to be done for the disabled in India.

Most public places are not planned with them in mind, making it very difficult for them to access these spaces. Equipment like wheelchairs are very expensive so most of them, being from poor backgrounds, can't afford it. Most of all, the prevailing attitude is that disabled people are dependent on others and will always be so. Most of them are not encouraged to study further or to aspire to a career, or to have any ambitions for themselves at all. At each stage, Ekta herself has faced this from various people, even though they were well meaning. She feels she has had to struggle to make people see her as a person first and a disabled person later.

She went on to win a silver medal in Berlin at the Athletics Grand Prix, and in 2017, she qualified for the World Para Athletics Championships in London. Her breakthrough year was 2018, when she won the gold medal at the Asian Para Games in the women's club throw event; and in 2019, she took part in the World Para Athletics Championships, where she earned a place on the team for the Tokyo 2020 Paralympics.

Before the Tokyo 2020 Paralympics, Ekta stepped up her preparations. By now, she had reached the status of World No. 5. In paralympic sports, each participant has a slightly different level of injury and motion, so there are many different categories. Ekta was in the quadriplegic, i.e., most seriously injured and least mobile group.

Fight, Failure and Faith

But then the pandemic began, along with the lockdown, preventing people from travelling. Given her condition, Ekta was among the category of those with highest risk because people with a cervical spinal cord injury have impaired respiratory systems. The breathing capacity of the lungs is severely compromised already. So she could no longer go to Sonipat for her throw sessions. She took the decision to bring all her training equipment home.

She set up the gym, and the therabands, and focussed mainly on fitness strengthening exercises.

'One thing was clear in my mind—that whether the Tokyo Games are happening or not, I will stick to my timetable, train six days a week and take care of my nutrition and mental health. No matter what, I will not give up.'

Though she was in touch with her coach, they could not meet because of the high risk to both. Every day, her family helped her exercise and videotaped her while she was doing so. In the afternoon, she sent the videos to her coach and they connected on the phone to discuss what she did right, and what could have gone better. During the pandemic, she rediscovered her love for writing and began penning down poems and started drawing.

After training for over four years, the day of the competition finally dawned. Ekta was very excited—she had psyched herself up for this day for so long. As she got ready, she did her visualization exercise, as she always did before every competition. She imagined her every move, from emerging into the arena on her wheelchair to turning round and round, to the moment she let go of the club, to seeing it land as far away as she could see, to the roar of tumultuous applause. Her coach wished her the best of luck—they both knew she could not be better prepared.

As Ekta emerged into the arena, she looked up. There were no spectators because of the Covid risk. She knew she would miss responding to the crowd. The sky was cloudy and grey. Drops of rain fell on her upturned face. The chilly breeze ruffled her hair and sent a stray strand flying into her eyes. She felt a pang of unease. So far, she had trained in dry conditions, be it cold weather or hot. How would the glue behave in humid, rainy weather?

Ekta brought all her focus to bear on the challenge at hand. Her attendant handed her the club. But it slipped out of her grasp. The attendant tried again. And again. Each time, the club slid out of Ekta's hand. The glue was not sticking because her hand was wet and slick with the rain.

Ekta and her attendant exchanged panicked glances. What to do? Then Ekta suggested adding a little powder to make her hands dry. This time the glue stuck and the club stayed in Ekta's hand. Ekta gathered her resources and turned, releasing the club with a powerful jerk of her body. She almost fell out of her wheelchair but managed to keep her balance. But her grip had become compromised because of the rain. She knew she would not place. After years of hard work, she ended up not being able to win a medal.

Ekta felt crushed with disappointment. She had dreamt of winning the Olympic medal for years. But the same grit that had helped her overcome all obstacles so far, made her feel all the more determined to keep competing and keep winning. She decided to set her next goal for the Paris Paralympics.

'Life is not in your hands, but living is,' she signs off.

Hacks to Storm the Norm

Norm: People with disabilities are burdens on their family and society and will always be dependent.

Life in India is difficult for people with disabilities, especially if they are from middle or lower income families. Neither our public spaces nor our private ones are designed to be inclusive, and most of the equipment or changes required to be made to the living environment are expensive. In addition, if one has acquired the disability later in life, it can be very challenging to get used to a new way of living, with a much more pronounced dependence on others. But while you can't go back to living life the way you did earlier, there are ways to make it as friction-free and productive as possible.

Hacks:

1. Set SMART goals

Rather than focussing on what you can't do, find out what you can do. Do your research, learn as much as you can about your condition and figure out what you can realistically aspire to. Then set goals for yourself—small, achievable ones that give you hope and the confidence to keep pushing ahead. Be patient and consistent and keep charting your path forward.

2. Be giving

'You may have had to accept help from friends and family as you cope with your disability. See what you can do as a form of gratitude. It can be something as small as sending a card or flowers, or being a listening ear to them, or helping them with some things you excel at. Try to find a cause to be passionate about and volunteer your time and effort. There are many ways to get involved even from home, and being passionate about a purpose will give you a great reason to wake up every morning.'

3. You are enough

You are not your disability. While your activities might be restricted by it, your personality, your values, your sense of humour, your warmth, your wit and your intelligence—these are the things that make you the unique person you are. List your strengths, especially those in the workplace. This is the value you add, these are the unique things you bring to the table that no one else does in the same way. Remember this when you ebb.

KIRTHIGA
Make the Most of Everything

Introduction

Kirthiga Reddy is the co-founder and CEO of Virtualness, a venture-backed high-growth start-up that's at the intersection of generative AI and blockchain, enabling monetization and fan engagement for creators, brands, sports, media and entertainment. Her personal goal is to change the stat of there being only 4 per cent women founders in blockchain technology.

Kirthiga is a woman of many firsts: she was the first employee of Facebook India, and their managing director for over six years, where she built a business that's now worth over $2 billion in annual revenue; the first female investment partner at SoftBank Investment Advisers (SBIA) and manager of the $100B+ SoftBank Vision Fund, leading a portfolio of over $5B; part of the first all-female, all-immigrant SPAC (Special Purpose Acquisition Company) management team to ring the NYSE bell in her role as president, Athena Technology II; and the first South Asian to chair the Standford Business School management board, and more.

She holds an MBA from Stanford University, where she graduated as an Arjay Miller Scholar (top 10 per cent of the class), an MSc in computer engineering from Syracuse University and a BE in computer science and engineering from Marathwada University, India, where she was a university rank holder, ranking second overall. She has been on *Fortune* India's list of most powerful women, *Fast Company's* list of most creative people in business, Stanford University's notable alumni and Syracuse University's notable alumni, among other recognitions.

Kirthiga lives in California with her husband and two daughters, and is passionate about educating the girl child, diversity, mental health advocacy, tech for good and entrepreneurship.

Why Kirthiga?

Women in STEM is a topic that has gained resonance worldwide. With the growing 'bro culture' actively discouraging women from entering and building careers in Silicon Valley, Kirthiga's track record is all the more remarkable.

As Facebook's first employee in India, Kirthiga cut a wide swath. Often featured in the media during her tenure, she was clearly extremely intelligent, accomplished and seemed to have the world by its tail. Then came the controversial Free Basics fiasco, followed by her move back to the US, and it seemed like the two were linked.

How do women, even the most shrewd and capable ones, forget to be their own advocates and brand owners? Why do they so often fall into the trap of believing that their work speaks for itself and doesn't need any further spotlight? And do women really see each other as rivals at work, or can they form supportive networks?

What Would You Do if You Weren't Afraid?

Kirthiga hugged her down jacket tighter as she walked across the tree-lined Stanford campus. It was December and the cold breeze characteristic of North California was making her shiver. Looking around at the groups of fellow students huddled around the courtyard in animated discussions, she suddenly felt out of sync with them. She didn't know whether to laugh or cry at the surprise life had thrown her way. She had just begun her MBA at Stanford Business School, trading a high-paying job to reinvent her career. But with incredible timing, a quarter through her degree, she had just found out that she was pregnant! Kirthiga and her husband had postponed starting a family for several years since they were busy with their careers. By the time they were ready, they realized it wasn't as easy to conceive and had eventually turned to IVF. This pregnancy was a much-awaited one.

Kirthiga's mind was already racing ahead to everything she had planned for the next year. Among the elective courses she had signed up for was the sought after 'Strategy and Action in the Information Processing Industry', taught by Professor Robert Burgelman and Professor Andy Grove, former CEO, Intel. This was a marquee course she knew she wanted to take even before she applied for her MBA. But it was so demanding that if a student skipped more than two classes, they were forced to drop out.

She would now have a new-born baby on her hands in the same semester as the course.

'How will I cope with this?' she wondered. 'Will I really be able to manage both a new baby and my MBA at the same time? How about the pregnancy itself? What if that doesn't go smoothly?' She spent a few sleepless nights mulling over her options. This or that? That or this? After racking her brain furiously, as always, she turned to the superpower of the 'AND'.

'When things are presented as this or that choices—and certainly there are times when one must make a choice—more often than not, some creative thinking allows for an AND solution.' That was because access to education was not something Kirthiga took lightly. Not only because she had been raised to value the power of education, but also because her homemaker mother had been denied the opportunity to study.

'Before she finished her high-school education, my mother's parents decided that she knew enough math to do the grocery and laundry bills so did not need to study any further. Her brother, on the other hand, went on to get a master's degree. While my paternal grandfather encouraged her to continue her education after marriage, mom conceived during her first year, and getting an education remained an unfulfilled dream.'

Her mother had always regretted not being able to study. She wanted to make sure her daughter didn't miss out on it as well. She got on a plane—her first solo plane journey ever—and travelled across the world to be there for Kirthiga's delivery. She stayed on for six months just so Kirthiga could complete her MBA.

Kirthiga's first daughter was born on 23 September. Kirthiga missed exactly two classes in her elective and went back to her MBA course two weeks later, bucking the Indian social norm that new mothers should not step out of the house for 60 days post-delivery. And the elective she had fought hard to be allowed to take proved worth the fight; she applies the learnings from it even today. Moreover, Professor Burgelman was so impressed with her that he said she had paved the path for him to be open to having pregnant women sign up for his course in the future. It wasn't easy, but with the support of her family, Kirthiga graduated in the top 10 per cent of her class. 'We partied more after my daughter was born than before! She would be up late anyway, so we'd go out with her. She had 365 aunts and uncles—all my classmates,' Kirthiga says with a grin.

God of War

Kirthiga's father grew up in a lower middle-class family, with few resources. The house was spartan—the bathroom was a pit with no running water, and food was cooked on wood stoves, until his kids were teenagers. It was a day for celebration when they finally got a gas stove. It was a typical joint family, where the sons, their spouses and children would live together with the parents, eventually taking care of the entire household.

Her father had opposed more than one tradition in his lifetime. When he decided to relocate from Chennai to Mumbai for better career opportunities, it was seen as a family betrayal. His father was so upset that he threw the cooking utensils out of the house and said, 'Take them. Take them and leave.' Years later, when he and his wife conceived their second child, the entire family was convinced it was going to be a boy this time and had picked out the name 'Karthik', after the popular South Indian deity, Kartikeya. When the child turned out to be another girl, his parents refused to go to the hospital to see the baby. Kirthiga's mother wept in grief because the family had rejected the baby. Kirthiga's father consoled her, saying, 'If we have a third child, I want her also to be a girl.' The baby's name went from 'Karthik' to 'Kirthiga' in a flash!

Making the Most of It

A cost accountant with a steel manufacturing company, Kirthiga's father loved being transferred to new places. The family led a peripatetic existence, and Kirthiga and her sister studied at many different schools across India, learning new regional languages— Marathi, when they moved to Maharashtra, and Kannada, when they moved to Karnataka. Deeply involved with the kids' upbringing, their father would iron their school uniforms and tie their shoelaces, while their mother took care of the home and kitchen. The kids were expected to roll with things, learn to adjust and make new friends wherever they went. Kirthiga was a carefree younger child who loved reading, academics and playing with her friends.

By the time Kirthiga completed her schooling, the family was based in Nanded, Maharashtra. She did not meet the domicile requirements for entry into the well-known or highly-ranked government colleges. She ended up attending a private engineering college which was so new that even the classrooms were yet to be built! Disappointed at not having the option to attend the higher-ranked colleges, she went moaning to her father. He gave her what would become her go-to mantra, 'Life is about what you make of the opportunity. You could go to the highest-ranked school and do nothing with it. Or you could make the most of the opportunity in front of you.'

Kirthiga opted for computer science since it was rumoured to be the next big thing. She found the small, close-knit community and the personal attention of the new college highly conducive to learning. At the end of her course, she was surprised to find that she stood second not just in the college but also at the university level. In fact, she had beaten students from all the colleges she had been ineligible to apply to! That was when she recognized the value of what her father had said.

On completing her degree, her only career goal was to get a

job—any job. She approached a well-known professor who ran a programming training institute. When she went to the interview, she was surprised to see the office space—a tiny room with barely any furniture—that looked like it hadn't seen a fresh coat of paint in years. She figured that the outfit was very small and was not doing very well, so she quoted a measly monthly compensation of ₹1,500.

To her shock, barely a month after she began working there, the institute shifted to their new office space, which had been under construction when she had interviewed. The new office was swish and swanky, leaving Kirthiga shaking her head at the life lesson she had learnt: never judge by appearances!

Stanford and the Baby

A year later, she wanted to apply to the US for her master's degree. Her father beamed and said, 'This is a matter of pride for the family. You will be the first in the family to go abroad for graduate study.' Her mother beamed and said, 'Get married and do whatever you want.'

A matrimonial ad the family spotted in the newspaper led them to a US-based engineer who was looking for a wife. Kirthiga was allowed to go to a single dinner with the potential groom, Dev, with his sister as the chaperone, before she had to make a decision. Four days after they met, Kirthiga and Dev were engaged and a year later, they got married. Fortuitously, it was the best career and life decision she made. He turned out not only to be a companion and soulmate but also someone who championed her ambitions.

When it came to her marriage, for the first time, Kirthiga found her father giving in to the traditional patriarchal norms. Perhaps he was afraid that Kirthiga was raised with so much freedom that she might unknowingly raise hackles. During her engagement, her father cautioned, 'Don't be too gregarious.' Kirthiga instantly worried that this feedback came from her in-laws. He also told her, 'Whatever you do, never hurt a man's ego.'

Later, Kirthiga overheard her mother-in-law asking Dev, 'How much does Kirthiga earn? I can't tolerate her making more than you.'

This question was par for the course for a traditional South Asian family. As Kirthiga froze in the background, Dev said, 'Do you know what I want? I want her to be so successful that I can retire and spend time with the kids.' Kirthiga grinned to herself—she had found the perfect match! It takes a man with a lot of confidence to have this conversation, that too with his mother.

Kirthiga applied for a master's degree so she could study right after she got to the US. Her father hesitantly took out a loan of ₹4 lakh, wondering if it would be worth it. Meanwhile, with advice from her then fiancé, Kirthiga managed to get a research assistantship that paid enough to cover her education.

When she landed in Syracuse, Dev came to pick her up from the airport. His last semester at Syracuse overlapped with her first. As they drove down the highway, Kirthiga got her first surprise. 'Why can't I see any people walking along the roads?' Coming from India, where there were few expressways at the time, and where people, cows, bikes, scooters, buses, cars and trucks all share the same road, she found it puzzling to see the roads so empty! Within a few weeks of her arrival, she also experienced something she had only read about or seen in the movies—snow. A massive snowstorm hit, with eight inches of snow in an hour. It struck her as magical and exciting, and she ran out to catch the fleeting snowflakes with her fingers, enjoying the dizzying whirl of the snow around her. Over time, though, the novelty of snow palled under the drudgery of sweeping it from the driveway and struggling into multiple layers of clothing for a simple grocery run.

When Dev graduated and relocated to Silicon Valley to find a job a few months later, it suddenly hit Kirthiga that she was more than 3,000 miles away from her family and friends. She felt alone in a strange new world that she hadn't quite mastered yet. She immersed herself in her academics with even more focus as a way to cope. As she made new friends, the loneliness subsided.

After she completed her degree, she began working for Silicon Graphics—among the hottest companies of its time. She received some instrumental advice from her first manager at Silicon Graphics, who told her, 'Kirthiga, focus on the success of the customers, the organization and your team. Your success is a by-product.' Kirthiga took the advice to heart. Job descriptions became largely irrelevant as she realized her job was really about doing whatever it took to make these three constituents successful. She shared that it also gave her the conviction and moral compass to advocate tirelessly for change when it was needed. 'Many times, people think they have done their part by raising issues. However, that's only part of the process. Change never comes easily, and it is so important to continue to advocate for needle-moving changes—and to do so respectfully.' Within six short years, she rose to the position of director.

In this new role, Kirthiga needed to contribute more to company strategy. She began to enjoy that aspect of her job and thought of pursuing an MBA to hone her business skills further. She wanted more training in marketing, finance and building a sustainable organization. She dithered between a part-time executive MBA, which allowed her to keep working, or a full-time one, which would mean giving up her job, the career progress she had made so far and her sizable income. Her husband encouraged her to go for it, saying, 'I can tell you really want to do the MBA. Get the full experience of a two-year full-time MBA. Two years is nothing in a professional career of many decades.'

Rule of 'AND' Again

One of the prompts for the Stanford Business School admissions essay was, 'What matters most to you and why?' After much introspection, Kirthiga's answer was, 'To live life fully and help others live life fully. To make the most of my potential and help others make the most of their potential.' That was one of the factors that shaped her career decisions.

Post Stanford, Kirthiga was deliberating a career move to a product role in a small start-up rather than a business role in a large, established firm. It was an unusual move and Kirthiga wondered whether it would impact her career negatively. Although the norm is that women find it harder to ask for help, Kirthiga decided she needed expert advice. She reached out to Jana Rich, then a partner at an international recruitment firm, Korn Ferry International, to think through the decision. Though it involved a 40 per cent pay cut from her previous salary and an individual contributor role, she opted for the start-up, as she felt she would learn more and grow faster.

'I look for three things in whatever I do. Firstly, a big bold vision. Secondly, people from whom I can learn every day. Thirdly, my skills and talent should uniquely be a game changer.' Within four years, the company was acquired by Motorola for half a billion dollars. If if one looked at her LinkedIn, they would see 'Director of Engineering' at Silicon Graphics and then 'Director of Product Management' at Motorola. It is important to remember that careers are often non-linear. Kirthiga has leaned into non-traditional routes and they have given her the best opportunities to learn and grow.

By the time she had her second daughter—also an IVF baby—Kirthiga had moved on to a role that involved frequent travel. For Kirthiga, as she did with her older daughter, it was important that she breastfeed the baby for a year. It was a personal choice—one that she acknowledges may not be the right choice for everyone—and encourages everyone to make their own choice. She wondered how she would be able to keep that commitment, with her days on the road. The 'AND' solution came to her rescue again. She decided to travel with the baby and schedule meetings around her feeding schedule. The universe conspired to make it easier—for instance, when she travelled to North Carolina, she found that her colleague's wife ran a day care where she could safely leave her baby, go to work and come back to nurse.

She also asked for a room at the office so she could pump milk for her baby. The firm converted an office room for her. It was right next to the CEO's office, and the loud pump noises were mortifyingly audible in his room! Instances like this made her aware of the real barriers that existed for women and made her determined to do her bit to bring down the barriers.

A few years later, Kirthiga and her husband moved back to India. She started a role with US-based Phoenix Technologies, while Dev worked on an entrepreneurial venture. As they experienced the rise of the Internet, Kirthiga was introduced to Sheryl Sandberg, the then COO of Facebook, through a business-school classmate. She expressed her excitement about helping lead Facebook's growth in India and they stayed in touch. A year later, Facebook announced its intention to open its operations office in India. A lengthy interview process later, she became the first employee that Facebook India hired.

The Facebook Journey

When Kirthiga joined Facebook India, it was an exciting chance to grow the company's footprint in the world's second-fastest growing economy. Kirthiga set up one of Facebook's four Global Operations Centres—and the first in Asia—in Hyderabad. Eventually the Operations Centres would go on to serve over three billion Facebook users worldwide. At Facebook India, Kirthiga brainstormed with the leadership team and they set themselves the '100-100-100' goal. Like most multi national companies, Facebook was organized by functions. While the operations and sales departments reported directly to Kirthiga, the different functions: growth, HR, policies, etc., reported directly to their regional or global counterparts. The '100-100-100' goal brought the different functions together behind a common vision. This meant 100 million people on Facebook, $100 million made in revenue and they wanted to impact 100 million people through community efforts. At the time, there were only eight million people on the Internet from India.

'It was a four-year target and we had no idea how we would reach that.' But the sheer audacity of that goal inspired the entire team to come together, achieving the goal more or less within a quarter of the set time frame.

'My favourite Facebook India story is when the founder of a large Indian fast-food chain walked up to me and said that many of her cooks did not know how to read or write but they knew how to use their phone, and they knew how to use Facebook. That is how they kept connected.'

One of the lessons she learnt on the job was to focus on company culture. When Facebook's head office executives first came to India, she was very excited with the business results the team had achieved. She began the interaction by showing them a PowerPoint presentation that listed the numbers. But she was taken aback by their reaction. 'No, no, you are getting ahead of yourself. I want to know how you are building the right people and the right culture. If you do both of those, business results will come. Focus on that first.'

Kirthiga took the feedback to heart and focussed on understanding Facebook's culture more deeply. She learnt that it was a reflection of Facebook's five values, 'Be Open. Be Bold. Build Social Value. Move Fast. Focus on Impact.' She delved into each of these and partnered with Human Resources and the head of leadership and development to invest in and build the right culture. Among the most important decisions she took to achieve this was a commitment to interview the first hundred hires across all levels—which meant a lot of work!

Learning from Failures

Kirthiga believes in the adage that failure is the First Attempt In Learning—an opportunity to reflect and grow.

Shortly after having her second child, she ran into a roadblock in her career. She had returned to work within six weeks of having the baby and was working hard towards a promotion. She found her performance rating that cycle to be surprisingly mediocre.

'I feel the impact I make isn't being fully appreciated. Am I really only mediocre? What is the point of working so hard and missing out on family if this is the rating I get?' she railed to Dev.

They both decided that it was time for a break. She decided to avail herself of paid family leave to bond with the newborn. In the first few weeks, Kirthiga loved the slower pace of life. She enjoyed being around for her new baby's every waking moment, puttering around the house, and picking up her older daughter from play school. She liked not having to be on the move every moment of the day.

That break also gave her some much-needed perspective. She

reflected on how much she loved her job and how deeply committed she was to the organization. It was time to show that she had what it took to rise to the next level. She had an honest conversation with her manager. Instead of questioning his commitment to mentoring and coaching her for the next level, she went in with the assumption that this was the case and made it explicit.

'I love this company, and I really love my job,' she said. 'I am coming back with the belief that you will invest in me and guide me to the next level.' The two of them jointly set measurable goals for the next six months. At the end of the time period, Kirthiga knew she had clinched the promotion.

A few years later, when she was with Facebook India, she was asked to move from Hyderabad to Mumbai to lead their business growth. She thought she had a strong succession plan for the operations centre. However, the plan she put in motion did not have the approval of the key stakeholders involved. As a result, the team was disgruntled, there was a huge disruption in operations and there was a loss of momentum for the centre. One of the lessons she took away from that was to ensure buy-in from all key stakeholders for critical business decisions.

A few years later, with her daughters in middle school and starting to think about college, Kirthiga wanted to relocate back to the US. This was something she and Dev had always planned, as they wanted their kids to attend college in the US. Since she was a prominent face for the company in India, the communications team wanted to carefully craft the announcement of her departure.

Around this time, the Facebook HQ team from California started lobbying for Free Basics, an initiative to provide free Internet in developing countries, including India. Free Basics would provide a stripped-down version of the Internet, with Facebook at its heart, to Internet-dark markets, thus growing its footprint in these areas. The initiative came up against fierce resistance from the intelligentsia. The company received widespread public backlash.

Meanwhile, the official announcement of Kirthiga's relocation plans kept getting postponed. Eventually, she got the green light to announce it the day after Free Basics was banned in India. Due to the unfortunate timing, the media assumed that her exit was due to the Free Basics debacle and widely publicized it as such despite Facebook's later clarification.

Kirthiga felt irritated. She had achieved so much in India, had had a brilliant six years, and now her reputation was linked to a crisis she hadn't even been involved in. She had a key epiphany: the responsibility for her reputation rested only with her. Nobody else would ever care as much. It was up to her to safeguard it.

A corollary lesson came over time; one can never take away the real impact and the sense of accomplishment. There is a simple principle: clear eyes, full heart, can't lose—if you have put in your best and created impact, and you know in your heart what you have achieved, no one else can take that away from you.

Work-Life Balance

Like many working women, Kirthiga struggled to balance her expectations for herself across her multiple roles. A close family member would regularly send her articles about how children need time—more than money—from their parents. He would make it seem as though she was making a choice between her children and money, treating her career as a vanity project. He didn't understand that the choice was much deeper—about independence, self-worth and impact—not at the cost of children but along with the children.

In her book *Lean In*, Sheryl Sandburg talks about how guilt management is just as important as time management. This specific social cultural belief was hard to tackle and internalize. For example, her team had once planned an outing to watch the movie *The Dark Knight* as a celebration for achieving a milestone. She felt torn. One part of her felt that she should celebrate with her team. At the same time, another part said she had been working round the clock and was not only tired but also longed to be home with her children. She kept going back and forth between both options, feeling guilty about letting down either set of people in her own head. She kept debating which one she should choose with her husband. Dev finally told Kirthiga, 'Whichever way you decide, you should be completely present. One night isn't going to define what you contribute, either at work or as a mom!'

Another time, she felt guilty that she wasn't involved enough in what her kids were doing at school. She kept wondering if she was doing right by her daughters. Every day, she would come home late, tired from a long day at work. She felt uneasy that she hadn't looked at their schoolwork and wanted them to show her what they had been studying. The kids would be winding down for the day and would resent having to dig out their schoolwork again. After a while, she took the time to stop and reflect—either she needed to do something different and act on that guilt or stop feeling guilty about it. She discussed it with Dev, 'Am I not giving them enough time? I'm never around to help them with their homework...' Dev said, 'I look after their schoolwork and help them whenever they need it. Do you really think it would be helpful for them to have two parents pushing them? Instead, find something else to do with them that might be fun for all of you.'

Kirthiga took the advice to heart. She concluded that the kids were on top of their academics. Dev was very involved and helped them where needed. Having both parents involved might feel overbearing. She started creating a continuing story about the adventures of two sisters and their dog, which became a cherished bedtime routine. As the kids grew up, she and her daughters would spend 40 hours a year doing community service together, something that was soul-satisfying for them all.

When she moved back to the US, Kirthiga carved out a new niche for herself at Facebook, focussing on emerging markets. But, by now, Facebook had become a very large entity. She missed the start-up ecosystem and could no longer feel the direct impact of her work. At a conference she attended, they spoke about how 95 per cent of one's face time with a child is already over by the time they go to college. That hit Kirthiga hard—her older daughter would be ready to join college in two years! She decided that she needed more time with her daughters and quit Facebook, planning to chill out for a few months.

It wasn't an easy decision. Kirthiga had built deep roots and friendships within the company. Tears rolled down her cheeks as she wrote out her resignation letter. But she knew this was something she just had to do for herself. Her friends and family members were aghast. Conventional wisdom held that your chances of landing a job are better if you start looking while you're still employed. Her well-wishers were convinced she would lose her negotiating leverage if she took unstructured time off. However, Kirthiga was adamant.

'I don't want to plunge into something else without thinking it through. And I don't want to look back at this time and wonder why I didn't spend more of it with my daughter. If I were to look back and regret that I was missing out on a career high then I am sure I would regret it more if I saw that I was not spending time with my kids,' she said firmly.

During her break, she ended up doing a second trek to the Everest base camp with her daughter, among other things. A year later, while dropping her daughter off to college, she received the best award of all.

'What about my parenting? What would you want to emulate and what would you avoid like hell?' she asked her daughter. Her daughter thought about it for a moment and said, 'I want to emulate how you always put us first.'

Lobbying for Equality

Upturning the belief that women are each other's worst enemies at work, Kirthiga found many women who helped her along her journey. Her first manager at Silicon Graphics helped her grow from individual contributor to team lead, and advocated for Kirthiga to be the one to take her place when she left. When Kirthiga was contemplating different career paths after her MBA, it was a female mentor that Kirthiga reached out to for direction. Later, while setting up Facebook's India operations, she learnt a lot from her female peers who were doing similar roles in other geographies.

Over the course of her career, Kirthiga felt the impact of gender not just as an individual, but also as a manager. Once, when she put up two deserving candidates for promotion, she found that the organization and stakeholders easily promoted the male candidate but held off the female candidate's promotion. Kirthiga was furious. Unconscious biases run deep. Women are promotoed based on performance, while men are promoted based on potential. The female leader was eventually promoted a year later; but the impact of such cumulative delays was a huge disservice to female executives, and needs to be tackled consciously.

When hiring, she always advocated for the long game. Archana Vadala joined Facebook India as the head of staffing when she was expecting her first child. During the hiring process, in many companies, the question would be, 'How would we meet the intense business demand for hiring if our head of staffing leaves for maternity leave within the year?" However, Kirthiga viewed it very differently. 'At my end, I was just so grateful that Archana was ready to embrace the Facebook India opportunity at a time when she was doing so well in her career at another Internet giant. She could have easily said, "I am having a baby. This is not the time to make a job transition."'

Sure enough, Archana whipped things into place in the first few months of joining and had processes and leadership plans in place to tide them beautifully through her maternity leave. She went on to have a career spanning more than 10 years and was promoted to lead staffing for Facebook APAC, being one of the senior-most leaders in the region.

Kirthiga is very glad they didn't let a six-month leave hamper judgement, and applauds the glorious impact Archana has had. 'She set the path for other women in similar situations to make the jump. We were also proud of bringing on board women who were returning after several years of break for parenting.'

Kirthiga also attended regular informal gatherings of women leaders committed to each other's professional and personal growth. She went on to participate in organizations like All Raise, which was committed to increasing the number of women investors, and Neythri, for South Asian Women.

At the same time, Kirthiga felt that men, as much as women, get defined by the social stereotypes around their roles. When her family moved to Mumbai, she found that the school parents' group consisted only of the mothers. She lobbied to add the dads to it as well, and many dads were thrilled to be involved.

After she left Facebook, she joined SoftBank as their first female investment partner. People would ask why she would join a firm which didn't have an existing track record of supporting female investment partners. But Kirthiga thought this was a great way to get back to the start-up ecosystem,

> ### Kirthiga's Success Hacks
>
> - One, the partner you choose is the most important career decision.
> - Second, there is no right time to have a child, everytime is the right time.
> - Three, think of the superpower of the 'and' versus the tyranny of 'or'.

something she enjoyed immensely, and create an impact. Moreover, if someone didn't take the first crack at the glass ceiling, how would it ever shatter?

While at SoftBank, Kirthiga faced her share of gender discrimination from the companies they were investing in. Once, a company CEO came in for a meeting, and was introduced to Kirthiga and a male colleague as the principal decision-makers on the deal. Much to her annoyance, he kept addressing all his questions and responses to her male colleague. Kirthiga had long ago decided that she would speak up for herself.

'So I raised my voice and said that it is probably an unconscious bias but you have to remember that you have two decision-makers on deck.'

She also realized how the system was biased against lending to or funding women. As a Harvard study showed, venture capitalists asked male entrepreneurs different questions than the ones they asked women entrepreneurs.

'For the men, they would ask what their plans were for the future and how they planned to grow, but for the females it was "what are you going to do about the tension?'" Kirthiga was the executive sponsor for Emerge Accelerator, which backs brilliant companies founded by under-represented founders. She was also the executive sponsor for Connect and Lead, an event to bring together rising leaders across portfolio companies. She invested deeply in the internal team, helping champion affinity groups for women, LGBTQIA+, parent groups and more. 'I am as proud of the work I did on the DEIB side as I am about my work on the investing side, deploying $1 billion across nine investments in fast-evolving sectors,' she says.

Future Plans

One of the thoughts that keeps her up at night is the desire to help create and scale sustainable businesses. That comes from observing the first company she worked for go belly up. Silicon Graphics was a $2 billion company with 9,000 employees. 'Our clients told us that no one could do the work that we did. Our products were used in the making of *Jurassic Park*, in the landing on Mars and the Human Genome Project. However, by the time I left, I had started witnessing the beginning of that decay. A decade later, the company went bankrupt. It was an important lesson that you could have the best technology and the best minds, but that alone cannot develop long-term sustainable businesses.' She believes that, 'When businesses succeed, livelihoods flourish.'

She is currently co-founder and CEO of Virtualness, a mobile-first platform designed to help creators and brands navigate the complex world of the blockchain and Web3.

'Creators are the ultimate entrepreneurs. My co-founder and I have been at the heart of the Web2 ecosystem, building and onboarding creators, brands, sports, media and entertainment, and we're on our journey to do it again for Web3. People are spending more and more time in various digital worlds and have the desire for customized experiences, individual identities, expressions and personalized commerce,' she says. Kirthiga is excited to see how various physical experiences will morph into digital forms in newer ways. She views Virtualness as enabling a new economy—unlocked by generative AI and the blockchain—to deliver unique experiences and drive monetization.

In addition to driving impact with her talent, expertise and time, she also funds important causes. She has established the Kirthiga Reddy Scholarship Fund at Syracuse, her alma mater. She also co-founded Liftery, a social-impact platform reimagining the landscape for working women, from young adults to empty nesters, with the goal of enabling 10 million moms across the globe to climb higher in their careers. 'With a 39 per cent drop off mid-career, if we don't stem that, we'll never get to 50–50 at the top.' Kirthiga recently rang the NYSE closing bell on National Equality Day to highlight the cause.

Looking back on her journey, she wishes she had been more exposed to entrepreneurship as a career option! During her undergraduate education in Nanded, someone asked her if she would develop a hospital automation software for his hospital. She had the skills and knowledge to do so but was only exposed to 'service careers', with her father working for the same company for 30 years. Anything non-academic felt like a distraction.

'I have learnt to treat every opportunity with an open mind, and to give it the diligence it requires, even if it feels foreign.'

Her favourite advice to herself—she got it printed on posters when she turned 49—is:

- F*** what doesn't matter
- Embrace the hard for what matters
- Love laugh harder

Hacks to Storm the Norm

Norm: Women see each other as rivals at the workplace.

It is considered par for the course that women at the workplace can't be friends and instead see each other as rivals. This stems from a mindset of 'lack', wherein we are led to believe that there is only one seat at the table, and therefore we jostle with other women for it. While full equality at the workplace is a long way off, at most workplaces, women are not there just to fill the diversity quota, but because businesses understand the value they bring.

Hacks:

1. Many seats at the table
Remember, there are many seats at the table! If you come at it from an abundance mindset, believing that there are always jobs for those who add value, you will stop seeing anyone else as a threat.

2. Unpack your biases
Understand your own unconscious biases—it's scary but natural that everyone has imbibed these from social constructs. Realizing what your biases are will help you be more open-minded about your colleagues.

3. Unity in strength
There is always strength in numbers. A group of women working together can help create more change and equality than one woman alone. Become a friend and mentor to other women at your workplace; help create space for them and make them your allies too. See what you can accomplish together.

LAVANYA:
Breaking Stereotypes

Introduction

Lavanya Nalli leads the e-commerce, private-label and expansion efforts at the Nalli Group of companies and expanded its footprint to 40+ stores. She started her career with the Nalli Group—a $100 million national retail chain—focussing on new business development, growth opportunities and operations, and expanding its footprint from 14 to 21 stores. She holds an MBA from Harvard Business School, and has worked at McKinsey & Company and Myntra (which was acquired by Walmart-owned Flipkart). To list some of her accolades, *The Economic Times* named Lavanya among corporate India's fastest-rising women leaders and in their 40 under 40 leaders in 2020, while *Forbes* named her among 'Asia's Women to Watch' in 2016. A frequent speaker at industry events, she is an ambassador for the Government of India's innovation efforts through NITI Aayog's 'Champions of Change' programme. Lavanya is also a published author of three children's books.

Why Lavanya?

Traditional Indian business houses are typically not accustomed to having the daughters of the family enter the business. Fifth-generation family scion Lavanya Nalli made her way into the hallowed Indian saree brand's team out of sheer determination. Having gained entry, what did she do to be taken seriously in a business where the senior management had seen her in her diaper-wearing infant days? Coming in from a tech-engineering degree, how did she navigate between being coddled and infantilized to being taken seriously as a professional and manage to convince a conservative retail business to launch brand extensions?

When we spoke to Lavanya, we heard about how she didn't just face this but used it to her advantage. With a pragmatic outlook on life, she also learnt to traverse common dilemmas that women face at corporate workplaces—such as not being a part of the smoke-break decisions. All this while taking the venerable family business into the exciting era of e-commerce. How? Read her story to find out.

#original

Believe it or not, despite being from the Nalli family—who own one of India's most beloved saree brands—Lavanya did not know how to drape a saree when she entered the business! Not only that, but as a daughter of the family, no one took her ambition of working in the family business seriously. How she used that to her advantage, changed things inside this venerable brand and built their e-commerce business is a story by itself. In her words, 'I see my life journey as a series of serendipitous successes. I was lucky to have been born in the family that I was, with the platform and opportunities I've had; I never forget how much that has had a role in the life I've led so far.'

Growing Up with Stereotypes

Growing up, Lavanya lived in the ancestral home located at the top of the building that housed the flagship store in Chennai. The four-storey building was a combination of home and playground for Lavanya and her cousins. The entire extended family lived and worked in the building that had been built by her grandfather. Lavanya's childhood was spent running in and out of the store, playing cricket in the street with the many employees who were long-term retainers and being babysat by them. Dinner table conversations across generations seamlessly integrated the personal and the professional, flowing from sales and business plans to family weddings, celebrations and report cards. 'That integrated work-life harmony and the free-flow of business talk at the dinner table was something I grew up with and has been formative in me formulating my own notions of work-life integrity. I witnessed up close the work ethic and how driven and involved my grandpa—and later my dad—were while growing up.'

The family was a typical conservative South Indian one. While the boys were encouraged to study and develop their skills with the objective of handling the family business one day, the girls were expected to study just enough to find a good life partner. The ideal was for the daughters to marry into a good, well-settled family that would not 'necessitate' them to step out of the house and work. At the same time, girls and boys were brought up with egalitarian expectations of excelling in their studies and extracurricular activities like sports, music or the arts. And it went unsaid that both boys and girls would marry at an early age, within their caste and within families of a similar background. 'Most of these norms felt true back then, with one major caveat: in our family, it was less an expectation of women alone, and more an expectation on all kids. It stemmed from a very strong notion of South Indian tradition.'

Lavanya had always loved the creative arts. Nothing got her more excited than participating in debates at school, writing, drawing and acting. With a deep interest in literature, she wanted to become a journalist. However, as is quite common in Indian families even today, her family felt very strongly that she should opt for a professional degree in science. Even worse, her school teachers, too, felt the same way and convinced her family to push her towards an engineering degree. This was the first of a series of incidents that slowly dawned upon Lavanya an understanding of the pressures to conform to societal expectations.

Once everyone had convinced Lavanya to study engineering, she was driven to excel at it and wanted to go to one of the leading institutes for her course. She was keen on taking the SAT exams to study abroad. However, her mother was afraid to let her only daughter leave the family home at such a young age. Lavanya was hugely disappointed. She had been excited at the thought of going abroad to study, being challenged by the best teachers in the world and finding her own wings away from the protection of the cozy family nest. But the thought of rebelling never occurred to her. The family ethos of stoicism eventually made her reconcile to the family's wishes.

Thirsting for Acknowledgement

While she was pursuing a degree in computer engineering, she decided to intern at Nalli. Until then, no girl from the family had worked at Nalli; in fact there were only two female employees there—Lavanya and her father's secretary. Her family thought it was a quixotic decision but treated it like a hobby. They indulgently let her go ahead and intern, thinking she would get bored by the end of it. However, working on the supply chain and overseeing the roll-out of inventory-management systems and software applications, she found the consumer and retail aspects so fascinating that she decided she wanted to work in the business after her graduation.

By then, Nalli was a large operation with stores in different cities around India. But the nerve centre remained the flagship store in Chennai. On her first day at work, Lavanya was a little nervous. She wanted to be taken seriously, but many of the workers were people on whose laps she had played as a baby. There was no possibility of anonymity since everyone knew her. At the same time. Lavanya didn't want any special consideration for being the daughter of the family.

For Lavanya, there was a curious sense of non-occasion when she merely walked down a few steps from the family home and into the store. The familiar smell of incense and flowers placed at the temple in the store greeted her. But, all of a sudden, she was seeing the store with new eyes. The sheer range of merchandise around her was bewildering, and she wondered how anyone managed so much inventory across multiple stores.

Since she was only 21, Lavanya was not taken too seriously by some of the long-term employees of the business, many of whom thought she was just doing this to keep busy until she got married. She decided to use that to her benefit. Lavanya would buttonhole anyone she met and ask a stream of questions about everything she saw. She didn't care if anyone thought she was stupid; asking questions was the only way to learn. 'I was able to learn from people who had been in the business for many years and were very generous with their time and their advice. When you don't know much, you're less curtailed and more open to trying different things. That kind of energy to do something and make a mark means you will end up doing something right.'

Since Nalli was a family concern, there were neither defined career paths, nor a structured induction or training programme. This proved to be a positive as well as a negative—Lavanya could put her curiosity to good use and learnt about all aspects of the business without any boundaries. Since many employees had been there from the beginning of their careers, they had just accepted that certain things were done in a particular way. Lavanya came to the operations with a fresh set of eyes and noticed things that people around her had thought were just everyday occurrences. Coming in with no expectations placed on her, she was free to learn and make her own mistakes without judgement. In contrast, the boys in the family would not have had that freedom and would have felt the burden of expectations from an early age.

'My being left to my own devices to learn on the job and neither expected to enter the family business, nor actively discouraged, was a boon in disguise.'

At the same time, there was subtle discrimination under the guise of protection. When she wanted to go visit the weavers from whom Nalli sourced their sarees, she would be dissuaded. 'It's a seven-hour journey and there are no clean bathrooms.' These were valid concerns, yet they prevented her from getting the same training as the men around her.

She travelled across all the branches of Nalli in different cities, observing, honing and analysing what was happening. The dinner table, where her grandfather would tell stories of how he had tackled various issues, became another rich learning ground. Unlike her father and grandfather, whose acute business acumen and gut-instincts were honed from decades of business experience, Lavanya was starting afresh. She needed a more observational and data-driven approach to inform her decisions and had to adopt a measured process rooted in research. Observing consumers on the shop floor and working alongside the star personnel, she would watch with a keen eye and ask why things happened a particular way.

'For instance, I used to see how people used to buy sarees at Nalli. The older women would buy but the younger women wouldn't. So I asked the VP why they wouldn't buy it. The VP said he did not know. I wondered if I was the only curious one.' She decided to employ unconventional means to dig into the question. She asked the guard to track how many younger customers accompanied the older ones into the store and how many came in on their own. Then, she asked the sales personnel to track how many younger customers bought something for themselves.

As she analysed the patterns of behaviour, she realized that the preferences of the two age groups were different. Younger customers didn't mind coming in to the store, but the store layout catered more to older women. So, the younger women got the feeling that the brand was for their mothers rather than for them.

She discussed her findings with the operations team at the store level and brainstormed with them. She recommended launching a brand extension—an additional brand under the umbrella of Nalli. This would be a store that targeted and tapped the younger audience by being designed around their preferences. Since she had invested in research, she had the data to back her recommendations in front of the leadership team. And, by involving the operations team in the strategy, she won their respect.

Nalli Next was rolled out and went on to expand to three stores across India. It was built with a different format and layout, meant for a newer market with a different way of shopping. The merchandise sold through Nalli Next was significantly distinct from that sold at Nalli to retain the identities of the two brands. During Lavanya's tenure, the footprint of Nalli expanded from 14 to 21 stores across India.

Now, since it has been over 15 years since the original concept was created, Lavanya and the team at Nalli are revisiting the brand formats holistically. They plan to revamp the offerings and consolidate the different formats into one or two catering to different segments, relaunching the new avatar ahead of their centennial celebrations in 2028.

Alongside her work at Nalli, Lavanya continued to follow the creative pursuits that made her heart sing. She acted in theatre and wrote articles and books that were published by the children's publisher, Karadi Tales. She also continued to have a deep interest in fashion and design.

The Harvard-McKinsey-Myntra

Four years down the line, she felt that she needed a jump up the learning curve. As a traditional business, Nalli could not teach her what she wanted to learn. The business was still run based on traditional patterns and followed instinctive patterns rather than process-led thinking like modern businesses do. She decided to pursue an MBA and got admitted to Harvard Business School. By this time, her mother had seen her travel extensively for work. Moreover, Lavanya, with four years of work under her belt, was no longer the sheltered young girl fresh out of school who had never lived away from home. Her mother had become much more comfortable with the idea of Lavanya leaving home to study.

Lavanya found her time at Harvard hugely inspiring, both through the quality of teachers and teaching it exposed her to and the peer group of classmates from around the world. During her time at Harvard, she fell in love with a young Marwari boy, and the two of them decided that they wanted to get married.

For her family, this was a huge step, as hardly anyone had married outside the community. Her family was initially nervous, but Lavanya was very sure about the decision and convinced her father to meet the man before taking any decision. Once her parents met Abhay, they realized he had all the qualities that they would have desired in an ideal husband for their beloved daughter.

After their marriage, Lavanya and her husband settled down in

Chicago. Lavanya began working with the leading consulting firm, McKinsey. Chicago, an area in the midwest of the US, is known for its family values and industriousness. McKinsey grounded Lavanya in the values of teamwork and a strong work ethic, while also teaching her a highly analytical and process-led approach to work. She got a chance to travel across the US and other parts of the world, and work on a variety of business problems across different business sectors.

While Chicago could be bitingly cold in the winter, it was a fun and exciting place to live and work in. The couple had flourishing careers and were doing very well financially. But both of them had very long work hours and lots of travel for their work. They hardly got to spend any time together and barely saw each other, even over weekends. They decided to look for other opportunities in line with their passions, which would also give them more time for themselves.

Lavanya found an opening at Myntra in India, then a new start-up—neither an established corporate, nor a family business. It sounded like an exciting new opportunity. Myntra's vibrant culture and ambition attracted her. She took up the role of VP of business. Competing against Snapdeal and Amazon, workflow tended to be dynamic, with speedy decision-making and quick implementation. The team would put in 12-14 hour days, with several meetings to brainstorm and strategize.

After some time, Lavanya found that team members would often come to her and state that they had made x or y business decisions. She wondered when the decision had been taken. 'There was a habit. Some guy would stretch and say, "I will go out for a smoke." Someone else would also tag along, and like this, all the guys would head out together. By the time they were back, they would have decided, for example, to do the rush hour sales. I noticed this a few times.'

Lavanya realized that she needed to be involved in the decision-making when it happened, wherever it happened, to be an effective leader. Moreover, she knew that the discussions where they debated one solution over another were critical to the strategy.

She had a choice. She could either take it up formally as an issue or figure out a way to be part of the decision-making process. The more she thought about it, the more she realized that it was just a matter of being at the right place at the right time when crucial decisions were being made. She decided to join the smoking gang on their smoke breaks, even though she didn't smoke.

'These natural power circles start to form, and you have to adapt to them.'

Back to Family

Two years down the line, her father approached her and asked if she would like to rejoin Nalli. By this time, Lavanya's brother had also joined the family firm. Given her previous stint, she knew she would be welcomed, but she still had the task of finding a way to be useful at work and adapting to their ethos and cultural codes. She wondered what she could do that would give her an independent identity and a sphere of work that was complementary but not competing with what her brother was doing.

With her Myntra experience, she knew that the Internet was shaping up to be a big opportunity. Nalli hadn't done much on that front. It was more of a product-focussed and operationally excellent organization than a marketing-driven one. Lavanya decided to take charge of bringing Nalli up to speed by launching their e-commerce business.

All business units at Nalli have been traditionally headed by a family member, although they employ several professionals. Since the other family members didn't know much about e-commerce, they were happy to let Lavanya take the lead. The focus was more on achieving the top line and the bottom line than on measuring her performance as a female leader.

Lavanya knew she would face many challenges in making the family understand new ways of doing business. For example, in a family business, cash is king. Growth can be sacrificed, but never profitability. The typical model of e-commerce which acquires customers through discounting products and frequent sales while ignoring profitability, was something that went against the grain and business values of

Nalli. Moreover, there was no second line of leadership from which she could readily identify possible employees for her business.

However, she knew this was a big potential opportunity and that Nalli needed to do this to continue to be relevant to younger consumers who were shifting to online shopping. In her vertical, she decided to set up things her own way. This ended up being an opportunity to set up a gender inclusive division. She knew that having gender parity in the workforce automatically helped iron out male-female power equations. Through concerted efforts, she ended up building a 45 per cent female workforce across functions from shipping and packing to finance. At the same time, the company invested considerably in training the workforce so biases wouldn't crop up. Having a merit-oriented culture allowed Lavanya to be uncompromising on performance without giving in to existing gender-biases.

She faced the usual gender bias, conscious or unconscious, at times. Occasionally, business associates would comment, 'Why don't we wait for your brother or father to join us?' She wouldn't understand where such comments stemmed from and just proceeded with the meeting unfazed, saying, 'I'm here, so why don't we just close this deal right now and then we can move on.'

The e-commerce business grew significantly, doubling in sales from 2018-2021. Currently, Lavanya is slowing down their e-commerce intentionally to focus on building systems and processes to scale, and looking to bring in professional talent so that she can move out of the operational work back into the strategic building of the business. Her plan is to focus on building an internal-design unit and expansion efforts in the next two years.

Getting the Help She Needed

One of the things she realized through her career was the need for both mentors and sponsors—mentors who would help her grow and sponsors who were not only invested in her growth but who would find opportunities for her. While she actively worked to develop sponsors for herself, even at Nalli, she found that it was crucial for women to find strong sponsors. 'You have to find someone who can take you under his or her wing and basically create opportunities for you. Trust me, there would be far fewer women who move out of the workforce if that were the case. A lot of women working in family businesses as well don't necessarily get that kind of support.'

While Lavanya had never rebelled against family dictats, she also did not cave in to social expectations to be a particular type of person or lead a particular kind of life. 'I never thought much about what society expected and I never put much stock into trying to impress other folks or conform to the mainstream. As a result, I've been able to live an original life. I've always thought, 'Okay, what's the worst that can happen? Someone's going to be disappointed in you—it's not the end of the world. We all have good and bad days...'

A Work in Progress

Some of the core values Lavanya swore by—a strong work ethic, which only got stronger through her many experiences. A good sense of self-awareness that was honed further after having a child. She felt that self-awareness brought a true understanding of what was important and what was not. That was a liberating factor. Third was self-acceptance, which gave her the kindness and freedom to allow for occasional failures and the resilience to come back after a failure as well.

'You cannot take risks and say, "But, I can't fail." I'm okay with telling myself, "I'm not perfect, and there are going to be cracks in the surface, but that's alright. I'm a work in progress."'

Shortly after becoming parents, she and Abhay had to take care of their child with little to no help during the pandemic. That further honed her ability to prioritize what is truly important and forget about the expectations that society places on mothers to do and have it all.

'Something has to give in order to make room for something else that has been added to your plate. Motherhood is a huge responsibility, and if that gets added on, then you have to take a few other things off your plate. You have to be okay with making certain trade-offs. I'm going to pick and choose the areas where I'm going to be an involved parent. If there are people who judge you for that, let them. You can't please them all.'

When it came to the topic of doing or having it all, she felt it was one of the biggest cons that has been perpetuated.

'If anyone says they can do it all, please don't listen to them, and secondly, if they can do it all, more power to them, but please don't feel compelled to do that yourself. We have a finite reserve of energy, and we have to respect that. It's important to focus on things that replenish energy rather than depleting it. A work-life balance is a myth but work-life harmony can be certainly achieved by any person, male or female.'

Over the years, she came to believe firmly in self-care. While her day was split between her child, her business, family and socializing, she ensured that she made time for self-care, be it fitness or doing something she loved.

'It's important to take time out for yourself, whether that's socializing, working out, reading a book or anything that you enjoy, because that is what will bring your energy levels up.' She also loves spending as much time outdoors as possible, with family and friends. Her mantra on tough days was, 'Focus on the basics, mundane as they sound—getting enough sleep and staying fit.'

'I see my life journey as a series of serendipitous successes. Similar to driving with high-beam lights on a dark road at night, I have a goal but only plan tactically for the next two–three years and keep an open mind to opportunities that may arise out of nowhere.' Lavanya says with characteristic humility. However, she is very clear on what she wants to leave as a legacy. 'I look at it as an opportunity to make a huge impact in the world by virtue of the position that I am in, the business that I am in, the number of people we provide employment to, the number of people that we can help upskill and our positive impact on the community at large by virtue of doing business the right way.'

Hacks to Storm the Norm

Norm: Women lose out for lack of access to 'water-cooler talk'.

It often happens that not due to any nefarious intent or purposeful manipulation but just happenstance, you could end up missing out on some critical decision-making meetings or access to the right people at the right time. If you feel there is a mal-intent behind this, by all means take it up with the human resources department. Otherwise, there are other ways to handle it.

Hacks:

1. Nurture deeper relationships

Women are good at making deeper bonds as opposed to casual side talk. But it doesn't have to take a lot of effort or struggle. All you have to do is make your networking feel human by nurturing through acts of service, being interested in other people, and simply putting yourself out there for others to relate to. When you're nurturing your networks, you're initiating opportunities to connect. (And don't worry; this will be reciprocated.) You need to initiate opportunities to connect where you can reach out to prospective clients, mentors, colleagues, volunteer associates, etc. And don't think of this as a superficial connection; remember that you bring a lot to the table too.

2. Find a female mentor

Having a mentor who can guide you through the ins and outs of the industry can be invaluable. Especially if they have already 'been there, done that, got the t-shirt'. They can provide advice and support and can help you navigate challenging situations that may arise. The trickiest part is in finding the right mentor, and that begins with you being clear on what your short and long-term goals are and then listing down some people who you really look up to or admire. You may or may not be able to get one of those people to be your mentor, but it gives you clarity on what type of a mentor will be the right fit for you.

3. Be confident in your skills

Easier said than done, right? But keep in mind: you were hired for your skills and ability to do the job. It's easy to succumb to imposter syndrome when you're the only senior woman in a professional space, so create a 'WINS' folder of praise and accomplishments as a reminder of what you bring to the table to boost your confidence daily.

MALINI
Outsider on the Inside

Introduction

Malini Agarwal was among the first well-known Indian influencers, the founder and creative director of MissMalini Entertainment and the co-founder of Good Creator Co. She is also the Founder of a community for women called 'Girl Tribe' by MissMalini.

Beginning her career as a dancer, she went on to become a radio jockey, a TV show host, a programming director for Channel [v] as well as an author and content creator. She has won numerous accolades, including being named on *Fortune India's* 40 Under 40 list as one of the top business leaders to watch, on *GQ's* 50 Most Influential Young Indians list, as one of World Marketing Congress's 50 Most Influential Digital Marketing Leaders, *Cosmopolitan's* Editors' Choice Awareness Influencer of the year 2020, one of the Top 10 Young Businesswomen by CNBC-TV18 at the Young Turks Summit and the #1 Digital Influencer in the world on SERMO's Digital Influencer Index 2016. She was also a part of YourStory's 100 Digital Influencers of 2020. She topped Impact's Most Influential Women in Media, Marketing and Advertising list in 2017 and was named Global Social Media Icon at the Malaysia Social Media Week in 2019. She is currently working on her second non-fiction book.

Why Malini?

In India, most parents dream of their child being good at academics and becoming a doctor, an engineer or joining the government or private sector. However, Malini Agarwal's parents were with India's Foreign Service. As the daughter of a diplomat, Malini grew up living in different countries, including Somalia, Lebanon, Germany, Greece, Ivory Coast and Bulgaria, and attending American and international schools. With a liberal education and wide exposure to social norms outside India, her career choices differed from the conventional medicine and engineering norms. Malini's exposure to global cultures influenced her life in very interesting ways. She believes it made her more expressive, more outspoken and gave her the ability to mingle with a diverse group of people easily.

'I am very grateful for the fact that I had such an eclectic childhood. My father was a diplomat with the Indian Foreign Service and the Indian Ambassador to many of the countries I grew up in. Growing up in different countries was an extraordinary experience. I am 100 per cent sure that studying in American and international schools gives you more than just an accent! It taught me to express myself freely, adapt to and thrive in new environments and make friends from all over the world with a robust understanding and appreciation for different cultures, even as a child.'

Growing up among diverse cultures gave her both a heightened appreciation for Indian culture and a desire to help the world appreciate it.

'I distinctly remember being nine years old when a Jewish friend of mine came over to play with my Barbies, and I happened to have a *rakhi* amongst my toys. While we were playing, it came undone, and she noticed the swastika that was part of the design and tossed it on the floor in disgust. But even at such a young age, I was able to quickly explain that this was nothing like the Nazi emblem; it was part of Indian culture, and the *rakhi* was a symbol of sibling love and support. She immediately understood, and we moved on effortlessly. Later that year, someone in my class asked me innocently if I used to go to school on an elephant in India (how cool would that have been, by the way!) which made me realize that the world has a vision of India that is somewhat limited to what they see in movies or TV shows about the flora and fauna. When I returned to live in Bombay, this was one of my motivations to lend my young millennial voice to my blog so people around the world would be exposed to a more current and complete version of modern India; the one I know and love so well.'

Dancing Queen

Opting for a career in dance was an unusual choice, involving an accident of fate. Malini began by wanting to be a lawyer like her sister. Like many kids, her career dreams were shaped by what she saw on television. A fan of American legal shows like *The Paper Chase*, she wanted to become a criminal lawyer. But her family worried that it would be too dangerous, especially in India.

With her father posted to a country that did not have an international school, Malini returned to Delhi with her mother at age 17 to complete high school. After Class 12, she attended Maitreyi, an all-girls college that is part of the University of Delhi. Used to co-ed schools and a very different system of education, college came as quite a culture shock. To combat that, she decided to try out almost every form of extracurricular activity possible, so she could make friends with girls who were equally creative. Among those activities were fashion shows and dancing.

As it turned out, the choreographer that particular year immediately realized that Malini had tremendous potential and asked if Malini would like to join her dance troupe. She enthusiastically agreed, and, while pursuing her college degree, began performing at public shows with Ronica Jacob and the Planets in 1995. She simultaneously emceed at events for pocket money.

Malini's mother, a huge fan of Hindi movies, had loved recreating famous Bollywood scenes when she was a teenager, leaping from terrace to terrace as Nadia Hunterwali. So she was always very enthusiastic about Malini's love for Bollywood and encouraged her passion, whether it was helping her make Bollywood fan scrapbooks for her favourite stars as a child or driving her to dance practice after college. She loved to come and watch Malini perform. As soon as Malini set foot on stage, her mother would burst into loud applause and be ready to record the whole show on her handycam to proudly show friends and family.

Making Her Own Luck-By-Chance

Malini knew that the hub of the entertainment industry in India was Mumbai. After six years in Delhi, though she had achieved some success, she knew that she would have to move to Mumbai if she wanted to become a bigger success. It was a huge and gutsy decision. She knew almost no one in Mumbai. From everything she had heard, Mumbai was at least twice as expensive as Delhi. And she would be facing a lot more competition—almost anyone from any corner of India who wants to work in the entertainment industry eventually moves to Mumbai, doing gigs to get by until their dream job comes knocking. But she knew she had to take the plunge.

'Aged 21, I arrived in Mumbai in January 2000, armed with two suitcases, a pager, ₹40,000 in the bank and just one dream—to live a life less ordinary.'

The yellow Mumbai taxi took her from the airport to her digs. A tiny 250 sq ft. room held just a bed, a desk, a lamp, a microwave and a wardrobe, with a shared bathroom down the hall. It was a far cry from the comfortable, airy place and home-cooked food she had left behind in Delhi. But she couldn't repress the throb of excitement—she was about to chase her dreams!

Malini knew what her dream job was at this point—to become a video jockey (VJ) with MTV or Channel [v]. Armed with a portfolio that had just five photos—those too shot by a friend and not a professional photographer—she marched into the MTV office for an audition. Sadly, the talent coordinator was just polite enough to give her five minutes of her time before sending her on her way. Both the music channels at the time were dominated by professional models-turned-VJs and were unwilling to experiment with someone who didn't fit the mould. With her bank balance dwindling, Malini knew she had to find a job quickly.

As it happened, one of her friends, Nikki, had moved to Mumbai as well and was working with a well-known filmmaker who made advertisements, Prahlad Kakkar. She set up a meeting between Malini and him for career guidance. Prahlad looked at Malini crustily and asked, 'Why do you want to become a VJ? Forget about all that. What else do you do?'

Malini hesitantly held out a notebook filled with her poetry, saying, 'Well, I write.' Prahlad flicked through the poems, even as Malini flinched inwardly, and surprised her by saying, 'Well, then that's what you should do.' The next thing she knew, he was calling someone at an ad agency and saying that he was sending over a new copywriter to work for them.

Though he had squashed a dearly held ambition in a moment, something about the easy way he created another opportunity for her got her excited. New doors were opening. While she doesn't remember if she got the copywriter job, she soon became a writer for a dot-com that had just been founded. They paid a meagre salary of ₹5,000 which just about covered her rent of ₹3,500, but it was a start. Malini decided to take up the job as a stopgap, something the dot-com founders were aware of.

She was assigned to work on a concept note for a website for Mumbai's second-largest tabloid, *Mid-Day*. Every day, she would think of all the various sections it could cover, from property listings to events to movie reviews. Every evening, she'd take a thick stack of printouts to her boss, who would approve the ideas and ask her to flesh them out further. The content bible for what would go on to be called ChaloMumbai.com grew inches thick.

Meanwhile, she had not stopped hunting for a better job with better pay. She moved to a job with a website called IdeasForYou.com, where they paid a salary of ₹15,000, plus benefits. Her job here consisted of visiting a home-appliance outlet to get specifications and information from the sales reps and writing reviews. Malini found herself having to become an expert at all kinds of products, from dishwashers to washing machines.

A few weeks later, her former employer called. They wanted her back to implement the content bible she had created. With another job in hand, Malini was able to insist that they not just match her new salary but include a small raise! As project coordinator, Malini had to make the content and technical team come together to create the website. Over the next six months, she worked day and night, getting the two teams to see eye to eye and working together to bring her vision to life. She ended up stationed at the Mid-Day office most of the time and fell in love with the buzzy vibe of a live newsroom.

Funnily, one day, her then-boyfriend's mother called Malini's mother, and relayed in tones of deepening horror, 'Your daughter entertains our son at four in the morning!' Malini's ever-supportive mother didn't bat an eye, saying coolly, 'Well, we're not there. Whatever they're doing at four in the morning, they could be well be doing at 12 in the afternoon.' It's a far cry from the norm in India where most families would be horrified at hearing something like this about their daughter and instantly bring her home or get her married off.

By the time the website was up and running smoothly, Malini decided that she'd had enough of Mumbai and roughing it out the way she had been. She had been debating moving to the US where her brother lived, and studying either journalism or dance. But one last job interview beckoned.

The company she was interviewing with was called Asia Content. The interviewer, Anil Nair, who would go on to be one of Malini's favourite bosses, said, 'Look, I'll be straight with you. We're looking for someone to run the romance section on MTV India online—not just a copywriter—but you have big shoes to fill.' One of Malini's driving forces in life is love—the romantic kind. She even has a tattoo from the movie *Moulin Rouge* that says, 'The greatest thing you'll ever learn is just to love and be loved in return.' She was thrilled that her job would involve writing about romance. Her new business card said 'Channel Head—Romance & Sexuality' and her role was to fill up the section with interesting content.

They say that if you enjoy what you do, it doesn't seem like work—Malini consistently carved out her career out of the things she enjoyed doing, and loving her job made it easier to excel at it. Malini had so much fun doing this job that she taught herself Photoshop and Dreamweaver and started experimenting with the website pages during her time off, trying to see how she could make them more interesting and engaging. It's important to note that Malini was continuously eager to learn and to experiment with new things, traits that helped her go very far in her career.

Three years later, the dot-com bubble suddenly burst. The division was downsized from 14 to four people. And the four people who remained, including Malini, were marched back across the office courtyard to a different office space—coincidentally, the very office space Malini had first approached to audition as a VJ! Over time, Malini began writing promos and scripts for MTV India. By now, her desire to become a VJ had died down, but she still had a great gift of the gab.

One day, her friend at MTV told her that someone he knew was holding auditions for RJs for a new commercial radio station. Malini figured her gift of the gab could be well utilized in this medium. Always up for trying something new, the next afternoon, Malini auditioned, with six content pieces that she had written around music trivia and entertainment news. She was allotted the night shift from 9 p.m. to midnight, so she'd spend her days at MTV and her nights at WIN 94.6.

At MTV, the content was all about the video and audio coming together to create an experience for the viewer. But in radio, the power of voice and music came together to enable the listener to create their own magical experience through their imagination. Malini fell in love with the medium that enabled her listeners to create their own imagery.

Outsider on the Inside

Unlike many driven people who chart out every move in their career, Malini's career was shaped by a combination of luck-by-chance and a willingness to try new things. Luckily, some interesting new opportunity or another always turned up.

As an RJ, she was supposed to invite celebrities from the movie industry and ask them to discuss their favourite Hindi film songs. Initially, she was hesitant. What did she—an ordinary girl from

Delhi—have in common with these huge stars who were treated like demigods in Indian households?

But then she told herself that they were just people. She would just be herself and try to make a genuine connection. Slowly, she built an identity, and her natural manner put her guests at ease. Since they were used to flattery or awe, it was comforting for them to meet someone who treated them like a normal person. Over a career of 15 years, she established good contacts within an industry notoriously difficult for outsiders to break through.

'I was an outsider but I was not in a rush to become an insider. I was enjoying myself. All I needed to do was let my personality shine and that is the reason why I have those friendships and relationships today.' One of the things she took away from the experience was that while networking may be important for career progress, it's more important to become an interesting person with whom people enjoy connecting. Networking on the basis of what someone can do for you or vice versa creates only a superficial connection that remains transactional. But, as an intrinsically interesting person who had many different pursuits and could converse on a variety of topics, she would forge a deeper, richer and more genuine relationship since people would enjoy interacting with her.

'I feel I have been very emotionally driven, and as long as I am emotionally happy, I am not that stressed about my career. I was always very happy that I had a career I loved whether it was dancing or emceeing or gigs.'

Since she had such an unusual career path, she had no role models, something that worked in her favour. She could not copy anyone else and had to chart her own path. As a result of her individual thought process, she was able to carve out a new space in the industry. Rather than follow tried and tested paths, she chose to follow the beat of her own drum, and that resulted in a career path that no one had imagined until then. A few years later, she had become a well-established name in the worlds of media, marketing and advertising.

It would not be surprising for someone who enters the entertainment industry to become very conscious of their appearance.

However, Malini had an innate self-confidence that helped her keep this kind of insecurity at bay. Being comfortable with who she was and more interested in cultivating the person she was becoming, rather than how she looked, gave her an inherent ability to withstand the pressure to conform, and helped her stay balanced in an industry that can easily push people into insecurity.

Interestingly, some members of the family could not break out of traditional norms.

'There was *nani's* sister who did not like being called nani because that made her feel old, so she would make us all call her Maya Mausi. Once, she was telling me many years later, after I returned from Mumbai, "Oh Malini, now you are looking so good, *pehle kitni kaali si aur sukhri si hoti thi*" and I really don't know whether that is a compliment or not. I never felt there was any problem with being dark and skinny, and so I always felt a bit of a problem with that comment and found it funny. This habit of commenting on someone's skin colour is so ingrained in our patriarchy, and I feel good that now it is slowly changing. We have to love the skin that we are in.'

This is a valuable takeaway from her story—to tread uncharted paths rather than follow tried and trusted paths. It is very easy to get drawn into herd behaviour and follow what everyone else is doing or believes is the right thing for you to do. It is harder, but ultimately more rewarding, to develop the self-belief to follow what your own instinct tells you is right for you. As the famous poem by Robert Frost goes, 'Two roads diverged in a wood and I, I chose the one less travelled by, and that has made all the difference.'

Universe's Plan

Malini firmly believes in both; that the universe has a plan and that you can't enjoy the sweet taste of success if you have not tasted the bitterness of failure. In fact, though she has had her share of ups and downs, she doesn't regard anything as a complete failure but rather as a learning experience. Even the low phases, she believes, happen for a reason, and always end up taking one to a better place.

'I am really a believer in destiny and the idea that the universe conspires to bring what is yours to you. I am also a firm believer in learning from the things that hurt you.'

Her MTV stint was highly successful, leading to a later move to Channel [v] as a digital content head. This was back when digital content was just beginning, so Malini became one of the pioneers of digital content in the country.

In 2008, she decided to start blogging, just out of interest. It was still a relatively new phenomenon around the world, especially in India. While she did it just as a hobby, she soon spotted the business potential. Taking an enormous chance once again, she quit her well-paying job at Channel [v] to run her blog full-time. Within three years, she had a team of 47 people working with her.

In 2012, she made the gutsy move of asking for angel funding to turn her blog into a professional content platform. Gaining inspiration from international celebrity content platforms like Perez Hilton, Malini's blog contained celebrity gossip, fashion titbits, celebrity lifestyles, international trends, etc. She started the company MissMalini Entertainment with her business partner, Mike Melli. Later on, her husband also joined the team as the third co-founder. Her husband, Nowshad Rizwanullah, had already completed his undergrad at Yale and was pursuing his master's degree at Harvard Business School when she started the blog.

Three tips to build a brand that you don't get in a textbook:

• Just be yourself, no matter how quirky or weird you may think you are! That's what makes you stand out.

• Show your vulnerability. It is okay to say you have acne, period cramps and other things. Be authentic.

• Communicate, communicate, communicate. It is not just you, but the audience you are reaching out to. It is all two-way communication, and you must be a brand that speaks to your audience.

Interestingly, they had both met through an offline social network she had started in Mumbai called Friday Club. Soon, the three of them began covering industry events related to entertainment and fashion. By 2014, the website was covering a gamut of content, from TV shows and awards to their own events. When asked if two people can wear the pants in a family, Malini refutes it heatedly, saying, 'It's all about the teamwork that both partners bring in.' More practically, she says that two incomes are a necessity in these days, and that if a couple can work it out, they can win the world.

It was time to shift gears because being an entrepreneur was unlike anything she had done before. Suddenly, there were lots of people to be responsible for, not just herself. She developed a new respect for her previous employers as she realized what it took to manage so many people and care for them. Even today, she thinks of herself as someone who has 75 kids in the office.

'It is really like running a family, and I have to worry about each person, their feelings, their life journey and how they are going to cope. As an entrepreneur you can't take leave.' The pandemic made it that much harder, but it's a journey she wouldn't trade for anything else.

Good-hearted Content

While MissMalini started by covering the same type of content that the paparazzi love, Malini slowly realized that she didn't identify with it anymore. Mean gossip and rude innuendo had never appealed to her. Many of the stars were people she had met and interacted with during her days as an RJ and later at MTV and Channel [v]. She had made a rule early on in her career, to never write something that you can't say to someone's face.

A few years later, another turning point came. Malini had spent her whole life online and had been among the early adopters of social media. She felt that the Internet had turned into a toxic place, especially for women. She wanted to leave behind a legacy and change the online culture. That's when she decided that she needed to craft a safe space for women to share their stories. Something synced with her belief that social media can be a place to craft great connections between people and build positive interactions around the globe.

'Social media can be used on a mass scale to connect with people, which is not otherwise humanly possible. So I wanted to prove that and get rid of the concept of likes and followers. I wanted people to feel positive. I thought if positivity was the new currency, what is one's worth?' She began a new online social media space called GirlTribe, which is now thriving and where conversations range from fashion to health to finance to parenting. 'I am so happy to see that women have so keenly come forward. We have so many GirlTribe meetings—see the energy there and it would prove to you how magical it is.'

Speaking Out

During her early days in the field of entertainment, Malini rarely faced the sexism or misogyny people tend to associate with the industry. Surprisingly and ironically, her brush with this came after she had become an established name.

She was named Impact's #1 Most Influential Woman in Media, Marketing and Advertising. When she was invited to Goa to speak at a conference about brand-building, she felt very proud of herself. She spent hours putting together a very detailed presentation. After she was done, there was to be a short Q&A on stage with the very well-known head of Zee—Mr Bhaskar Das. He was someone whom she respected a great deal and thought of as a role model, and she was looking forward to the interaction.

But his line of questioning was shocking and very far from what she had expected as a professional.

'His first question to me was, "I've heard you're very expensive?" I let that slide because I know people assume I get paid lakhs for a tweet and perhaps he was alluding to that (albeit poorly). But then he said, "I've always wanted to ask you this question..." and I thought, great! He's going to ask me about my incredible journey, how I built a brand from scratch in a male-dominated industry, or perhaps he's going to ask me about the book I'm writing...and he said, "I've always wanted to ask you, how have you resisted the urge to have an extramarital affair with a Bollywood actor?" I was taken aback and, at the time, tried to laugh it off with a joke about, "Have you seen how cute my husband is?" But as I walked off the stage, I was fuming; equally with myself for not having said something right then about how insulting, inappropriate and downright idiotic the question was. Reducing my hard work and career into a suggestive one-liner for his own amusement. I tweeted about it, and the entire conference went into a tizzy!'

She called her closest friends and confidantes to discuss the matter. In hindsight, she felt she should have done more and spoken up more strongly but her conditioning all these years not to 'make a scene' most likely prevented her. The entertainment industry is notorious for closing ranks against 'troublemakers'. Her friends told her she had done the right thing by not making an issue of it. But the feeling that she should have stood up for herself stayed with her. She vowed that if she ever faced such a situation again, she would not hesitate to call out sexism.

If someone as successful as she could still face this kind of behaviour, it spoke volumes for what freshers must face. Now that she has become a well-known influencer with a following of millions, she believes she owes it to newcomers to speak out and correct this kind of toxic behaviour.

'I remember two instances where I felt quite proud of speaking up and was glad to see that the audiences in attendance quite wholeheartedly agreed with me. I was invited to speak at another conference, and when I arrived a little late (as I was waiting for my outfit to be steamed), the male moderator introduced me, laughing, "Malini's here, she had a wardrobe malfunction." I thought that was unnecessary but let it go.

'In fact, before the event, I was waiting upstairs in my room with my entire team, and they wanted to brief me. I said the moderator could brief me in my room, and my manager called him, and he said that's fine. Since everyone was running late, we decided we'll skip it. But on stage, he says, 'Malini invited me to her room,' with a smirk and zero context. Not mentioning that this was for a briefing in the presence of my entire hair, makeup and management team.

'That was when I was giving the example of how people trust recommendations from people they know or admire, hence communities and influencers are an important part of the branding ecosystem. I said, "If I wanted to buy an AC and I asked you (moderator) what AC I should buy what would you say?" He said, "I'd tell you don't buy an AC, just be naked!"

'That's when I shut him down. I explained how *this* exact sort of thing is what filters up, down and around. While men think it's okay to say things like this in jest, they do not realize that, tomorrow, our sons will follow in their footsteps and make the same joke with some girl in school and on and on goes the macho merry-go-round. (Turned out *he* has a daughter. So I'm *extra* glad that I said what I did.)

'Another time I was invited to Sweden to speak on a panel about women in various leadership positions, and our moderator was an Indian man who decided to ask the pilot before me (a woman, of course) if she finds all the buttons on the plane intimidating. To which she replied, "No, because I know how to fly a plane." When he came around to ask me a question, I had to stop him and ask, "Would you have asked a male pilot the same question?" To which the audience erupted in applause. So now I take these things in stride and use them as "teachable moments". I won't lie—I enjoy it very much!'

One of the things that gives her the strength to do so is her circle of friends. 'That is why I surround myself with people who love, support and guide me—like GirlTribe—so that they can lift me up.'

Learnings from Looking Back

Malini has suffered from her share of imposter syndrome, something that tends to haunt many women. They feel they are not good enough, qualified enough or smart enough, and thus end up with a lack of confidence in their own abilities, even if the rest of the world can see their worth. Despite her achievements, Malini suffered from imposter syndrome for years.

She also resents the cookie-cutter set of qualities that is associated with leadership, often derived from the 'strongman' model of leadership. She feels the softer set of skills, which can be seen as fluffy and not contributing to business, is actually critical to being a good leader. 'I think people often discount the qualities women bring to a business by calling them 'soft skills'. Empathy and having a high EQ (emotional quotient) have clearly become the needs of the hour, where the millennial workforce expects more from their employers than just a pay cheque.'

In a career filled with remarkable achievements, Malini counts writing her first book, *To the Moon: How I Blogged My Way to Bollywood*, as one of the most significant ones. She had dreamed of being an author since she was little. To be able to fulfil the dream and have it become a bestseller was a sweet moment.

The sweeter triumph? 'I can say writing a book is something I always wanted to do, but the greatest achievement has been building a brand name. I am so proud that MissMalini, being an Indian brand, appeals to so many global women, so many millennials and even the Gen Z now, and so this name resonates with positivity for young India.'

She loves remembering all the people who mentored her over the years. In a way, she believes people like Priyanka Chopra, Sushmita Sen, Arianna Huffington, Michelle Obama and Oprah, who all spread joy and happiness, are her mentors, who inspired her to do what she does.

Like many driven people who enjoy what they do, Malini doesn't know how to switch off. She often stays up late, chasing yet another idea. Sometimes she feels she can't simply enjoy her success without thinking about the next thing to be accomplished. But she also feels that what she revels in is not work-life balance but work-life integration. Since her job involves doing so many fun things, it doesn't feel like a constant push and pull between work and leisure.

Malini's life hack: have fun. Spend time with your friends, family and pets, and have game nights. Don't spend all your time waiting to have fun, and don't wish time away.

Hacks to Storm the Norm

Norm: Life without a plan is seldom successful.

You would have heard most people tell you that to reach your destiny you need to plan your life. A simple Google search will lead you to almost a dozen self-help pages ranging from three steps to 100 ways in which to get your life on track. It is an accepted norm that life without a plan is a chaotic, meandering, directionless life. However, going with the flow can sometimes not only be liberating, but bring serendipitous surprises your way that you would otherwise not experience. Being open to whatever comes your way and learning to cope or triumph is one of the best lessons you can learn, because life is unpredictable, and sometimes sticking to a rigid plan leaves one unprepared for this unpredictability.

Hacks:

1. Trust your instincts

The first thing is to know and trust that wherever you decide to go, you will land somewhere that is right for you. When you don't follow the same path as everyone else, you have other milestones and achievements. You will do things that are just as important to you as getting married or having your first child is to them—but society won't recognize them the same way. You won't get the same support and encouragement. Not because people don't care, but simply because they don't know. There is no beaten track for your life. So your gut is your best friend; that inner voice that gives you the courage to head out into the wilderness without a track to follow.

2. Start to embrace uncertainty

It is important to put yourself in situations completely out of your comfort zone sometimes, where you are forced to rely completely on your bravery, gut instinct and resourcefulness to get by. It is equally important to have times in your life when you don't rush to make a plan. Experiment with changing one routine at a time.

Always start small. For example; go a different route to work this week. Don't watch TV for one evening. Order a different meal at the restaurant. See what happens.

Learn to see the uncertainty as part of the adventure of life.

When we practice these qualities, we keep them acute. When we don't, they lie dormant. It is no use to have a rusty sense of self-belief, determination and resourcefulness when shit hits the fan in life, which it is sometimes bound to do.

3.   Minimize your to-do list
Only aim to do the vital thing that needs to get done. Use your free time to be flexible and explore.

MEENA
Maximize Your Potential

Introduction

Meena Ganesh is an entrepreneur, business leader, independent director and mother of two grown-up children. Coming from a conservative South Indian family, Meena transformed personally and professionally over multiple decades of her career. Starting out as an IT professional, to becoming an entrepreneur, to building multiple businesses, she has had a very varied career spanning multiple industries and domains. She did all this while managing a home with two children who are now well on their own career trajectories.

For the past few years, she has been focussed on building multiple start-ups, while spending a lot of energy in building her healthcare start-up that is very close to her heart. She is also part of the boards of large, listed entities as independent director. Apart from her professional life, she also spends substantial time on her foundation that is focussed on creating sustainable livelihoods and improved healthcare for the rural population.

Now that her children have grown up, she has doubled down on learning skills she had always wanted to earlier—music, dance, bridge and swimming have come back to the fore. Post Covid, she has been spending more time travelling, both within India and abroad. Meditation and spiritual growth are also focus areas for her.

Why Meena?

There are far too few women who have turned into serial entrepreneurs with a multimillion-dollar business to show for it. With Meena, you get not just one, but several businesses that she has started or groomed to success. At the same time, she comes across as the epitome of the traditional ideal of the Indian woman, soft-spoken and courteous. How did she manage the tough negotiations and interactions that are a part and parcel of a high-flying multinational career and of successfully running a business?

In addition, she started her first business with an infant in her arms and a young daughter. She and her husband plunged into the business together. Given that a business is considered no less demanding than a child, how did she manage the time for her three children? And did she manage to keep her personal and professional lives apart, as society advocates, or was it all one glorious mish-mash?

Keep Learning, Keep Growing

Unassuming, but with a calm self-assurance and a twinkle in her eye, Meena Ganesh confounds almost every norm we can identify—not not rebelliously, but with decisions born out of deep inner conviction. Brought up to be a '*chamathu ponnu*' (good, well-brought-up girl) and groomed to be the traditional ideal of wife and mother, she, however, is the founder of multiple start-ups and has always worn the pants in her family, right alongside her husband Ganesh. Meena's life journey has been about happily doing the expected and then going beyond to do the unexpected!

After getting married the minute she graduated from business school, Meena went on to build her entire career post marriage. At one time she was the main breadwinner, as her husband had been bitten by the entrepreneurial bug. Later, she moved to Bengaluru with her daughter for a high-level job at Microsoft, while her husband remained behind in Delhi to manage his business. She went on to have a second baby and dived into the start-up world almost simultaneously, the first of her many entrepreneurial babies.

Born to a typical middle-class Tamilian family, her father was a Railway employee while her mother was a homemaker. There were no career women in her family or neighbourhood who could have been role models, and certainly no one, male or female, who worked in the corporate sector. In hindsight, Meena feels this obliviousness and lack of knowledge worked in her favour, as in many ways, the path chose her and drove her to pick the riskier but more rewarding route over the safe and well-trodden one.

Interestingly, Meena was not an assertive person growing up. During her childhood, she grew up with a sense of inferiority to her sibling, which was innate and took her many years to overcome. She was neither clear about what she wanted to do, nor particularly adamant about her decisions. However, saw women of substance in her family, with innate intelligence, entrepreneurial abilities and effective managerial skills. Without being highly educated or career women, they ran their households like tight ships, managed the extended families and were fantastic problem solvers and programme managers. She grew up with the sociocultural norm that as men might be busy with their careers, all other situations, problems and challenges could and should be managed by women. While this could be seen as posing a double burden on women, Meena chose to see it as an empowering vision of women. This, '...created a strong sense of ability that was gender agnostic. There was no reason why I would not be able to solve any problem posed to me, because that's what all the women I knew did, and I came from that stock too!'

In fact, a sociocultural norm she had been brought up with that had worked to her advantage was that women should help to be the bond and build consensus and move things along. One can see that norm playing out in her personal life as well as her professional one.

Growing up, while both she and her brother were expected to excel at their studies, her brother was expected to go to a top engineering college and then study further to set up a solid base for his career. Meena, on the other hand, was expected to complete her master's and settle down to a life of quiet domesticity. Her family dissuaded her from pursuing courses like engineering or medicine into which she had got admission—because what was the need for a girl to do that? It was her brother, then completing his PGDM from IIM Calcutta, who suggested that she appear for the CAT exams. Though she got admission at IIM Ahmedabad, Bengaluru and Calcutta, the family felt most comfortable about her going to IIM Calcutta, as they had lived there earlier. It was easier to travel to than Ahmedabad, and, moreover, her brother had studied there.

Standing on Her Own Feet

Meena agreed with the family consensus and went off to Calcutta to study. The IIM at Joka was on the outskirts of the city. A verdant campus ringed by lakes, it was a world in itself. Connectivity by landline phones in the late '80s was very poor, while mobile phones hadn't been invented yet. Trunk calls were expensive for a middle-class family, so she called her family at best once a week for a designated three minutes. Meena had to cope with everything on her own, good or bad. The years away from her family at IIM Calcutta helped Meena learn how to stand on her own feet and cut the umbilical cord.

The move to Kolkata changed the course of the rest of her life! Meena echoes Sheryl Sandberg in saying that her choice of spouse was the best career decision she made. On campus, she met and fell in love with a classmate. Ganesh, brought up by a working mother, did not just support Meena's right to work but helped her refine and grow her career aspirations throughout her life. He was as invested in her success as his own, and ensured that the two of them worked together to achieve both dreams.

Given the conservative family she came from, Meena was very nervous about telling her family about Ganesh. She knew that this was a step out of character. Hesitantly, she told her parents about him during a holiday visit home. Her parents were aghast. This was not what they had bargained for when they had sent her to Calcutta. She was supposed to be getting an education in management, not romance! The prospect of a love marriage itself made them uncomfortable. They had always dreamt of getting her married to a groom of their choice from the same community, whom they would first suss out. Being presented with someone whom their daughter already preferred was a spanner in the works. In addition, he was just a couple years older than her—just 23, and they would have preferred a more traditional set-up where the groom was better settled. He was too young to be ready for marriage. Moreover, he had a single mother and two younger sisters, whom he would have to take responsibility for and get settled in life.

Arguments raged back and forth, followed by silent resentment from both sides. Meena had never rebelled until now, never even thought of asking for something she knew her parents will disapprove of. She almost gave up the notion of marrying Ganesh and told him that they should break up, because it was making her parents so unhappy.

Ganesh was made of stronger stuff and had already seen tragedy in his life. He was not ready to give up on his dream of happiness with Meena. He pleaded with her to give him an opportunity to meet her parents and convince them. Meena didn't think that it would work— her family was so adamantly against the relationship. Ganesh didn't give up; and finally, Meena agreed to let him meet her father once.

Her father was accompanying Meena back to Kolkata when she asked if he would agree to one meeting with Ganesh. 'Just meet him with an open mind. After that, if you don't like him, I won't insist,' she said. 'Alright, I will meet the boy once,' her father said sternly.

On the day of the meeting, both Meena and Ganesh were too het up to eat breakfast, though Ganesh put on a brave face. Meena went over the details of her family again and again, tutoring him on their likes and dislikes. They proceeded to Coffee Corner, a small first-floor shack on campus that served tea and snacks. Her father walked in and nodded a hello to both of them. After a few preliminary remarks, he signalled with a lift of his eyebrows that Meena should leave the two of them alone.

Meena paced up and down on the road outside, wondering how the conversation was going and praying everything was going smoothly. Half an hour later, she heard a shout from the balcony above. She looked up to see Ganesh gesturing to her to come upstairs. When she joined the two of them at the table, her father said, 'So, when shall we fix the marriage?' Meena couldn't believe her ears!

Ganesh joined his new job in April, as soon as they completed their degree, because her parents were worried that when someone asked them what their son-in-law did, they could not say he was unemployed. 'So he had to join soon for everything to look decent, so it does not look like I married a loser,' Meena says with a grin. The two got married in June. Meera opted for NIIT as an employer, because that would take her to Delhi where her husband was posted.

The first couple of years, the couple had plenty of tiffs as they learnt to live together as a unit. 'I do not remember any specific incidents of our fights, other than the fact that you sometimes want to kill the other person, but yes, it's a part and parcel of a matured married life where after the night is over you move on and begin the morning with a smile.' But poor phone connectivity and the cost of trunk calls meant that there was no ready listening maternal ear to listen to her complaints or grumbles. She had to figure out things, learn to negotiate, compromise and adjust to a new family and new job by herself. She feels this is something today's kids miss out on due to the constant connection with their families with the ever-ready mobile phone.

The couple made their home with Ganesh's mother and his sisters. This arrangement worked out beautifully, since her mother-in-law— who lost her husband at 35 and brought up three children on her own—not only sympathized with Meena's career ambitions but also knew how important it was for women to work.

'I was very lucky, though I know these kinds of arrangements may not work for everyone. Many families are dysfunctional and that makes it hard to adjust,' Meena acknowledges. Since there were four women at home and Meena was brought up to be the homemaker, Ganesh didn't chip in with the housework, but Meena feels he would have had there been a need.

Evolving Her Career

During one of her placement interviews at IIM, one of the questions she was asked was, 'Where do you see yourself in the next five years?' Even though it was a frequently asked question, she was not prepared for it at that point, and just spoke the honest truth, 'I have no idea.' Her initial plan was to work hard and enjoy her married life for five years before quitting to raise her children. The social norm that dictates that men should be the providers for the family gives women more freedom to experiment with career choices, she feels. However, by sheer chance, she had landed in a great place to begin her career. She might have struggled to find her way in a large firm. But NIIT at the time was a nascent start-up in the IT education space and allowed a lot of space for independent thinking and intrapreneurial spirit. Anyone who put their hand up found an opportunity to grow, regardless of gender. It was there that she found her wings, encouraged by her husband and his family.

Meena's family training demanded that she should excel at whatever she had taken up, be it homemaking or her career. She travelled frequently for work and volunteered for tough assignments. When they had been married barely a year, Ganesh moved to Mumbai for work while the four ladies stayed back in Delhi. It was challenging, especially for Meena who was still new to the family and striving to adjust and get to know them. She would try and travel down to Mumbai on weekends by Rajdhani, since flights were unaffordable for the young couple. Sometimes she was lucky enough to have to travel to Mumbai for work. In those days, when there were no mobile phones and only expensive 'trunk calls', as they were called, old fashioned snail mail came to the rescue of the couple. As Meena says, 'I wrote prolifically, but didn't always get the same quantum of responses!'

A year later, Meena got a transfer to Mumbai, but, coincidentally, the same day she moved, Ganesh got transferred back, so she ended up staying in Mumbai by herself. It was the first time she had stayed by herself, that too in a new city. But she managed to adjust and delivered a great project before moving back. Many years later, when she moved to Bengaluru with a six-year-old daughter in tow for her role with Microsoft, things had changed to some extent. Mobile phones enabled the couple to stay in touch regularly, while their schedules at work didn't leave them too much time to miss each other. Ganesh travelled down as often as he could. Moreover, their relationship had deepened and matured after so many years of marriage, so the long distance was easier to manage.

Her drive to excel made her constantly push the boundaries and go beyond what was expected to create impact—traits that remain constant. Though she was very young, she didn't hesitate to take on outstation and remote training assignments. These involved travelling by train, carrying 10–15 PCs packed in large wooden containers, and often travelling to new cities that she didn't have much knowledge of. Motivated to give her best and to learn, she was happy to take on whatever work was required, be it consulting, training, client facing or back-end work.

'A few years into my career, I realized that I was excellent at my job and the company recognized that by promoting me and featuring me in one of their advertisements. So that showed me that this is something I can do; it gave me a calling.' Once she had tasted the joy of professional success, there was no looking back.

She often worked weekends to get reports out, without any hesitation. She also eagerly took on projects that pushed her out of her comfort zone. For example, at PwC (a multinational consulting firm), she got assigned to a project involving financial re-engineering, though it was not her skill set. It needed a lot of reading, learning, working with experts and building a model along with an expert, all things that were new to her; but she was able to do it effectively, to the delight of her client.

She joined Microsoft to set up and build a consulting practice, which was a very tough ask. In 1995, Microsoft's database, SQL Server, and their mail server, Microsoft Exchange Server, were not very popular, so getting consulting assignments was super tough. Meena struggled with this uphill task for the first year, until eventually she was able to make some breakthroughs and the road became easier. Her success with this led to her getting promoted to set up newer business units for the company.

Mothering and Careering

The birth of her first child is something she ribs her husband about. Her mother took the first train out from Chennai as soon as Meena's labour pains began, but Ganesh was busy in the throes of managing his first start-up. He dropped her off at the hospital and calmly went back to his office, only turning up that evening after everything was over to coo at his newborn daughter!

They say it takes a village to bring up a family. Meena's village included her mother-in-law and mother, who sprung into action whenever Meena needs their help with the kids. Meena gratefully remembers her mother-in-law taking early retirement when Meena's daughter was born, so that a family member could look after her while Meena headed back to work. Later, when her mother-in-law needed surgery, her mother travelled across the country to help out. Meena says that her mother, despite her traditional upbringing, has always been her cheerleader and support, her only complaint being, 'Why do you have to work so hard? Why struggle so much?' This is born out of concern and affection rather than gendered expectations.

At the same time, Meena acknowledges that not everyone may have a village, and, at times, women may have to take a step back from the workforce temporarily. Her advice to women about how they should approach their careers when there are testing personal demands at home is pragmatic. She believes they should hang in there, taking a necessary break or a slower track for some time. During the break, they should continue to stay in touch with their field, and when they return, be realistic about possibly starting from a lower position and working their way back up.

Returning to work three months after her daughter was born was a necessity, since Ganesh was a fledgling entrepreneur at the time. Like any career woman, she struggled to balance her own expectations of what being a mother entailed with her career ambitions. She worried about being put herself out there, making sure that she was visible and not relegated to the background.

Without the benefits of mobile telephony, email or WFH workplaces, the only way to be visible was to show up, in person. Even during her maternity leave, she attended a few meetings that she deemed critical. When she was still nursing her baby, she attended long meetings, taking small breaks so she could attend to her daughter. She took on projects that were high-visibility, even if they entailed more hours, and learnt to consciously draw attention to her work, rather than waiting for it to be noticed. Years later, when her son was born while she was at Microsoft, she had technology that could help. Email and mobile phones helped her plug into work just 30 days after her son was born. But the work culture was still male-dominated, and didn't take kindly to maternity leave. When Meena missed a work trip overseas during her leave, it raised eyebrows.

At the same time, travelling or long hours at work induced the guilt that was almost a by-product of motherhood. When her daughter went to Montessori, Meena's mom-guilt racked up. Many mornings, she was in too much of a rush to drop her daughter off to school. The days she could, she saw the other kids carrying in projects that had been slaved over by their mothers, or dressed in beautiful costumes, painstakingly made by homemaker mothers, for school performances. She wondered if she had made the right choice for her daughter, worried that she would grow up and resent Meena for not having had enough time for her. She overcompensated at both ends, feeling anxious and on edge.

'I wanted to be always in touch with my children, so, even during trips abroad, I would find appropriate time slots to connect with them every day without fail. There were some interesting moments, when the schools where I wanted to admit my first child really frowned upon a working mother.'

Later when she turned entrepreneur, it was personally stressful in multiple ways, since Meena had a young baby and a small daughter to take care of. Since the BPO worked through the night, Meena often attended client meetings during the day, came home for a few hours to be with the children, went back to work after dinner, returned home by 3 a.m. and woke up to send her daughter off to school in the morning before beginning the grind all over again. Having an excellent set of household staff, supervised by her mother-in-law, helped ease the load.

'Having a small kid and starting up a 24/7 call centre was very challenging. It was physically very taxing and I used to keep going back and forth from office to home and back again every day so that I didn't miss time with the little one who was less than a year old when I started. Once I set up the Mumbai operations, travelling every week to Mumbai with a young family was emotionally draining, and physically too; I would take the earliest flight and minimize nights away by flying back by the last flight.'

Then, one day, watching her mother-in-law chatting with her sisters-in-law, she saw what a great role model she had been for her daughters. She understood how much this lady had shaped her husband to be the egalitarian he was. And she realized that she herself was a strong career woman whose daughter was going to appreciate her for those unique strengths one day.

'I realized I need to be a stable and happy mother for the sake of my own children, or else they will be impacted. And I would not be happy without my career.' It's a valuable lesson that children will appreciate a happy and fulfilled parent more in the long term, even if they sometimes resent the forced absences in the short term. Once she got over her guilt, she felt a sense of freedom that improved her relationships both at home and at the workplace.

Looking back with the benefit of hindsight, she wishes she had taken herself less seriously at this time, particularly the pressure to do certain things or do things a certain way, and to try and be a superwoman. Meena has come to believe it's not about work-life balance but work-life flow—at times work is in the driver's seat and at times life needs to be.

'Work and life are not two separate entities, they flow and merge; and I need to be able to do the right things on both fronts at the time they deserve to be done, which could mean leaving early, working late, working after kids sleep, whatever is appropriate. Taking days off if a child is sick, working through weekends during stretch times. I have tried to remove guilt so that I can do what feels right on both home and work. I have also found that prioritizing is deeply critical; focus on only those items that truly matter to you. Stop worrying about expectations of others and do the right things. I have tried to establish a work-life flow, rather than a balance. This means focussing on the element that is important at that point in time. It also meant treating my children as responsible beings and not over-monitoring them.'

Betting on Herself

After having her daughter, well set in NIIT, she could have chosen continuity over change. But Meena had an innate drive to constantly challenge herself or, as her mother puts it, 'to struggle'. Her career was something that needed to give her joy. If she was bored and had stopped learning and enjoying herself, she would move on and find something else to do, either in the same organization or another one. She preferred taking the risk to staying stuck and feeling stagnant.

Meena consistently bets on herself and encourages other women to do so. She moved to PwC, a multinational consulting firm, and a few years later, joined Microsoft.

'In PwC, having a woman boss was helpful, and also offered a role model. The time at Microsoft was more challenging from a gender perspective as there was very low diversity and the culture was ultra-competitive. I tried very hard to make sure that I was heard and given the opportunities that I deserved.'

At certain points, she felt that her own personality traits may have possibly hindered her. She was brought up to be quiet and in the background, which gave her innate resistance to calling attention to herself or making small talk. She often expected her work to speak for itself, rather than spotlighting it. In addition, the workplace norm of socializing and networking was difficult for her as an introvert. This prevented her from forming those invaluable connections that help smooth the way.

It was only with time that she realized that people need to feel comfortable with their co-workers as people, not just their work. So she set out to build bridges. When setting up Tesco's India centre, she was conscious of the need to create a good impression, firstly, because the company was white and male-dominated while she was a brown woman, and secondly, because she was moving job opportunities from the UK to India. Empathetic by nature, she began speaking to her overseas customers and colleagues about their families and personal lives. This was not a thought-through strategic choice but something that came most naturally to her. Tesco employees found this so unusual that they ended up being disarmed and charmed by her.

A year and a half later, she took the leap and went to Bengaluru on a big promotion, moving there with her daughter while her husband remain in Delhi to run his start-up. At Microsoft, she was appointed head of the Application Developer Customer Unit, where she worked with various software development start-ups.

In 1999–2000, the dot-com boom was the talk of the town, and there was a lot of excitement around the world of start-ups. Having seen her husband go through his start-up times before angel funding and VCs abounded had given Meena a view into what it could mean, both in terms of the challenges and the wins. She was intrigued by the idea of having her own business to run and mould as she wanted. She had been bitten by the entrepreneurship bug!

The Twists and Turns of Entrepreneurship

A couple of colleagues and friends were equally enthusiastic about the thought of starting their own business. The idea of a BPO business struck them—these were the early days of the BPO sector. Nights and weekends were spent brainstorming the strategy for an Internet BPO business with her two co-founders. Between the three co-founders, no one had put up their hand for the role of CEO. Since Ganesh had experience running a successful start-up, the team naturally turned to him for advice on many points.

'It was funny—Ganesh constantly provided ideas and was our sounding board as we drafted our strategy. When it was time to approach investors, the conundrum was who was going to occupy the

CEO's seat, as none of us had any experience in that position. Literally the day before our pitch, we invited Ganesh to come on board.'

Luckily, funding fell into place by March 2000, and with an eight-month baby son on her hands, Meena and her team launched CustomerAsset. They planned to provide outsourced services for Internet businesses in the US. Unfortunately, their best-laid plans went awry. With the 'dot-bomb' and later 9/11, US companies suddenly became more conservative about spending abroad. The company had to pivot and become a call centre BPO, which required a completely different set of skills and a different order of investment—enough to dampen anyone's enthusiasm. But Meena says with her characteristic composure, 'As long as one has no ego and is willing to admit you don't know everything, you can learn what you need to know to succeed. In any situation, I am positive that we will find a way out of it and make it work.

'To cope with the challenges come leaps of imagination and innovation that go on to set the course of the industry. Each venture has its share of amusing incidents, unexpected reactions, and dramatic moments that add an extra sprinkle of excitement and charm to the whole experience.'

In 2000 BPOs and call centres in India serving US clients were a new concept. The team wondered how Americans would deal with an Indian customer service executive on the other end of a phone line.

'The idea of introducing US customers to an Indian customer service representative on the other end of the line was akin to a delicate dance, particularly with our lengthy Indian names. Picture this: minutes ticking away on precious international leased line time, simply because the customer was wrestling with how to pronounce "Srinivasan" or "Jayalakshmi."

'To circumvent this, we introduced a workaround—aliases. Our agents adopted easy-to-pronounce, familiar names that fit seamlessly into an international conversation. The strategy was so novel at the time that it was picked up by *The New York Times*, splashed across the front page as though we had pulled off a great masquerade.'

That clever innovation went on to become the modus operandi of

BPOs thereafter! In 2005, Meena and Ganesh launched TutorVista, a personalized one-on-one tutoring service that brought Indian teachers to American students through a digital platform. Completely unique, the idea piqued the interest of leading global media outlets like BBC, NBC, Fox News and more.

During a media interview, a particularly feisty journalist decided to dig into a potential problem he believed could pose a formidable challenge—the Indian accent. With the camera rolling, the journalist asked the parent of a student, 'How does this work for you? Even I find it hard to understand Meena. How does a 12-year-old like John follow along with such a thick accent? Isn't that an issue?'

Meena held her breath, knowing that her vision could be marred by a damning headline like, 'American Students Confused by Indian Tutors!' But the parent's response defused the tension.

'Yes,' the parent replied, 'John had some trouble understanding his tutor initially, but in the past six months, he's not only mastered Math and Science but also picked up the Indian accent!'

The room erupted in laughter. The following day, TutorVista was front-page news again. This time, though, it was about how their tutoring service gave American students an unexpected bonus—a free crash course in the Indian accent.

Reflections on Her Journey

Looking back at her journey, Meena wishes she had known her own aspirations and priorities better at the start; that would have helped her prioritize at many points. She also feels that if she could advise a young Meena, she would tell her that it's okay to have a zigzag journey that meanders along the way, as long as it's going in the right direction.

She admits that she could have progressed faster if she had been better at networking or spotlighting her work in the right fora. In fact, women who are shy are often perceived as arrogant, and she faced a little backlash from batchmates after she became a successful entrepreneur. She wishes that organizations would have mechanisms

'As an entrepreneur, each venture is its own unique adventure, filled with colourful characters, twists, turns, and surprising revelations that often take you by storm. For me, these surprises were an integral part of my entrepreneurial journey that not only taught me the importance of resilience and adaptability but also served as entertaining anecdotes. The world of start-ups, it seems, is nothing if not full of surprises!'

in place so that women would not feel left out in the network—the norms of networking, including late nights or drinks at the pub are often difficult for working mothers to cope with.

Some of the self-beliefs that helped her on her journey were her ingrained values of doing her best to excel at everything, and perseverance. At the same time, one of the self-belief norms that hindered her was imposter syndrome. At IIM Calcutta, she didn't apply for some of the top jobs due to her sense of inadequacy that took her several years to overcome. However, having seen her own journey, she says that one of the pleasant surprises in life is how much things can change. 'It is possible to keep reinventing oneself with a growth mindset; I didn't see myself at this place today. And I am sure my 20-year-older self will be very different from my current self.'

Of course, there were times along the way when she experienced failures. Not getting a coveted promotion or having a person hired over her were demotivating moments while she was an employee. As an entrepreneur, there were multiple situations when things were not going according to plan—be it achieving revenue targets, business turbulence or external circumstances.

'However, I never considered giving up or quitting. I looked for ways to fix the situation, or else, in the case of corporate, move on to a different role or company. Quitting my career or taking a break never really was part of my plan at any point in time. When things looked bleak, I turned to my husband and a few other family members for support and counsel. Over the years I have developed some level of spiritual muscle that helps me get through tough times.'

One of the things that keeps her charged is the desire to learn and innovate. 'Every business that I have built looked very different from where I started and what I had envisioned. This constant evolution of my businesses and me as a consequence drives me to do more.'

The norm of women being consensus builders who help people to work together cohesively

> Top three takeaways to help you succeed:
>
> • The starting point does not define the journey or the end point, it's the effort that you keep putting to move forward.
> • Each of us owe it to ourselves to maximize our potential while taking the rest of the world along; it's not one at the cost of the other.
> • Grit, relationships and continuous learning are essential ingredients.

becomes a key strength for her at the workplace. Building teams; helping others grow; building consensus across various parts of the organization, or even across countries; understanding the agenda and needs of others, and, hence, ensuring win-win solutions; and mentoring youngsters to access their potential are all intuitive skills for Meena.

One of her joys as an entrepreneur and leader has been mentoring young women. She feels many of them come from a very different place today, in comparison to the norms that Meena was brought up in, laughingly quoting the example of her own daughter, 'Whom we are all scared of; she can argue successfully about anything', and that of one of her male managers, who, at one time, had five smart young female subordinates and used to say, 'I can't even open my mouth, these girls are always telling me what to do.'

She does feel some men are lagging behind compared to the progress women have made, claiming that women will join a job and then take leave or go off on maternity leave, and she has had no qualms in calling them out. She reflects practically that at a time when employees typically move jobs in less than three years, a six-month maternity leave period is no big deal, as long as the employee comes back with a genuine desire to make an impact and contribute, citing her own experience.

Over the years, Meena and Ganesh have founded or invested in and scaled more than 12 businesses together, apart from being angel investors in over 20 start-ups. While being married to someone for close to 40 years is difficult enough, they have negotiated the additional challenge of running businesses together with equanimity, always being each other's cheerleaders and sounding boards. As they started their entrepreneurial journey together, they divided up responsibilities as per their skills and experience. Ganesh handles sales, marketing and raising funding while Meena runs the business and leads human resource management. He is the big-picture visionary while she is the hands-on details person who thrashes out operational glitches, manages the scaling up and so on. Each relies on the other's expertise without needing to tread on each other's toes.

Meena wears her incredible success lightly. For her, it is all about the impact she can create through her work. She thinks of each of her start-ups as additional babies that she needs to mother and bring up to be independent. She is now on the board of large listed companies as an independent director, bringing her many years of corporate and start-up experience to the table in these entities.

She feels India has a huge number of problems that need to be solved and is excited about playing a role in doing so, while building successful businesses along the way.

Going forward, she wants to create large-scale social impact and has just set the ball rolling with her foundation. As she said elsewhere, 'We are seeking excitement and happiness in doing things that money can never buy.'

Hacks to Storm the Norm

Norm: You should keep your personal and professional lives apart.

It is often believed that husbands and wives working together is a recipe for disaster. They will not only be unable to keep their business and personal lives apart, but will end up screwing up both. Be that as it may, one of the arguments for why they should work together is because building a business involves taking risks and having trusted partners. Who else is more likely to have your back than your spouse of many years, and to understand the diverse commitments you both have to manage across family and work? Some handy hacks for ensuring you can manage this successfully:

Hacks:

1. Colleagues at work, spouses at home
Remember that your equation as co-workers is different from that as partners. The way you interact, your style of communication at home, will not work for the office. Once in office, speak to each other as co-workers and colleagues do, with the same degree of respect, leaving aside the personal nuances and familiarity that you use at home.

2. The office avatar
Unless your relationship began at the workplace, seeing the office 'avatar' of your partner can sometimes be disconcerting or unsettling. However, it is important to remember that each of us has a workplace demeanour that is different from our demeanour at home. At home, you're not stressed about achieving targets, managing a team or reporting to a boss. At work you have responsibilities and a certain style of doing those things. At work one of you may be a big-picture person while the other may be driven by the small details that can snag execution. One of you may be better at running one part of the business than the other. It's important to learn to adjust to each other's style of working. Your differences can be complementary and contribute to a better business outcome.

3. Don't micromanage your teammate
Just like at home, leaving your partner to execute their part of the work without micromanaging is one of the best strategies. You're both on the same team, but teammates don't do their work identically. A good question to ask if you find yourself becoming hypercritical is, 'Would I react the same way if this person weren't my partner?' It's a good idea to ask your partner to keep the same question in mind too.

NIMRAT
Beyond the Shores of Success

Introduction

The daughter of an army officer who was killed by terrorists, Nimrat Kaur is an Indian actor who has acted in movies as well as on American television. Beginning her career as a print model, she honed her craft in theatre. Her first starring role was in Anurag Kashyap's production *Peddlers*, screened at the 2012 Cannes Film Festival. Her breakthrough came in *The Lunchbox*, co-starring Irrfan Khan, which was screened at Cannes in 2013 and went on to win worldwide acclaim.

She has starred in mega Bollywood hits like *Airlift* and played recurring roles in *Homeland* and *Wayward Pines*, widely viewed dramas on American television, as well as acted in several OTT series and films.

Why Nimrat?

To those of us from typical middle-class families, Bollywood seems like an alien world—one in which we can't expect to get ahead through hard work or academic attainment but something much more intangible—a combination of sheer talent and immense luck. So, when we first saw Nimrat light up the screen in *The Lunchbox* and read about her backstory, we were intrigued. And when she went on to act in arguably one of the world's most successful TV series, *Homeland*, our curiosity grew. How did a girl from an army background break into this notoriously difficult industry without the beauty pageant route? How did she survive and succeed in a place known, fairly or unfairly, as a hotbed of nepotism? With unusual choices of vehicles, including OTT series and movies like *Dasvi,* where she plays a rural politician's wife-turned-CM, how has she carved this space for herself in the entertainment world? Born in a country with no social security systems, Indians are brought up to have a fallback option, especially when they are trying out something as risky as a career in film. What was Nimrat's Plan B?

Over and above what she has achieved professionally, Nimrat has stormed several norms in her personal life as well. One is the norm of marriage being the lynchpin of one's life. Across the world, unmarried women are called spinsters—a term that brings to mind decaying hopes, a la Miss Havisham—while men are referred to as bachelors, a term that brings to mind a swinging lifestyle. Nimrat is arguably anything but that—a woman who remains happily unmarried. How has she managed to confound expectations both professionally and personally? Read on to find out!

Her Story: 'Unplanned, Blessed and Layered'

After nine years of struggle, it took only nine days of work for Nimrat to find her place on the global stage. But this is not the first time her life had changed on a dime!

Nimrat's father was an army man, while her gentle, docile mother is a homemaker. The family traipsed across India, Arunachal Pradesh to Punjab, moving from army cantonment to army cantonment. Her parents brought up their girls in a gender-neutral environment and encouraged them to try out all kinds of activities and pursue whatever interested them. Nimrat grew up unfamiliar with the fact that most girls are subject to a different value system than boys. 'My life was absolutely carefree, fearless; and it is almost like you are bungee jumping without a rope because your father has got your back.'

Her father pushed the girls to try new things, even things they didn't know they could do, and they flourished. He made it a point to enrol his daughters in co-ed public schools and convents rather than army schools, so they had exposure to all kinds of people around them. At school, Nimrat's class consisted of kids from business, government service and other civilian backgrounds, while at home, her friends were army kids.

The army cantonments in Pune, Bhatinda and Patiala gave Nimrat and her sister a very sheltered upbringing. There were constant social activities celebrated with people from different states and religions—festivals, birthdays, anniversaries and special dates for the regiment. Everyone earned more or less the same and had lived the same cantonment life. They all had similar housing, and a similar set of belongings that could be quickly packed up in big iron or wooden trunks, and taken from one posting to the other. There was a sense of neatness and order to the homes that was also reflected in their daily routine. Nimrat grew up with an egalitarian outlook and a feeling that the world proceeded with a certain order and structure.

Living with Flux

Since Nimrat was reserved and sensitive, she found it difficult to move from school to school and break the ice with new sets of classmates. However, when she was called to perform on stage in the school plays, she experienced a high that was different from anything else she had known. It was her natural space, where she found the freedom to express herself. Over time, the stage became her conduit to establish her presence and form a connection with her peers. 'Being on the stage was a safety net for me as I got to see how people reacted to me.'

Nimrat's father had complete faith in his daughters and their ability to achieve whatever they wanted. At one point, the family suddenly got transferred to Bhatinda in the middle of the school year. The girls were late for admission to the Army Public School. The session had already started for the year.

When the family reached Bhatinda, they found that the school was holding an entrance exam. There was just one seat left in the fifth standard. 300–400 students were said to be competing for it. The family was still in the unpacking-their-boxes stage of settling in. Army-issue trunks and suitcases were strewn around the house. Despite the military-ingrained precision and discipline the family had imbibed, Nimrat couldn't find her notebooks or pencils to practise her sums.

Her father's colleague dropped by amid the chaos. Sipping a hot cup of tea that Nimrat's mother managed to rustle up despite the disorder of the house, he commented, 'It is going to be very difficult for Nimrat to get in, the competition is enormous. What's your back-up plan for school, buddy?' Her father fixed her with a gimlet eye and said, 'There is that one seat, and here is that one girl. She is going to get it.' Sure enough, Nimrat qualified for that one last seat. That statement by her father has echoed in Nimrat's ears all her life, and it keeps her going at her lowest and darkest times. And she was going to need this memory.

A Jolt from the Blue

Suddenly, into this peaceful, orderly life, came a disruption of epic proportions. Nimrat was eleven years old. Her father had been posted to Kashmir while the family stayed back in Patiala, because it was not a family posting. He was a major in the army, an engineer posted on the border roads between Jammu and Srinagar. The family visited him that winter, during school holidays, eagerly looking forward to outings and activities—horse riding, skiing and snowball fights. They loved the snow, the beautiful scenery and, most of all, loved being together again. The small, tight-knit unit had missed the head of the family.

One morning, while Nimrat, her sister and mother were relaxing in the house, her father went on army manoeuvres. But he didn't come back!

Nimrat, her sister and their mother waited. And waited. And waited. Then the news came. He had been kidnapped by the Hizb-ul-Mujahideen. They had asked for some terrorists to be freed from prison in return for his freedom. The girls and their mother were frantic. They didn't know what to do. They could only pray helplessly and hope for the best. Day after day passed by. They were told the army was doing everything they could to rescue him. Each day they went to the army headquarters, asking for the latest update, but nothing changed.

Seven days later, they got an update. Nimrat's father had been executed by the terrorist group. He was just 44!

The family flew back to Delhi with his body in a coffin. Delhi was where Nimrat saw her father for the last time. He was later awarded the Shaurya Chakra, but the family had the ground cut from beneath their feet.

Their grief for the beloved father figure was intense. But his death also unmoored them from everything they had known. They had to move out of the cantonment. Not only had the family lost a beloved father and husband, but they were about to lose the protective shield of the army. While they would continue to receive his full salary since he was a battlefield casualty, the idyll was behind them. Gone was the bustling social life of the army cantonment, with its round of parties and social gatherings and the mix of people from across India mingling on equal grounds. 'In every way, life was over in a week.'

Despair and Disorder

The family moved to Noida to live with Nimrat's grandfather, who took on the role of paterfamilias. The sudden flipping of life left Nimrat disoriented, helpless and abandoned. She did not understand how life could change so quickly. She found it difficult to pretend that everything was normal and march on without such an important pillar in her life. In India, at the time, there was no concept of grief counselling or PTSD. The norm was that one picked oneself up and carried on, with little time to grieve and come to terms with the situation.

As the elder daughter, Nimrat felt that if she grieved openly, her mother would feel even worse about the situation. After all, her mother had lost her life partner in her thirties. So, Nimrat quickly gathered herself and got into a combative mode with life. With hindsight, she feels that the scars that were left because of the abrupt change and the lack of space to grieve openly had not healed completely. Advocating for mental health is something that comes from her personal experience. 'It is something that has not healed but was just covered up for a really long time. In my life, after the incident, so much has been built over it without properly acknowledging it, it has brought cracks in my personality itself. That is why I love it when people talk about mental health.'

The change pitchforked Nimrat into a completely different life. Unlike the army, civilian life was much harsher. The sense of egalitarianism was gone, and differences in wealth or social status were much more pronounced. Most of the kids did not understand army life and had known each other for a long time. They were less accustomed to letting new kids join their circles, unlike army kids. She felt isolated, off-balance and was not able to deal with the varied emotions of her situation.

Express, Explore and Expand

'What seemed like the end of the world is probably a beginning which you can't see right now.'

As a good student, Nimrat had been thinking of a career in engineering or medicine. Even the military had been an option at one point in time. But the emotional strain caused by unexpressed grief led her in a new direction. Getting involved with creative activities gave her a way to express herself. The stage came to her aid again like an old friend, giving her some catharsis. Now she felt impelled towards life as a performer. Additionally, having had to suddenly grow up beyond her years, she developed emotional intelligence which enhanced her performances. She enjoyed reading scripts and roles, and dug deep into the motivations of characters, analysing their development and understanding their perspectives.

'My father's death was a sharp turn in my life and any choice I made after that was mine. Had my father been alive, I would have had a very different life but I might never have chosen the things I chose today. I think I would have been brought up just like other kids to be a doctor or an engineer, as I was very good at studying as well. But the senses that were brought to me at the age of 11 due to the loss of a parent were huge. The vacuum that was created gave birth to artistic needs in me and a way to express myself. Somewhere, after such a complex loss, you lose the ability to express. So I started to live like a performer.'

Although she got admission into and pursued the coveted BCom course at Shri Ram College of Commerce in the University of Delhi, Nimrat knew that she needed to do something different in life. 'I figured that the regular life was not for me and I needed to make a turn that would keep the fire in me alive. I knew Delhi was not the place for that. I hosted gigs and started earning and saving in my first year in college. So, I had enough to survive for five–six months.'

She decided to move to Mumbai in 2004, where she felt her calling would find the right environment. It wasn't a conventional or easy move for the times. Many well-wishers warned her mother about the notorious world of ads and films, and advised her against letting Nimrat move. However, though her mother was soft-spoken and docile, she was strong. She believed that Nimrat should be free to pursue her heart's desire. So, off Nimrat went, armed with her savings and a portfolio clicked by a friend. Nimrat was full of excitement and trepidation in equal measures. On the one hand, she was moving to a city where she knew no one. She was planning to try and break into an industry that was notorious, to say the least. Moreover, coming from a middle-class background, academically fuelled careers were what she knew. She wondered if she was throwing away a chance at a secure life by not pursuing the obvious choices of an MBA or CA. Moreover, if Noida was a culture shock to a girl from the army cantonments, Mumbai was like Noida on rocket fuel.

But, on the other hand, she had a fire in her belly, which drove her to at least try. This was her chance to fulfil her dream of becoming an actor. For all her fears of failure, she knew her biggest regret would be if she didn't give it a shot and didn't give it everything she had, at least once. Having come to Mumbai in April 2014, she gave herself six months to find her ground or go back. She deliberately didn't have a back-up plan in mind, and was determined to succeed. Funnily enough, the advice she got from family and friends was that if things do not work out in six months, she could always get married—as if that was a fallback career!

'I always thought—are they serious? Are they afraid? Is it because they do not know better and they are actually wishing well for you? And this is all they know, and so they impart this unsolicited advice? Or sometimes, people are afraid to see what the possibility of a different kind of life might be. Because what if work is my first love and I want to have a man in my life who does not include paperwork and does not follow the norms set up by people over time?'

The Days of Struggle

While staying with distant relatives, Nimrat found life lonely. She didn't have friends in the city. Incredibly naive, she didn't know anything about how films were made. But she had done her groundwork before moving to Mumbai and knew the big production houses and where they were.

It took immense patience and persistence to try and break into the film industry—not recommended for the faint-hearted. Nimrat traipsed the length and breadth of the city, knocking on doors, handing out her portfolio. Her shoes got worn out from pounding the pavement, and her ears hurt from hearing polite rejections. She wondered if she had made the right decision. But a stubborn streak wouldn't let her quit.

'No one else knows your capabilities and the heights you can achieve for yourself. They might say you are not the right person or don't have the right face or colour, but believe in yourself,' she says.

She decided to audition for ads, both on TV and print, as a way of keeping herself afloat. After over 85 auditions for ads, and three months in Mumbai, she finally bagged her first ad campaign. A short while later, through serendipity, she heard that a UK-based production crew was looking for a new young female talent.

'My cousin was working at Star News. Rajeev Masand was working at Star News at the time, and he used to host something called *Masand ki Pasand*. And they were friends. And Rajeev's friend, Apurva Asrani, was the director and the producer of the music video. Rajeev told my cousin that there's a production team here from the UK, and they're looking for a new girl for music videos.'

Nimrat turned up for the audition, nervous and excited—this was the closest she had gotten yet to showbiz. She hadn't done anything apart from theatre in school and had to learn the vocabulary and grammar of screen acting and screen tests. She didn't know what a set looked like, or what a camera looked like.

'I didn't know that there was a separate person operating the camera.'

But she brought a fresh prettiness to her audition, which got her the part. The music videos she did for *Tera Mera Pyar* were a great learning experience. From then on, she was like a sponge, absorbing the intricacies of the camera with every shoot and from each new director.

A Steep Learning Curve

Naturally observant, she learnt to use her lived experience and people-watching to portray her characters. She started acting in local theatres to hone her craft. She wanted to learn how to emote her lines better, how to react, and not just act. Through her experience in Hindi and English experimental theatre, she learnt from the best in the business about how to plumb emotional depths and express herself better as a character on stage or screen.

Over the next nine years, Nimrat led a busy life in Mumbai, juggling print ads and TV ads, theatre performances and small roles in films. She loved her work in theatre and found it an incredible thrill to be able to connect directly with the audience. But the big break eluded her. There were many times when she wondered if she had made the right move in picking this career and whether her time would come, if at all. Often, projects were announced and came to nothing or turned out very differently from what she was promised.

There are so many stories about people who come to Mumbai with Bollywood dreams only to end up as bit players. When they don't find opportunities coming their way, some of them try to take shortcuts, or succumb to the casting couch. Nimrat acknowledges that this was a fear that was spread by others when she decided to move to Mumbai. But her mother had faith that Nimrat had been brought up the right way, with the right values and that she would never give in to pressure or compromise her values.

And yet, the joy of performing in a theatre and forming that immediate connection with the audience was tremendous; it was rewarding in itself. Should she be content with that instead of aspiring to greater heights? Or should she pack her bags and go home?

At times, she felt low enough to cry. She wanted to call home and speak to her mother or her sister every day, but in those early days of mobile telephony, calls cost a lot. Public Call Offices (PCOs) were around every corner, but even those calls cost quite a bit, so she kept her chats short, fought back her tears and provided for herself.

'There were days when I wanted to pack my bags and go back home. 100 per cent. You know, I was very, very down on many days. I felt like nothing was working out. And I couldn't see the light at the end of the tunnel. I didn't know where my next pay cheque was going to come from. For those of us who've grown up in homes, where everybody has a steady job, it's very hard to cope with that feeling.'

Money was tight. She had to carefully budget it for everything she needed, from rent and food to travelling to auditions, without the freedom to splurge. She couldn't afford to take cabs from one audition to the next, so she would travel by trains, buses, autorickshaws, and even walk if needed. She remembers one occasion when she was heading for an audition, dressed and made up, in an auto, when a bus splashed dirty water from a puddle all over her. She was in tears, her make up was smeared and her clothes were a mess. It would have been easy to call it off, but she made it a point to persevere and go to the audition.

'It was very difficult and very trying, but never enough to break me and to actually send me back home.'

Despite the mental see-saw, even in her lowest moments, Nimrat never felt like it was pack-up time. One of the things that helped her stay on course were her memories of her father. She remembered how he believed in her all the time and had a strong conviction that whatever she wished for, or her father wished for her, would happen. It was just a matter of time.

'As they say, there's a good wolf and a bad wolf inside us. And it's about which one we listen to. The positive voice has always been the loudest voice in my head—always. Something in me always told me that I was destiny's child. And you know, it may take a little time, but what I want will happen.'

Perhaps it was her upbringing and what she had seen, the army attitude or the example her parents had set—her resilience and her persistence carried her through in a field that was unpredictable and unstable.

While movies were being produced to launch star kids and many of them were getting projects without having done a day's work on screen, Nimrat never paid attention to it.

'Whatever happens, happens for the best. I feel like that narrative has always served me greatly. You do what you can and leave the rest to God, destiny and other forces above.'

She felt that many opportunities had fallen into her lap as well. So she continued concentrating on enjoying what she was doing and got better at it.

In a way, it was easier for Nimrat, as a woman, to deal with the uncertainties and the unpredictable income of an acting career. The norm that men were the breadwinners gave them less flexibility and less room for experimentation.

'I feel like, that way, women have it easier for sure because you are not really expected to wear the pants and so you can actually live the dream.'

The Big Break

One day, a dear friend, Seher Latif, (who has since passed away) told Nimrat that she was casting for a film. It was an indie (independent) film, not bankrolled by a studio and hence the small budget. Seher invited the director Ritesh Batra to watch a play in which Nimrat was performing. Ritesh and Nimrat met afterwards for a coffee. After their chat, he handed her a script, and lo and behold, Nimrat had signed her first film as the lead—without even a screen test! It had taken her nine years to get there. Interestingly, one of the things that worked in her favour was the fact that she was not overexposed as an actor!

She was going to co-star with Irrfan Khan, who was already well known and well-regarded. But she didn't let that faze her. With three-four months of preparation, by the time filming commenced, Nimrat was ready with everything she needed for the role. As it happened, Irfan and she had no scenes together; most of the film involved Nimrat on her own. But she felt the pressure of having to perform to the same standard. It was a short, nine-day shoot and before she knew it, the film was wrapped up.

Playing the role of a simple housewife, she channelled the women she had known from childhood, and the one social norm she had heard and seen in the women around her—that of the self-sacrificing woman. From her great grandmother to her grandmother and mother, women had been expected to live like this and have complied.

'If you're a mother, a wife or a daughter-in-law, you are expected to put everyone and everything else ahead of you and your needs. Your husband's happiness, your kids, your in-laws—they define your happiness. Women who put their needs first and who care a little bit more about themselves than they should are considered selfish.'

The World's Her Stage

There was a special screening of the film in Delhi, and the only people who attended were Nimrat, Ritesh Batra and Irrfan Khan's family and close friends. But then, the film went on to premier at the Cannes Film Festival in 2013. Nimrat had been to Cannes in 2012 for her film *The Peddlers*, in which she had a small role. But this was a big occasion. Still a newbie to the industry, she didn't know what to wear. She reached out to designers like Sabyasachi and Abu Jani Sandeep Khosla, who designed her outfits for the red carpet and the premiere.

As an indie film, *The Lunchbox* didn't afford her an entourage so she had to change in some random rooms and get into her second outfit with some help from the production team.

On the red carpet, the lights were blinding. There was a series of flashes as photographers unleashed their cameras, and Nimrat could hardly see clearly. She walked slowly, holding on to her outfit for dear life. She prayed that she wouldn't trip over her saree and have a wardrobe malfunction. The entire hoopla felt a little surreal. Once the day wound to a close, she was exhausted. She and Irrfan Khan decided to let their hair down at a small café. As she kicked off her heels to get comfortable, she realized that she hadn't eaten all day, buoyed by excitement. She asked Irrfan, who had been through this routine before, how he coped with it all. He laughed and gave her a piece of advice that she took as a life lesson. He told her to go ahead and soak it all in, enjoy it thoroughly and never waste a good moment, because it was all ephemeral. She took it to heart.

At the festival, the film became a sensation overnight. The film bagged the Critics' Week Viewers Choice Award at the 66th Cannes Film Festival. No one, including the director, had anticipated what a rage it would become around the world.

As she walked down the streets of Cannes, people were screaming out her name from the film, 'Ila! Ila!' There were hoardings with her face splashed on them all over town. Amul Butter did its signature take on the film. Suddenly, she was known and recognized as a public figure. As part of the film's promotions, she found herself travelling around the world, visiting beautiful places she had only read about in magazines. She was in the thick of things, interacting with the finest minds in the business. And she knew that this was her moment.

'I feel like I was hit by a tsunami. Your soul knows it, you know it; now life is not going to be the same.'

While Nimrat was in Croatia to promote the film, her agent called and told her that she needed to fly to London for a screen test for a TV show she had never heard of. The makers of the series had seen her play the part of a lonely housewife in *The Lunchbox*, had been incredibly struck by her performance and thought that she would be great in the role of a spy. They had reached out to her agent to ask her to take a screen test for the role.

Nimrat felt like it was a huge headache to rebook her travel. She almost backed out but her agent was persistent. After a late night of partying with other film folk in Croatia, fatigued and with a severe headache, Nimrat landed in London and headed to a cousin's house.

She asked her cousin to rehearse lines with her. After reading a few lines, her cousin felt the script had a familiar ring to it.

'What show are you auditioning for, Nimrat?' she asked.

'I don't know. I don't remember. Wait, let me see my agent's message.' She looked up from her phone to say, 'I don't know much about it. Something called *Homeland*.'

Her cousin's shriek of glee almost shattered the windows.

'It's a world-famous show. It's among the most watched shows of all time, di!' she told Nimrat. 'Is this real? Are you really up for a part in this show? You HAVE to get it!'

Now equally excited about the role herself, Nimrat prepped hard for the rest of the day. That afternoon, as the taxi weaved in and out of the busy London traffic, Nimrat thought what a coup it would be if she were to get the part. It was a major US TV series. And it was a terrific, if small, role. She reached the studio for her audition and muttered a prayer under her breath. She could almost feel her father's hand upon her head, giving her a blessing.

But when she reached the set, the showrunner came to greet her. Pulling her to the side, he said, 'We have already finished casting for the role you were sent, so we don't need you to audition.'

Nimrat's heart sank. Not wanting to show her disappointment, she turned to leave when he continued, 'But I've seen *The Lunchbox*. It's terrific. And I think you would make a great addition to the cast as a spy!'

Nimrat couldn't believe it. It was a coup to be part of such a huge, internationally acclaimed TV series. But even as the news sank in, Nimrat knew that there was something missing—her father. As soon as she returned to India, she decided to visit Kashmir all by herself. It was the first time she had been back there since he died.

She started a journey of healing and closure by revisiting all the places they had been to together years ago. She got a tattoo on her wrist that says 'Zenab'—a father's precious jewel.

Shortly after, she left for South Africa to shoot for *Homeland*. Working with an international crew, that too for a TV series as opposed to a film, was a completely different experience. *The Lunchbox* had involved only nine days of shooting, and, on an indie film budget, it had felt almost like a long play. *Homeland* had well-oiled international machinery. No character got the script in advance, so the actors never knew what was going to happen next. There were different directors every day, so it felt like a fresh challenge all the time.

Homecoming

Shortly after completing the shoot for her first season of *Homeland*, Nimrat flew home for another new experience—her first Bollywood film. *Airlift* was made on a huge budget, with superstar Akshay Kumar as the male lead. Produced on a large canvas, it was a different kettle of fish from what she had experienced so far. True to the types of roles she was comfortable with, it did not feature her as the typical romantic heroine. The movie was unconventional as a subject for Bollywood.

'I used to joke with Akshay, telling him that it was an art film for you.'

It went on to win both critical acclaim and box office success. With a bona fide Bollywood blockbuster, a clutch of roles in various other international series, including *Wayward Pines,* and becoming a series regular in *Homeland's* final season, Nimrat's career achieved lift-off. Along with that came a love that she had never expected.

'In bits and pieces throughout my life as a performing artist, so many people have loved me unconditionally—that love has come to fill the vacuum left by my dad's death. Love is love at the end of the day. Probably not the one I would have had from my father; but I think life has been really kind, and God has been really generous to me. I am living my life doing what I love; no day has been boring apart from the dull lockdown days. So I feel like I am living the most extraordinary version of the life that was given to me, and I am very grateful for it. It brings so much joy to my family and, in turn, to me.'

Success and Beyond

With success, one of the things that Nimrat had to learn is how to handle money. With a profession like acting, there was no guarantee about when the next pay cheque would come. There were times when she struggled to pay rent. And then there were times when she was flush with cash and tempted to go overboard on luxuries. Given her days of struggle and her middle-class upbringing, Nimrat knew that she needed to be prudent with her money. At the same time, the advice from Irrfan also rang in her mind, to enjoy the good moments. She neither wanted to be a miser nor a spendthrift. She learnt how to balance the two, saving and investing enough and yet retaining enough to have a good time.

'I don't squander away my money; I invest well. But I like to have the good things in life. I enjoy knowing how to enjoy my money. I'm not someone who saves everything and doesn't know how to enjoy it. I established a fairly good system, in that sense.'

Among the things that constitute a good time for Nimrat, one is spending time outdoors and at wildlife resorts. She loves to travel and explore new places. With a love of adventure, she enjoys driving huge cars, especially SUVs, and has even gone skinny dipping. In her own words, she 'never says no to a dare'.

While the film industry is largely male-dominated, Nimrat has been lucky enough not to face the infamous casting couch. But she says pragmatically, 'It is, after all, a male-dominated world due to the sex ratio. I know it is a struggle for every woman because all industries are male-dominated. I do not know of any industry that is dominated by women. So I have never looked at myself as a woman in a man's world but as a professional interested in pushing the boundaries, and that is all I am out there to prove.'

While different roles and opportunities keep coming her way, her family and friends are eager for her to get married and have a conventional family life. The norm of women having an 'expiry' date for getting married does come up a few times. She believes that relationships have nothing to do with happiness and that no external person can give one constant joy.

'To someone who has signed for [a] conventional life, marriage is probably the key to happiness. But, as we all know, relationships have nothing to do with happiness. I really believe that, because I feel there is no other person outside of us who can give us joy constantly. So, the biggest challenge for me is to be in a good relationship with myself.'

While she enjoys being on set and getting to know her colleagues, her personal life is largely spent away from people in the industry. She feels socializing with people in the same industry would limit her worldview and prevent her from expanding her horizons. Her biggest cheerleaders remain her grandmother, mother, sister and a few close friends.

Her definition of success has changed with time. She says reflectively, 'My definition of success was awards, bank balance, a certain image and a house somewhere. But today, while I enjoy all materialistic aspects of life, I know that success is not the depth of your wallet but the depth of your understanding of life and to derive happiness from the smallest thing in your life—the rainy day, your pet, the plant you water, things like that...'

> **What would your message be to the young girls reading your story?**
>
> 'Live your life as an individual. Forget whether you are a boy or a girl, whichever way the society recognizes you. You are a soul with a goal. I would quote Mark Twain when he said, "There are two very important times in your life, when you are born and when you realize why you are born."'

Hacks to Storm the Norm

Norm: You have to be a part of the insiders' club to succeed.

Outsiders are like strangers; they know neither the ways of working nor what it takes to succeed in a competitive industry. They're those within a tribe but not of it. Uncomfortable in their own skin, they are socially awkward—loners in the crowd. At first glance, such an outlook seems unconducive for success.

Hacks:

1. Bring in fresh ideas to the table
Outsiders can bring in a new vision and new ways of doing things that can prove to be game changers in the industry. Outsiders and misfits have the opportunity to combine the status quo with something new and lateral, yielding some awesome creative outcomes.

2. Trust your gut
To be a successful outsider, you need to be super brave! To many, it can come across as bravado—even recklessness—but it's actually a willingness to take risks: a strength born from the frustrations of being a misfit, bearing the constant tag of an outsider. If there's a defining characteristic between successful outsiders and those that remain alienated and frustrated, it's pure guts and inner strength.

3. Create connections
Let your empathy and creativity be your strength. Continue to listen, understand and let others know more about you. Be true to yourself. Be trustworthy and stand up for your values. Instead of being wishy-washy, hold strong to your convictions. This matters greatly to those watching you. Do not make yourself smaller in an attempt to belong; you will lose all respect. And finally, always, always remember the bigger picture of why you are here in the first place!

RAGA
Closets Are for Clothes, Not People

Introduction

Raga has had a multifaceted career—from advertising, to becoming the first woman elected to the board of the India New Zealand Business Council, to setting up a speakers' network in the UK exclusively for LGBTQIA+ women and those who are non-binary. Once married to a man, she later married a woman. When her same-sex partner of 15 years suffered a serious brain injury in 2020, Raga decided to slow down. She now spends her time on social projects within the LGBTQIA+ community in India and with Indians abroad.

Raga fights for causes such as domestic violence against women and violence in intimate same-sex relationships through advocacy, activism, writing stories and screenplays and speaking at diverse forums. She is on the EDI boards of several companies, a trustee/chair of trustees at the London LGBTQIA+ Community Centre and a trustee on the board of Enfield Saheli—a charity that focuses on empowering women who have suffered domestic abuse and violence. In 2022, Raga received the prestigious Woman of Courage award at the Houses of Parliament, United Kingdom, and was also shortlisted for the 'Woman of the Year' award at the Asian Achievers Awards in London. Recently, she has been shortlisted from among 90,000 nominations for 'Positive Role Model—Age' by National Diversity Awards, one of the most prestigious awards in the UK.

Why Raga?

From a chawl in Bombay, India, to a glittering advertising career in India and New Zealand, to setting up India's first speakers bureau, becoming an LGBTQIA+ activist in India and London, and now setting up the UK's first speakers' network for LGBTQIA+ women and those who are non-binary—the story of Raga's life is one of constant reinvention. Despite the grit she showed throughout her journey, she became fully herself only at age 50. Dressed in defiantly rainbow-bright clothes, forthright and opinionated, she spent years hiding a big part of herself from the world.

'It took me 50 years to love myself, so how could I have been fully me until then!'

Social norms end up ingrained in our minds and hearts and are sometimes the hardest to overcome, because, as humans, we are social beings. Homosexuality has been taboo in India for generations, and even today, it does not enjoy social sanction despite court rulings. How much more conflicting would it be if one discovered one was gay—something we are brought up to despise and regard as unnatural—after being married to a man? In Raga's story, we hear about how she traversed the journey through many different social norms—from those about sexuality, to those that assume that working women neglect their kids, to living an immigrant life and finally coming to an acceptance and unapologetic celebration of her multi-hued personality. We also get to hear a Cinderella story about how a girl from the chawls of Mumbai went on to become a much-lauded global professional and activist, but with a twist—she was her own fairy godmother!

Not So Sweet

When Raga was 13, she got a job at a coaching centre. Every evening, she'd be at the registration counter enrolling new students for three hours, earning ₹300 a month. That money was very precious for Raga and her family. That first Diwali, her employer handed over a box of *mithai* to each employee. Raga was excited that apart from her earnings, she would also be taking sweets home to her family—until she saw that ₹53 had been deducted from her salary. She asked her colleagues why that was so.

'It has been deducted for the cost of the box of sweets by the owner,' they said. 'It happens every year.'

'Why do you accept this? If it's a Diwali gift, he shouldn't cut our pay for it. If it's not a gift, then we should choose if we want it or not,' Raga said indignantly. The other workers shook their heads and walked away.

Raga hesitantly marched into the boss's cabin and questioned him. 'Either give it as a gift or I don't want it. Give me my money back,' she said. Her boss was furious. 'You're ungrateful. I've given you a job, now I am giving you sweets for Diwali and you are questioning me? Yes, your salary will be deducted for the sweets. And this is how it works here!' he raged and carried on shouting at her at the top of his voice. Colleagues and students gathered around, watching the drama, yet no one said anything. Raga was shocked into silence. Then she gathered her courage. 'You're a bully,' she said to him finally. 'I do not want the sweets; I want my full salary. I worked hard for it.' She stormed out, throwing the box of sweets at his face. Even at 13, Raga knew that she had to stand up for what she believed was right and found the guts to speak her mind.

Survival of the Fittest

Raga and her two siblings were brought up by their hard-working mother, with little money for food, clothing and shelter. They lived in a Mumbai chawl, cheek by jowl, with several other families. Neighbourhood gangs waged daily battles for supremacy. Life was a struggle for survival. A bucket of water, whose turn it was to use the communal toilet, walking through the by-lanes without touching each other—anything could spark a quarrel. The daily wrangling was caused by people's frustration and hopelessness at their situation.

Raga learnt to read from the scraps of newspapers that the peanut seller's basket held for wrapping his customer's parcels—her mother could not afford books. Her mother, however, managed to enrol Raga in a nearby convent school a year early, so that Raga was taken care of while she was out working and she did not have to leave her in the care of her drunk father. It was a difficult childhood. The teachers had no understanding or sympathy for her home circumstances. Often, Raga and her sister would be late for school because they had to wait in line for a bucket of water. The sisters owned one school tie between them and took turns wearing it. The teachers would make the girls kneel for hours for coming late, shame them or cane them in front of their classmates for not wearing the tie.

When Raga was six, her father passed away, leaving the family destitute. But despite her home circumstances, Raga never lost hope. She didn't feel she belonged in her environment; she felt like a misfit. She always knew that there was something better out there for her and had an inner fire to do something different. She loved Bollywood. To help herself cope, she would often pretend that she was an actor and that whatever was happening around her was happening to that character.

'It helped me immensely; although I lived a fictional life in my head, my story was being created by me, as I wrote my own script. I chose the character I would play each and every day.'

She recollects a defining moment in her young life, as a neighbour took her to a tall building in Pali Hill, Bandra, a wealthy suburb in Mumbai where many of the city's glittering movie stars live. The neighbour knew the maid of a film star who lived there. When she entered the palatial apartment, Raga took it all in.

'I was around eight years old and I remember that moment so distinctly—watching the star's child, the house they lived in and thinking how it would feel to live in a place like that and have that life. Never in my little head did I ever doubt its possibility.'

As she grew up, Raga's mother sent her to a secretarial school so she could become a secretary like many good Catholic girls did. After college and with a secretarial diploma, Raga began her career in advertising, as an assistant to the personal assistant of the then

CEO of Lintas, a leading ad agency in Mumbai. But she was very keen on becoming a copywriter and wanted to write ads. One day, she mustered up the courage to appear for a copy test. This could be her lucky break into advertising, she thought.

Advertising back then was considered the preserve of So-Bo—the South Bombay kind—people born with silver spoons in their mouths and sophistication on their tongues. They dressed well and spoke a kind of global slang. She didn't have the same networks and neither did she come from their kind of background. She failed the copy test. A very senior manager, who conducted the test, mocked her, 'I think it is better you stick with your day job. This is not for you.'

While Raga was disappointed, to her, this only meant that she had to find a different way to break in. She enrolled in Xavier Institute of Communications (XIC) to study advertising and marketing. When she confided her ambitions, her teachers and colleagues laughed in scorn. But she was not just determined; she was confident that she would be able to do it. During the day, she worked hard at her PA job, and in the evenings, she studied advertising.

Her quick wit and sense of humour, as well as genuine interest in people, helped her build a network of close friends at work. She also entered into a relationship with a successful man from another agency. This network and her relationship—which quickly became serious— gave her the security that she finally had many people who had her back. With the agreement of both families, Raga got engaged to the love of her life (or so she thought at the time). Life was looking up. However, one day, she discovered that her fiancé had been cheating on her. Devastated, she called off her engagement. Both families were shocked and surprised. In those days, it was a huge stigma to break an engagement. To get away from the clamour of this, she asked for a transfer to Lintas, Bengaluru.

However, after some time, she realized that although she had credentials in advertising and marketing now, she was being forced back into the role of PA. That was not what she was aspiring to. Moreover, she found it hard to be away from her mother and her family. By this time, she had become friends with Ravi, who worked at Lintas, and later went on to become her husband. With his encouragement, she interviewed at Ambience Advertising in Mumbai, and got hired as a junior account executive.

Here, she was assigned one of the most prestigious accounts the agency handled. It was a huge stepping stone for her. However, life continued to be a challenge, with the class divide in advertising often making her doubt herself. Interestingly, it was here that she discovered she had a knack for client servicing and building relationships. A born raconteur with infectious zest, she was a charismatic person. She learnt the ways of that world very quickly and began doing well in her career. Long days and nights at the office only charged her up more, and life was beginning to settle.

But that was all about to change. During an off-site visit with her colleagues, the group was playing cricket on the lawns. Rushing to catch the ball, Raga didn't notice a tree in her path. She hit the tree so severely that she lost consciousness. On her return to Mumbai, she discovered that the injury was quite serious. She had a crack in her neck and other accident-related health issues. It took months of hospitalization and rehab for her to get back on her feet again. Getting back to advertising seemed too hard then, so she decided to take a break.

A Time for Discoveries

After a long and difficult recovery, Raga joined a film crew that was filming a television series in Rajasthan. In a crew of 75 technicians, she was the only female. In the early nineties, life was very different in India. Very few women opted for such jobs. There were no mobile phones or emails. When she encountered difficulties, she had to face them on her own or go back home, which was not an option.

The crew was extremely patriarchal and misogynistic and didn't know what to make of a smart, educated girl in their midst. The director of the series was friendly at the outset, but when he asked her out and she said no, he turned antagonistic. Every day, there would be some leering or a sexist comment. Some technicians would try to grope or bully her. Someone else would sarcastically talk about how delicate girls were not useful. It was a humiliating and isolating experience, one that still makes her scowl in disgust. When she complained to the head of the unit and the director, she was made to feel like this was her fault. No one took any action to make things better for her.

In this hostile setting, she became friendly with the female lead of the series, Kavita*. As they spent more time together, Raga started getting attracted to her. Long ago, at school, she had been attracted to a female teacher, while all her friends were crushing on male teachers or schoolmates. At the time, there was no representation in pop culture or the media for the LGBTQIA+ community. She didn't even have the language to understand her feelings. Raga had been too ashamed to discuss how she felt with anyone. Now, so many years later, similar feelings surfaced, but in a deeper way. She worried about what this meant but couldn't ignore what she was feeling. The two young girls just organically started a process of discovery. They began a relationship without giving it a name, and soon they were deeply in love.

The constant sexism and bullying led to Raga moving into Kavita's home, which was a safe place for her. This gave the young couple an opportunity to become closer to each other. However, when the shoot was over, Raga returned to Mumbai. Continuing to be together was not something that had even faintly occurred to either of them. Raga knew the relationship had changed her profoundly but pushed it to the back of her mind, where it would stay locked up for years. Everyone thought and believed that she now had a close friend called Kavita.

'Growing up, none of us knew the word "lesbian". How would we know? The language did not exist. We cannot be what we cannot see, as we know. And with no representation around me, I had no clue that being attracted to someone of the same sex was normal.'

She returned to the world of advertising. Bright, curious and

---

*Name changed to protect the identity of the individual.

always up for a challenge, this time she had a proper role as an account manager. Rather than doing clerical work, she got to interact with senior clients, discuss branding and marketing challenges, and spearhead the development of ad campaigns. The interesting part of this move was that some of her peers from XIC had already become managers, and, yet again, she had to start from scratch. She didn't let this bother her, and focussed on working hard to deliver the best results for her agency and clients.

Over time, Raga made her mark in advertising. Having proven her capabilities, she quickly rose up the ranks, becoming the vice president and branch head of Lowe Lintas Direct in Mumbai. She was recruited to join the agency in 2000, when it was struggling. Only 29 years old, Raga was tapped by the agency to rebuild the Mumbai branch. When she joined, there was one creative director with a small team, one other senior person and one executive assistant. There seemed to be a lot of conflict within that small team. Raga had built a reputation of bringing people together, and, in fact, her relationship skills had been a key reason why she was recruited. 'I remember asking Raj why he recruited me for that role, and he said, "Your relationship skills—we need that for LinDirect Bombay."'

It was a difficult situation—some of the team members were senior to Raga and resented her elevation. Their insecurities led to them not cooperating or understanding the need to pull together. It took a lot of work to rebuild the team first, and bring them together to work towards a common purpose. In the span of a few months, the team started working together well and winning new business against agencies who had been far ahead of LinDirect. Within a year, the team started getting a lot of respect internally, within the agency, and externally, with clients. The team was continually growing. By the time Raga left in 2001 to emigrate to New Zealand, it was in a much better and healthier place than when she had joined.

Meanwhile, her mother had begun looking around for a good Mangalorean Catholic boy for her. 'There was no way I was going to get into a stereotypical marriage,' she says. She decided to get married to her ex-colleague and dear friend, Ravi. The two shared a great zest for life and loved and respected each other. Within a few years, they bought a flat on the thirty-second floor of a posh apartment complex in the suburbs of Mumbai, the city of dreams. This building was even taller than the one she had seen as an eight-year-old. They worked hard and partied harder, and were seen as a charming couple. Twin children, a son and a daughter, came along to complete the cosy picture. This was the fairy-tale life she had envisioned for herself as a child.

'Inside, I felt like a magician and that anything I touched would turn to magic.'

A Fresh Start

But with the arrival of the twins, the long hours that advertising demanded began getting to Raga and Ravi. They felt this was no life for them or their young children. They took a bold call to emigrate to Wellington, New Zealand, in 2001. They thought that they would have better work-life balance in New Zealand and be able to give more time to the children.

'I chose an interesting life for myself. Not only did I come from nothing, throughout my life, I made choices that put me in situations of great stress where I had to restart my life again and again. I came back to nothing many times in my life.'

Back then, not many people in New Zealand knew much about India, and many assumed it was a very backward country. The 'charmed' family had to start over from scratch. Raga had to overcome not only gender stereotypes but also stereotypes about India. When Raga made her first presentation at an agency, her boss asked her, 'Wow, your presentation skills are so good—where did you learn to use PowerPoint and Excel? You actually had access to computers in India?' For one job, she underwent eight interviews, including one with the CEO's wife, who wanted to check whether she would fit into the culture of the organization.

Neither her educational qualifications nor her many years of experience at a senior level at a multinational ad agency in India counted for much. Eventually, she had to take a job that offered her the salary she had earned when she first began her career in India. Her job was so junior that it included tasks such as taking letters to the post office. She had to become a different Raga now. 'All my ego about being the vice president of India's largest advertising agency came crumbling down. It taught me humility and reminded me that nothing is permanent.'

Supremely confident and focussed, however, she did not let this change of status bring her down. She grabbed every opportunity to prove herself and succeeded. 'There is one thing that I have always followed. I never hesitate to make a cold call and put my credentials forward.' This particular trait helped Raga immensely in her career.

But the struggle in New Zealand was real. It was very hard to be away from home without family support, with two small kids and an immigrant life. Her husband struggled even more and could not hold down a steady job. As a distraction, he began spending most of his time golfing. To sustain the family financially, Raga worked three jobs. Unlike her fairy-tale expectations, she was immensely overbooked in terms of time and hardly had any time to spend with her kids. While her husband supported her as much as he could, the traditional norms of motherhood didn't leave her. She found herself waking up at the crack of dawn for housework before heading in to a full day at work and getting back to home life to cook, clean, put the kids to bed, work and sleep again.

'If I had to travel due to work, school lunch boxes for the twins were packed in advance. Breakfast, lunch and dinner were put in the refrigerator, boxes marked and details put on Excel spreadsheets. Their uniforms and clothes were washed, ironed and kept ready for the time I was away. That was my life, and I was exhausted. I was constantly feeling the guilt of working so many hours. But I was the one who brought the income home, so I had no other choice; I kept going.'

In New Zealand, there was no one to support Raga, apart from her mother, who came to stay with them from time to time and used every opportunity to remind Raga of what she had left back home. It was a complete contrast to the privileged, pampered life they had left behind in India. Sometimes, Raga wondered if it was worth it and whether they had made a mistake.

Her marriage to Ravi was beginning to crumble under all these pressures and challenges.

A New Awakening

Around this time, Raga noticed something in New Zealand that she had never seen before—same-sex couples who were openly living their lives. Dating someone of the same sex was not frowned upon as much as it was in India. At her workplace, a few girls would discuss their dates with women. In India, homosexuality was an absolute no-no, not just frowned upon but actively shunned. In New Zealand, while homosexuality was not commonly or easily accepted, at least there was some space for homosexual couples. It was not completely hidden away.

Raga finally dared to open a forbidden box in her mind a little bit to see what was inside. She began wondering how life would have turned out if she could have been with Kavita.

'I gave myself permission to do it without actually going there. Kind of exploring in my head. Even in my head, the idea of it felt scary. Very scary.'

But she wasn't yet ready to open the box all the way. After all, she was still a married woman and a mother with young children. Having lived a heteronormative life thus far, it was a shock to her system. From a simple, conservative background, coming out and accepting her sexuality was neither a simple nor a natural progression. In some ways, she was homophobic, even towards herself. Given her manic work schedule, she was also too fatigued to have much time to think beyond the daily drudgery.

'I was too tired to even think of what was even beyond my marriage.'

Some of her hesitation also stemmed from a natural concern for her family—how would her family, let alone her extended family, react to a separation or her sexual orientation? How would it affect her and Ravi, and their children? Her mother who was proud of her daughter's coveted 'NRI life', and who had sacrificed her life for her children— how could she disappoint her? Raga kept worrying and kept trying to make her marriage work, putting patches on the holes and tears.

With hindsight, she says, 'Live your truth. If you know in your heart that this isn't working out, then do not prolong a dysfunctional marriage. Do not use your children as a reason, because they will grow up with time. Children only understand love.'

Yet, the box in her mind would no longer stay closed. Every once in a while, it would open up a little and tantalize her with the possibilities. Tentatively, out of curiosity, Raga went to a couple of gay parties. But she felt uncomfortable. They spoke a language she did not understand. Yet again, she found herself not fitting in. What Raga was looking for was ways to find the answers within. Who was she? What did she want? What was right for her and her family? While people in

'If the agency I worked with in New Zealand had offered me support in any way during those tough days, I believe my story would have turned out differently, professionally.

'Companies need to realize that people need to carry their full selves to work, to get the most from them. When there is homophobia, transphobia and no sensitization within the organization, it can be a huge burden for us. Often ending in traumatic ways.'

New Zealand were a little more tolerant of varied sexualities, they were far from embracing them; heteronormative lifestyles were still seen as the accepted way to live. There were still many employees who were homophobic or transphobic and did not hesitate to pass rude comments. There was a perception that being openly gay could lead to discrimination in terms of promotions at work. That made it much harder for someone who was still coming to terms with their own sexuality to be able to open up about it in the workplace and work their way through it.

Raga feels that companies need to have more inclusive DEIB (Diversity, Equity, Inclusion, and Belonging) policies for acceptance and sensitization of the entire workforce as to LGBTQIA+ people. Counselling and HR policies that advocate acceptance and help employees come out as openly gay will help them bring their whole selves to work.

Forced Out of the Closet

By now, Raga's marriage was effectively over. She and Ravi had nothing in common beyond the children, and the distance was only growing. Eventually, they decided to live separately, but Raga continued to feel responsible for Ravi. She supported both homes financially. Her kids, who were very young at the time, often reacted to the separation by blaming themselves for the break-up. The family was in deep emotional distress, and Raga was trying hard to hold on to her sanity, as well as keep her family together. Loneliness, fear and guilt all ate away at her, and she retreated into a shell. So vociferous at work, but in her personal life, Raga had little self-confidence.

'When I was going through my own stress, I did not want to be a gay woman at all. I fought against it a lot. I did not want anyone to know that my preference was for women, I did not want anyone to know my life. I was still holding onto my family and whatever little I had but it was slipping away from me.'

One morning, her mother, visiting her in Wellington, was cleaning a closet when she discovered an unsent letter from Raga to her best friend. In it, she confessed her sexual orientation. But, worried about her friend's reaction, Raga hesitated and had hidden it away till she felt strong enough to post it.

Her mother read through the letter. Words leapt out at her that she had never thought she would hear about her daughter. 'Attracted to a woman', 'sexuality', 'divorce', 'date women'—each of them taboo and considered a sin in her culture.

That night, as Raga was putting the kids to bed, her mother sprang at her, holding a sharp knife to her chest!

'What have I done to deserve this? I wish you were dead. I wish you were not born. This is a sin. A huge sin. You are a sinner. What will people say? You've destroyed your family for this? Have you no shame? I will kill you!' she roared in rage. 'You have to get back together with Ravi; put your family together. You have become too *firang*. You should go back to India immediately. How can you destroy them all for your shameful desire?'

Shocked at the aggression her mother was showing towards her, terrified of what may happen and still not wanting to hurt her mother in any way, Raga denied her sexual orientation. With tears rolling down her cheeks, she sobbed, 'I'm sorry, Mummy; I never meant to do this. I never wanted to let you down. That is not going to happen. Nothing is going to happen. Do not worry. That letter was nothing; I am not gay.'

Three Lives

Though she and Ravi were separated, she continued to try and rebuild bridges. But gradually, the conflict between her truth and the life she was leading only began to intensify. And the harder she tried, the more fragile the relationship became, until finally she decided it just wasn't working out between them. She then decided to explore her true sexuality. She gave herself permission to date women.

Raga was being wooed by a woman at that time, and she decided to give it a go. She hoped that this was something that would help her move forward in a life where she felt stuck.

But her euphoria about finally being able to live her truth was short-lived. Her same-sex partner turned out to be possessive and suspicious, with anger and alcohol issues. She constantly threatened to 'out' Raga—publicly revealing her sexuality to everyone. She would regularly beat up Raga severely over trivial issues.

'I was so ashamed of myself, of being with a woman, of being abused, that I would not talk about it to anyone. I lived in shame. Often, I would go to work with bandages on my face, pretending the cat scratched me.' Raga felt imprisoned by the threat the woman was holding over her head and unable to leave.

The NRI community tends to be close-knit, which could be a boon as well as a curse. Soon, word got around about her broken marriage and her sexuality. Many of the people she had thought of as close friends now ghosted her. Her kids stopped getting invited to parties and sleepovers. Overnight, Raga was completely ostracized!

Ravi was becoming less of a friend and going through his own issues—with friends and colleagues doubting his masculinity. 'So your wife has run away with a woman?' they would ask him. He continued to be financially dependent on her and spent money recklessly, running up debts everywhere.

'We struggled through this phase. I kept on paying for his groceries, yet some days when I picked up the kids from his house, they would say they were hungry because their father didn't have food at home.'

Raga was doing what a lot of women do—they protect their husbands and overcompensate. She had also made the classic mistake that many women make—her finances and those of her husband were intertwined. Her husband was in charge of the money even after they had separated. She didn't even know her bank passwords.

'I would buy a McDonald's burger for my kids, and a $2 bill would get declined while I was making $200,000 a year. I had to face the fact that he was a huge spender. All kinds of things were bought with my very hard-earned money. It took me a long time to get a hold of my banking; not because he did not want to hand it over to me, it was because I had no clue how to manage banking and my money.'

Raga let him get away with his behaviour because of the guilt she felt over breaking up the family.

The one bright spot was work—professionally, Raga was doing really well. In 2006, she was elected as the deputy chair of the India New Zealand Business Council, the first woman ever to be elected on the board. But this didn't mean the end of challenges. A traditional old white boy's institution, the council had no idea how to operate with a woman on the board, that too one with a voice. Often, Raga would only be asked a question as a mere formality, and the male voices would take over. She had to be vociferous to ensure her voice was heard, no matter how hard they tried to shut her down.

Her sense of self-respect and boundaries remained intact at work. She was very clear about what she would accept from clients and colleagues. She would not hesitate to walk out if someone was over 15 minutes late to a meeting without informing her. Never hesitating to call a spade a spade, she would come up with a smart quip or a quick retort in every situation. 'Your handshake is as strong as a man's,' a well-known wealth consultant in New Zealand told her. Raga looked him straight in the eye and said, 'No, actually, my handshake is as strong as a woman's!' Her repartee became her trademark, and people she met would look forward to her zingers. With recognition and numerous accolades and awards, in less than four years, she had worked her way up to a great position in advertising and was among the highest paid professionals in New Zealand.

But she was beginning to feel exhausted from trying to lead three different lives—the first, that of a successful, in-demand professional woman; second, of a victim of domestic violence who was beaten up and abused most days by her same-sex partner; and third, of a mother pretending to be happy around her children.

'It was a really dark time. I did not want to get out of bed in the mornings but would only do so because of my children and my work. There were times when I really wanted to end it all. I couldn't see a way out of my misery.'

She would cry every day in the privacy of her home. Yet, she presented a mask of positivity and cheer outside the home.

One night was particularly traumatic. Raga's partner flew into a violent rage and abused her more severely than she ever had before. Raga was gravely injured. The house was badly broken. That was one of the most traumatic nights of Raga's life. Lying alone for weeks, Raga wished she had succumbed to her injuries.

The trauma from that night continued to haunt her long after the relationship was over, and she suffers deeply from it even now. Her biggest regret is that she actually stayed in that relationship for two and a half years, which broke her self-confidence entirely.

She has shared this as a story in her book, *Untold Lies*. Her advice to women who find themselves in a similar situation—be it with a same-sex or opposite-sex partner—is to call it quits as quickly as possible rather than keep trying to make it work out. They need to find the strength to let go of their own limiting beliefs, because the vicious cycle of hope, despair and the humiliation of being at the receiving end saps the victim's self-confidence and makes it harder for them to leave, subjecting them to more abuse. At the same time, she advocates that women should be financially independent, because that is one of the key factors enabling one to make strong decisions.

Breaking Free

After this incident, she broke up with the woman, regardless of her threats. It was her love and sense of responsibility towards her children that gave her the motivation to carry on. She owed it to the kids. And somewhere at the back of her mind, a small flicker said that she also owed it to herself.

By this time, her sexual orientation had begun impacting her career. Though overt homophobia was forbidden by law, Raga found herself suddenly being passed over for prestigious projects. Snide comments were made. Her workplace began excluding her from social events. The accolades and awards stopped. Raga didn't know how to cope and had to continue working at the agency as she had a financial responsibility towards her family.

One day, during a work meeting, she realized she couldn't work there any longer. The job was no longer giving her joy or a reason to survive. She quit her job the same day. She still had bills to pay and no other job to go to. But it was tiring to be surrounded by constant homophobia demonstrated through actions, not just words. It was time to get out!

Raga decided to use her experience of being a part of the India–New Zealand trade relations to start her own consulting company. She began supporting local companies with their market entry into

India. She could take on the clients she felt like and refuse those she didn't want to work with. Now she was free!

Once, a potential client gave her a blank cheque, trying to sign her up to support his business to make an entry into India. But despite his eagerness to enter the Indian market, he kept voicing his poor opinion of India. Raga was taken aback by the negativity. She didn't want to work with anyone who thought poorly of her country.

'I kept asking him to stop that, but when he did not, I returned the cheque and said, "I really don't think anyone will work with a person like you in India and you really should not come to India."'

On another occasion, at an event, a senior person from New Zealand kept insulting India. 'I kept thinking—why isn't anyone stopping this man? Even the top business people kept nodding their heads, but I challenged him, I said, "You are being a fuck," and walked away. We never spoke again, but I think it is important to call out such people, and even if it seems too shocking, it is okay. We need to stand up for ourselves and for our country, no matter where we are. It is as simple as that.'

During this time, Raga had a contract with an event company that hosted top management speakers in New Zealand and Australia. Through this agency, Raga learnt a new business—that of running premium business events around the world. She supported this agency in hosting several top management leaders in India, China, Hong Kong, Singapore, Malaysia and other countries. Incidentally, it was this business that nudged her out of her shell. She was hosting an event with Deepak Chopra in Bengaluru and serendipitously happened to walk into the room while he was speaking. 'He was talking about the limiting beliefs that we have. How women try to tell themselves that this is it. They do not leave marriages that are not working; they do not leave a job that they are unhappy with; they will put up with dysfunctional friends and hold onto things.' Raga realized that until and unless she jettisoned her limiting beliefs, she would always lead half a life. 'I thought if I am not happy, my children will also not be happy.'

Finding Love

In 2008, she met Nicola, a New Zealander who was very much a part of the change in New Zealand's attitude and laws towards women, particularly gay people. Nicola was a professional, intelligent and strong woman who lived her truth. Raga and Nicola were soon in a relationship. The children were young when they met and recognized love when they saw it. They accepted Nicola into their lives happily. Slowly, Raga began getting her life together again. Over time, Ravi and Raga started building a new way of being—not just for the sake of their children but also because they really cared for each other.

'Just because we were no longer married did not mean that I had stopped loving or caring for Ravi. He was still my best friend. He was still my pillar. I was always going to be there for him.'

Raga realized that Nicola was keen to experience and work in India. They decided to move to Mumbai together with the children, even though Raga knew it would disrupt their lives. To her surprise, she found that her children not only adjusted, but they learnt many things.

In India, life was no different than before—both Nicola and Raga felt the need to hide their relationship. Raga's mother had come around to the extent of moving in and living with the family for over four years but never mentioned the fact that Raga and Nicola were partners. She grew to love Nicola and even taught her how to make the Mangalorean curries Raga loved, but would always introduce Nicola as Raga's friend. The schools, too, pretended that Nicola was a family friend and an 'emergency contact'. In their social life in India, they made a lot of friends, but their relationship was swept under the carpet. The extended family kept pretending that Raga was still with her husband and constantly asked about when he would be back. Raga herself was not ready to completely accept her sexuality publicly and come out.

Finding Her Voice

During this time, Raga and Nicola were also invited to set up a speakers bureau for a large publishing company in India, after which they decided to emigrate to the United Kingdom.

Driven by her childhood experiences and her professional expertise in hosting large-scale business events and speaker management, Raga set up a speakers bureau in India, operating out of the UK. Having grown up without access to books, she knew how it felt to be alone, without information or inspiration. She had seen the impact storytellers and subject matter experts like Edward de Bono, Stephen Covey, Mark Inglis and Deepak Chopra had on people, including herself. For the first year, they managed with just one speaker. The concept of paying a speaker to address a gathering was nascent in India. Eventually, though, Raga scaled up her business, bringing in partners, and they went on to represent a large range of speakers from India and around the world. Nicola and Raga started spending more time between India and London.

Raga had always had a passion for writing and would pen poems and short stories all through her life to manage her internal homophobia, struggles and the pain that she was carrying. As time went by, Raga started feeling suffocated, leading a dual life. She had a loving partner, the twins had grown up beautifully, she had a good friendship with Ravi and she was fully independent financially. She decided that it was time to come out of the closet she had buried herself in. With the encouragement of Nicola, the twins and Ravi, she revealed her true sexuality in her first book. In September 2019, Raga's book *Untold Lies* was unveiled by Dr Shashi Tharoor.

Her story started getting noticed in India, and Nicola and Raga's interview on Humans of Bombay and Brut India created a new world for them. Suddenly, Raga found herself being interviewed by media across India and being invited to book launches to share her story. One day, Barkha Dutt offered to showcase their modern family and invited Nicola and Ravi to her prestigious event, 'We The Women'. While Raga had always been behind the scenes, as someone who built other people's personal brands, this was a whole new game. One thing led to another, and, to her surprise, Raga found that she soon became a sought-after speaker on a range of topics. Her characteristic mix of candour, caustic wit and humour helped her connect with her audience in a unique way.

She also began helping LGBTQIA+ people who turned to her for advice. One interesting case was referred to her by a friend in India. A gay man married a straight woman with a mutual understanding that he would continue to live his gay life and she would continue to live her life. However, a few years into the marriage, the woman started threatening to tell his family that he was 'gay', trying to extort money from him. Raga found a lawyer to help resolve the case.

There was another case recently of domestic abuse faced by a woman from her same-sex partner. They were not out to the family so the woman was facing this on her own, scared and ashamed to tell anyone. She reached out to Raga, who intervened to support her, first of all, to get out of a very volatile and aggressive relationship, and then helped her get therapy.

Because she was not out, the woman was unable to seek any legal recourse. These kinds of stories of abuse are sadly quite common in the LGBTQIA+ community as well, and the lack of legal remedies makes them harder to resolve.

On a panel, Raga challenged the award-winning filmmaker Onir that all his stories were about gay men. She wrote a lesbian love story that is loosely based on her life. This story is now being made into an international film, and Raga realizes the potential to write stories that can change narratives.

When Life Gives You Lemons

But, like everything else in Raga's life—things kept changing. In March 2020, the lockdown was announced, and Nicola and Raga had to move back to London overnight. Their business took a huge hit, and things started falling apart again. During this time, Nicola had a brain injury, and life stopped for Raga. She put everything aside and spent two years caring and tending to Nicola.

At this point, Raga, who was still learning a new way of being a publicly out 'gay' woman, decided it was time to make peace with her life. Nicola, who had graciously, kindly, gently put Raga's broken pieces

Success Mantras

So, one is that we must learn to share our experiences. That is something we do not do, and I am beginning to. Two is to call out. We see people around us speak about horrible things, and we participate. We do not need to participate in that negativity or toxicity, and we should speak out. And three, what has personally worked is that every time I have some problems, I get my 'me' time, I go away, as it is very important to reflect. I think, as women, we do not do that very often, and we feel guilty and selfish when we spend time by ourselves, and I think that is critical.

together over the years and who had hidden away from living her truth, deserved better. She decided to surprise Nicola. When London opened up after lockdown, at a live London event, Raga proposed to Nicola with the full excitement and support of their now adult twins.

In August 2022, life truly came full circle. Raga married Nicola in a beautiful, intimate ceremony, surrounded by a few close friends from the LGBTQIA+ community whom they consider their chosen family and their two children. Her current focus is to make their marriage status legal in India as well, and she is now an intervenor in the current marriage equality petitions in India.

In 2023, she set up the UK's first speakers' network for LGBTQIA+ women and those who are non-binary. There are already people saying that it is going to fail.

'Fail or pass, it doesn't matter. I have to continuously keep doing the right thing—making space for women is critical. What is even more critical is making space for women who are marginalized.'

When there are dark moments, particularly with trolls and bigots, Raga does wonder why the universe presented this kind of life to her. Why couldn't she just have stayed married to Ravi and lived that fairy-tale life? But she realizes that she was given this life for a higher purpose, to challenge the norms of a heterosexual world, where the marginalized do not have the privilege of living their lives freely, loving whom they want and holding their heads high as they walk.

She sighs as she says, 'I am a part of this wonderful community. I was allowed to marry my same-sex partner and live a life of love and respect. I want this basic human right for the LGBTQIA+ community in India. My life is now fully devoted to community work. This gives my life meaning. I have finally found my purpose in life—a reason for me to wake up every morning. Maybe when I go to India, I will get a few *chappals* and tomatoes thrown at me, and that is okay. I am no longer afraid.

'I see a new India. From my lens and from how it was for me, the younger generation has representation and role models that they can access. Society is slowly hearing our voices; cinema and other platforms are giving our voices space. No longer should we have to force marriages, use conversion practices or do inhumane things to people just because we do not understand. If I were to live my life again with the freedom I now have, I believe I would have become one of the top CEOs or entrepreneur[s] of Indian origin. But it's never too late. I have started a new venture at 53. I have only just begun.'

It took Raga 19 years to feel comfortable with her sexuality and come out! It involved dismantling a lifetime of heteronormative, patriarchal messaging and internalized homophobia. But looking back at her life journey, she feels she would not trade any of it—neither the highs nor the lows—because that made her who she is. The only thing she wishes she had known was to take herself less seriously. Her advice to other LGBTQIA+ people is to 'get rid of the internalized homophobia. Accept yourself first. Once self-acceptance happens, be kind to the people who do not understand and give them the time they need.

'Closets are for clothes, not to hide our truth,' she says with a grin.

Today, Raga seems completely at peace with who she is. Her joyous confidence is evident as she speaks. With two nose rings, rainbow-streaked hair and a unique sense of dressing, Raga is at last unapologetically herself.

Summarizing her journey from not knowing to fully embracing every aspect, she says, quoting the value enshrined in Lintas's annual diary, "'To know and not to act is to not know at all." I knew this all along, but it took me 50 years to act on it!'

Hacks to Storm the Norm

Norm: Homosexuality is a taboo for even the most evolved people in a society.

While the term LGBTQIA+ has entered common parlance, it is still to become widely accepted as the way some people are. Even today, there is a lot of misinformation about whether it's a lifestyle choice that some people make or whether it is some kind of perversion or sickness that needs to be 'cured'. Given the aversion with which homosexuality is viewed in society at large, it can be very hard to acknowledge to yourself that you are homosexual. But the sooner you come to terms with it, the more peace of mind you will have.

Hacks:

1. Frame it differently
Did you choose to have black hair or brown eyes, for example? Did you choose to be short or tall, fair-or dark-skinned? These are all traits you were born with; it is in your DNA. So, too, is your sexuality. You don't choose to be heterosexual or homosexual; your body is born with those impulses. It's inherent and natural. Tell yourself this mantra, 'The fact that I am gay is just another facet of who I am, just as being creative, optimistic, or having brown eyes is. I choose to live my life authentically and happily. I have the right to be happy.'

2. Get professional help
Consult a reliable therapist at an early stage, when you are struggling to identify your sexuality, before you've even put a label on it. Therapists are trained to help you think deeply and cope with your emotions as you undergo changes. A good one can be a great support,

especially when you yourself or your ecosystem—friends, family—are not accepting of your truth. Think of it as an investment in your lifelong mental health.

3. Come out in your own time

Don't come out till you're ready. You're entitled to your privacy, and you don't have to reveal your sexuality until you're ready. Nor do you have to reveal it to everyone. You can choose trusted friends and family when you feel you've reached some stage of self-acceptance.

RAMYA
Move On to the Next Arrow

Introduction

Ramya Venkataraman is an alumna of IIT Delhi and IIM Calcutta. She began her career with McKinsey & Company and worked with them for more than 15 years across different sectors. In the last five years of her stint there, she built and headed McKinsey's education practice in India, pursuing her long-standing passion for education.

Ramya took the plunge into entrepreneurship in late 2014, setting up CENTA, a company that assesses and certifies the competencies of teachers, creates career growth and earnings opportunities for them and supports their professional development. CENTA currently works with over 1.5 million teachers—probably the world's largest platform for teachers—from more than 1,00,000 schools and more than 7,000 locations, the majority from across India, but with 140 other countries also represented.

Why Ramya?

> What are little girls made of?
> Sugar and spice,
> And everything nice.
> That's what little girls are made of.

Most countries have specific norms around femininity, and India is no exception. Girls are meant to be demure, self-effacing and cooperative. Their life story begins with marriage as the key milestone. Every major life event is defined by this milestone, including having a family.

Ramya Venkataraman, a motorcycle-riding IIT and IIM alumna who was a finalist on popular singing show *Close-Up Antakshari*, has broken every one of these norms and more. While she doesn't describe herself as a rebel, she hasn't allowed norms to stop her from pursuing what she cares about. Be it standing for student council elections at IIT, working with clients in the manufacturing sector, or going on to adopt a daughter as a single mom, she has written her script on her own terms. Born into a traditional South Indian family, what enabled her to buck the norms?

Girl on a Motorbike

Ramya wanted to contest campus elections for the post of the general secretary at IIT. This would be the first time that someone from the girls' hostel contested this election. Typically, candidates had to have a two-wheeler to get around the city for fest sponsorship meetings and other activities. She didn't have one. It was a costly purchase of ₹35,000 at that time. Ramya had grown up in a middle-class family where the budget had limitations. It wouldn't be easy to find such a large amount all of a sudden. But she didn't hesitate to ask her father for help.

She and her brother had been brought up to do everything they do wholeheartedly, be it academics or extracurriculars. Moreover, they had been taught that they should do whatever it took, ethically, to excel and win. Ramya's father didn't have that much money readily available. But he, too, didn't bat an eyelid once he understood why she needed the bike. The thought of her gender didn't even occur to him as an obstacle.

Ramya's maternal grandfather had kept some money aside, which he planned to give to each of his grandchildren at their weddings. Ramya's father went to her grandfather, explained the situation, and said, 'I am sure we can figure out her wedding gift at the right time. Why don't you gift her a motorcycle instead now?' Her grandfather agreed. Ramya got the bike she wanted. Although she did not go on to win the election, she enthusiastically rode the motorcycle for the next ten years.

Choosing a Career

Ramya's father worked in a bank, while her mother was a homemaker. While they both had stereotypical roles within the family, it was framed as a division of labour rather than gendered roles. Ramya and her brother did not grow up with gender-defined stereotypes. Brought up in Mumbai, Ramya grew up sporty, noisy and outgoing. Academic success came to her easily; she never needed to study much to do well. It was a family rule that the kids should be outdoors after 5 p.m., so Ramya spent much of her time playing with friends. Ramya's mother herself learnt to cook only as an adult because *her* mother thought children should not enter the kitchen. She followed the same principle with Ramya. So much so, that when Ramya went away to IIT, she didn't even know how many spoons of sugar she liked in her milk!

When she turned 10, her father was transferred to Delhi. Ramya began attending Mater Dei, a reputed school. Delhi was a culture shock for the kids. Torn from her childhood buddies and unused to the more aggressive environment in Delhi, it took her a few years to build strong relationships with her peers. She started spending more time reading. By Class 10, she also began formulating career plans and dreamed of doing something big.

The family carried a deep sense of patriotism, and Ramya was filled with the notion of directly being of service to the country. 'My dad was passionate about India as a country and I also heard a lot of stories about how my paternal granddad (whom I have not met) participated in India's freedom struggle.' Ramya thought that getting into the IAS would be a great way to contribute to nation-building.

Her father believed that she should take an unusual route to get there.

'My dad told me that it is good to be an IAS officer, but you should not be that type of IAS who does not have a proper technical background. So complete your engineering from an IIT, then do your MBA, and then study for your IAS.'

Her mother joked, 'Then any prospective bridegroom will say, "Let me go and study some more."'

But the family rallied around Ramya's career path and the preparation for the IIT JEE began. Her mom cleared up a whole room in the house, set up a table and even gave her the choice of having meals there or coming to the dining room. To add to it, a school teacher, Mr Khilnani, pushed her hard every time he thought she was wavering.

Incidentally, by the time she got accepted to an IIT, Ramya no longer had the aspiration to join the IAS, though the keenness to do something for the country—that something still to be defined—continued.

The first time Ramya observed gender discrimination was at some weddings. At pre-wedding gatherings, young men were praised for not asking for dowries. And young women found that many of the potential grooms they met asked for dowries. At wedding ceremonies, Ramya saw the difference in the way the boy's side was treated and the girl's side was treated. The girl's side was expected to be at the beck and call of the boy's side and fulfil their spoken and unspoken demands. The importance the boy's side received made it very clear where the power lay. Though Ramya grew up expecting to have an arranged marriage, she vowed to herself that it would not take place in this manner, on these unequal terms.

A Young Leader

In higher secondary school, even though she was preparing for the JEE, Ramya was busier with other aspects of life. She was elected head girl and had many responsibilities to fulfil.

During her tenure as head girl, the school decided not to participate in a prominent inter-school event that students had enjoyed for many years. The student body was distraught. As the student leader, Ramya organized a signed petition by the students to the principal to convince her of their arguments. However, the school finally stood firm in its decision. In anger, Ramya said, 'If I had to decide, I would decide differently... ', but her own statement made her wonder, so how *would* she decide? What would she value, and what would she compromise? That incident triggered a series of questions in her mind on what she wanted a school to look like. She often discussed these with her cousin Usha, a teacher.

Ramya loved participating in inter-school events and competitions. Through these events, she met students from many other schools. Some of her friends at school were interesting people who did well in many activities but not the things that the school valued. As a result, they always felt a little out of place and didn't enjoy it to the extent that Ramya did. This made Ramya feel that kids only enjoy school if they are good at academics or involved in extracurriculars. This epiphany would go on to shape her later career. 'So, the simple dream was that I wanted to start a school that would be fun for children of all kinds.'

Ramya cracked the IIT entrance exam and got into the prestigious IIT Delhi. At IIT, more than discrimination, gender stereotyping was common. Be it in a debate or a sport, girls were not considered competition but as extras. During freshers' ragging, the seniors showed the batch the honour board featuring the names of the hostels that won trophies each year. There was only one girls' hostel among seven boys' hostels. It did not appear on the board.

'Why is the girls' hostel nowhere on the board?' Ramya asked curiously. 'Because we didn't win,' said a senior, adding, 'now you people have to get us on the board.' The senior probably didn't realize that her one sentence would define Ramya's aim for the next four years! Almost immediately, Ramya and many of her batchmates started participating earnestly in freshers' events, gunning to win.

One of the girls, Nishi, was a state-level table tennis champion. She was to play against one of the boys' hostels in the freshers' match. Normally, girls were given seven points at the beginning of the game to level the playing field.

'Let both teams start at zero,' Ramya said, knowing her friend's skill with the game. The boys were surprised.

'No, it's okay, we're happy to let you get a head start with seven points. We will still win,' they smiled.

Ramya and her friend tried again to convince them.

'She's a state level player, it's okay, let's start out with both sides at zero,' they said. But the referee, a senior boy, didn't want to change any norms.

The match was soon under way. Both sides waited to see what would happen—there was far more at stake than a simple game of ping-pong. Shrill cheers rang out from the two hostels for their respective players. Unexpectedly for the boys' hostel, right from the beginning, the female player dominated. The boy she played against was no match for her. He found it impossible to return her serve or anticipate the direction in which she would return the ball.

Slowly, the boys' voices died down. They hadn't expected such a turn of events. Meanwhile, the girls got more and more excited, louder and louder.

By the end, it was a complete rout. Nishi won 21–0! The boys were shocked and upset. They tried to cover up for the sake of their egos, claiming, 'You won because you started with seven points.'

'Arre, but we didn't beat you by seven points, we beat you by 21 points,' Ramya huffed.

'Yes, but the seven extra points right in the beginning gave you a psychological advantage,' the boys stated, walking away quickly before they were challenged to another match.

The girls won the freshers' trophy. Winning the inter-hostel competitions did more than just win the girls a trophy. It started breaking the stereotype and helped them be treated as equals, even in the face of 'benevolent' patriarchy. The boys started respecting their female classmates as equals and stood up for them.

'In my department—mechanical engineering—there would be professors and lab assistants who would say it was difficult for a girl to use the heavy machines and lift them and stuff. But because of this new equation with them, I found the boys in my class standing up for me and saying, *"Nahi sir, woh sab kuch kar sakti hai, usko karne do!"'* (No, sir! They can do everything; let them do it!)

Ramya's four years at IIT became about ensuring the girls' hostel won trophies, rather than academics. Ramya was not the first person to think this way. In each of the three batches senior to her, there were a couple of girls who pushed for the girls' hostel to go out there and win. 'That was a great starting point for us,' says Ramya.

'There were already a couple of things we were doing well at—like dramatics and music—so it was all about, how can we now do this consistently and extend it to all of BRCA (Board for Recreational and Creative Activities) as it was called? It also made it easier to rally people, saying, 'We need to continue what our seniors have started.'

Call it chance or like minds coming together, Ramya became close friends with those few seniors—Jo, Nalini, Lavanya and Pooja. 'That was like my apprenticeship,' she says, 'I understood bits and pieces of this whole dynamic in a protected environment.'

By the end of her second year, Ramya had started rallying the hostel behind this objective. When you ask her, 'What objective?', she says, 'My underlying objective was for us to be accepted on campus as equals, to stop the stereotyping...but the tangible objective became the BRCA trophy—because without that, the goal was too vague.'

As a first step, she understood the points' system behind the trophy in great detail. While some events had one team from each hostel, others had participation points that were based on how many individuals from the hostel joined in. The girls' hostel had just 15 people in a batch, compared to 50 people per batch in each of the boys' hostels. For the events with participation points, Ramya pushed as many people as possible from the hostel to join—including master's students, who were often more focussed on academics. She remembers a Scrabble event that saw 24 girls participating—the highest from any hostel!

Some of the girls would be reluctant.

'But I don't even know Scrabble. I have never played it.'

Ramya would argue, 'It doesn't matter. Most of the boys who land up haven't played it either. You are just going to get participation points.'

'But what if I get a zero score?'

'How does it matter? We know you are going only for participation points. You would have still contributed.'

As participation grew, some of the boys also started cheering for this spirit. For example, one afternoon, the girls found out about an inter-hostel bridge tournament taking place that evening. None of the girls knew how to play bridge. Ramya asked one of the boys, 'Can you quickly teach a bunch of us how to play?' He was willing but surprised, 'How can you learn this in two hours?' But Ramya insisted, 'We will learn quickly. And we will play as much as possible.' In the evening, the other boys were surprised to see a bunch of girls at the game of bridge, something they had never seen before.

'But why did we get to know only in the afternoon?'

One of the girls found out that, with the girls' hostel being at the other end of the campus, event posters often reached there late. There was no negative intent, just that someone would try to club the poster delivery with another trip.

'But someone must be deciding on the event date even before the posters are created—how do we get to the source?' was the next question. This root cause analysis led them to a diary in the students' activity centre, where planned events were recorded. They set up a process to take turns getting details from the diary each week, so that they could plan in advance.

'For me, the only answer to stereotyping was to win,' she says. She managed to convince her father that a high rank at IIT was not a prerequisite for an MBA. It was years later that Ramya questioned whether that approach was correct or whether the right way to go would have been to protest or educate against the stereotyping itself, rather than pushing to prove themselves.

A True Victory

By the time Ramya started her fourth year, there was more acceptance on campus. Until a few years earlier, the norm had been that only boys contested college elections. But a couple of Ramya's seniors had broken this norm—thinking that it was time that a girl contested and won, they jumped headlong into institute elections and started occupying a few posts. Taking this one step further, Ramya decided to contest for the post of general secretary. Interestingly, some girls thought this was not the right move. But that was not because they felt there was a gender issue. They believed that their time at IIT should be spent on more important activities like learning, rather than trivial things like campus elections.

In hindsight, Ramya feels she should have spent more time studying and getting to know her professors; but, at the time, proving her hostel's mettle in campus elections and fighting for equality seemed far more important. Despite procuring the all-important motorcycle and the high energy campaigning, Ramya lost. She was defeated by a handful of votes.

'I lost by some 10 votes, and very interestingly, there was a guy who locked up some people in a hostel room because he did not want them to vote for a girl. Though the rest of this whole story now feels like a part of childhood or growing up, this is one thing I still feel a grudge about and still find it a little bit hard to reply to this guy on Facebook.'

After completing her engineering degree, Ramya qualified for entrance into IIM Calcutta. At IIM Calcutta, Ramya found that the gender ratio, while better than at IIT, was still skewed—19 girls in a batch of 332. However, she did not find the stereotyping she had experienced at IIT, though there were a few classmates who discriminated against women.

Ramya's hostel had a ratio of 75 per cent boys to 25 per cent girls. The students were free to come and go to each other's rooms as they wished. Groups of boys and girls routinely hung out and studied together. There was also more diversity in other ways. 'Among my friends were people like Munira, Tulika and Kumudha who came from non-engineering backgrounds and brought a different perspective and a different kind of confidence.' Ramya took her motorbike to IIM, which gave her a certain street cred. At an inter-hostel competition dubbed World War, Ramya was elected commander-in-chief for her hostel, the second woman to be chosen for the post until then.

Determined to succeed on her own merits rather than being pigeonholed by gender, her keenness to be treated as an equal continued and she refused to accept special treatment.

'At IIM Calcutta, Nestlé announced two awards: 'Best Young

Business Manager of the Batch' award and 'Women in Management' award. Though the intent was very positive—to encourage women who did not receive family support to pursue management—I felt it would not be appropriate for someone who had received *all* possible family support (like myself) to apply for it; so I applied only for the first one and luckily also received it.'

A Detour to a Dream

All through her years at IIT and IIM, Ramya's dream of starting a school hadn't left her. But some volunteer projects with a couple of NGOs made her realize that she needed more skills and a certain amount of money. She decided to think about this dream, say, 10 years into her career. After her MBA, she joined the prestigious consulting firm, McKinsey. Since the firm hired mostly from premier MBA schools, the gender ratio at the firm was similar to that in these schools at entry level. However, there were far fewer women at the higher levels of the organization.

'During my time at the entry level, it was 15–20 per cent women while at leadership level, it was 5 per cent.'

Consulting involves a lot of travel and working from a client's office or factory location for much of the week. While at the entry level, women were able to cope with the demands of travel, as they got married and had children, it was no longer doable.

'The biggest reason why a lot of women opted out was the travel. It was not the long hours; it was the travel. The home situation was such that during the day they could still get support, but when it came to the night, staying away from home multiple nights was not as acceptable for married women with kids as it was for men. As a partner, you work with five–six clients, and you have to travel to different locations. For example, it was very common for me to be on five–six flights in a week. Most women do not have the luxury to be able to do that. In consulting, it was difficult to find many career opportunities without travel.'

She noticed an interesting principle in the way the firm treated men and women. They were both expected to put in the same quality and quantity of work. They were both expected to pull all-nighters when required. They were both expected to travel to and from client sites. However, her mentors at the firm believed in equity. When women had to travel or go home late at night, Rajat and Ramesh took care to ensure their safety.

Specializing in manufacturing and heavy industries in her later years in the firm, Ramya often travelled to client sites. Their manufacturing sites were so male-dominated that they sometimes did not even have a separate bathroom for women. Once, she ended up asking a male colleague to stand guard outside the men's restroom! Both she and the firm ensured her safety through some standard protocols they developed.

'You have to be careful that you are not left alone in the plant and that some of your colleagues are with you. That you are not stuck in the middle of nowhere, and you are travelling together. If you are travelling very late at night, you are using only an office car.'

Meanwhile, her parents had begun the hunt for the ideal groom. Though her parents were very progressive, they expected her to get into an arranged marriage as soon as she finished her degree from IIM. Ramya, too, was keen to get married. Friends tried to set her up. But, somehow, none of the potential matches worked out.

As her friends slowly got married, she started becoming the odd one out. Her parents became anxious. Over time, the stress of it began to weigh on her. With most people around her in pairs, she began feeling like a third wheel in social gatherings.

When she came across an opportunity for a transfer to Chicago, she jumped at it. The move ended up being a welcome break from everything. She enjoyed setting up an independent home in a different country. There was less pressure around her single status. The work culture was different, as were her clients. She started making new friends.

Homebound

A couple of years later, Ramya was ready to move back to India and live close to her parents. They had missed her a lot. They were so happy to see her back that the topic of marriage became much less frequent in conversations. In her own mind, it continued to cause a niggle. And then one day, she still remembers how everything changed in a moment.

A couple of complex projects at work and the role of heading teams now had forced Ramya to introspect and start working on a new set of skills for herself.

'I used to think I was good at what I did. And then I really struggled with a couple of projects, which hit me hard. The initial reaction was to think that something was wrong with the project. But then I started understanding what I needed to do differently. And gradually, it became great fun trying to practise that every day.'

In the midst of a busy day at work, when she barely had time to draw breath, a thought occurred to her. 'I am liking this moment, and that's all. Why does anything need to change to be happy?' She understood that if you choose to be happy, you are happy.

'I feel trying to learn and improve yourself puts you in a different zone.'

Meanwhile, her desire to work in education had resurfaced. In a couple of years, Ramya began writing down the dreams and ideals of what she wanted to do in education. She shared her document with a couple of confidantes to bounce her ideas off of them. Her mentors were intrigued by her ideas and would ask provocative questions that made her think more. Slowly, she began to get more and more obsessed with her plan. She would sit in client meetings, ostensibly paying attention, but her mind would be busy refining her ideas. When she reached home from work, even at 11 p.m., she started a second shift working on her plan.

Around this time, the daughter of a close friend was diagnosed with terminal cancer. Soon afterwards, Mumbai was attacked by terrorists. Several people died in the attack. While no one she knew personally perished, Ramya was suddenly hit by the reality that life is fleeting and uncertain. She couldn't afford to keep postponing her dreams and waiting for the right time. The right time was now.

She decided to speak to her bosses at McKinsey. As it happened, McKinsey had been exploring the education sector as a new opportunity. The managing director suggested, 'Ramya, why don't you help build McKinsey's education practice? That will help you gain experience and give you the contacts you need to succeed.'

Ramya was intrigued; this sounded like a great plan. 'Okay, I'll try it for six months,' she said.

'No,' Adil Zainulbhai, the then chairman of McKinsey India, refused bluntly. 'Change like this isn't possible in six months. It will take at least a year. You'll have to give it that length of time at the minimum; otherwise, don't take it on.'

Ramya reflected on it and finally agreed to lead the practice for a year. But once she started working with clients, the projects took on a life of their own. Ramya worked on a wide variety of projects with different clients, whether it was with a large municipal corporation to set up India's first public–private partnership for government school transformation (variants of this model were used in many other states over the next several years and are in use even today), helping build the National Skill Development Corporation or creating the strategy for organizations like Teach for India, Azim Premji University and The Education Alliance. On the more commercial side of education, she worked with global private equity firms on evaluating their education investments in India. She felt deeply passionate about each of the projects and wound up working with McKinsey for another six years. Later, she realized that she had gained unprecedented exposure to the sector at all levels. Her position gave her a ringside view of the problems and the opportunities in education.

A Systemic Change

One day, her entrepreneurial bug started biting her again. 'It was particularly during a late-night karaoke session with one of my favourite teams. A young associate's comments made me feel that a different approach is needed. And while that partly informed our project, I also started once again thinking about what I want to do in education.'

While she had dreamt of setting up a school from the beginning, she now wanted to design something that could change the ecosystem as a whole. Otherwise, her influence would be limited to a handful of students. Ramya had looked into content as well as training as a means of improving teaching quality. But there was a lot of content available for teachers, and she found that the training wore off in a month or two. Then, it was back to business as usual. Teachers were demotivated to improve because there were no incentives for them to change. They didn't see a career path; there was no possibility of promotion. The system didn't even offer a pay difference between good teachers and indifferent ones.

"'What would happen even if I improved?" they asked me. "Everyone gets the same salary and bonus.'"

Ramya understood that in order to motivate adults, there had to be a tangible pay-off—some reward for self-development. In any profession, there are too few people who study for its own sake. Her idea evolved to make teaching aspirational by creating large-scale external recognition of teachers' skills and rewarding the ones who were more competent.

After brainstorming various ideas to help improve the quality of teaching, Ramya hit upon an idea that would be a win-win for teachers, schools and parents—an accreditation system. Centre for Teacher Accreditation (CENTA) Private Limited would provide accreditation for teachers, certifying their competence. Schools that hired CENTA teachers would be able to use this to showcase their own quality as compared to other schools that did not have CENTA teachers and therefore attract more pupils—for example, even EducationWorld's India School Rankings now have CENTA teacher scores as a parameter in school rankings. Teachers would see career growth and earning opportunities as a result. These opportunities would motivate a large number of teachers to keep improving their teaching skills, and, as an outcome, students would benefit.

Society giving aspirational value to professions correlates with the primary wage earners opting for those professions. Teaching is no exception—the reduction in its aspirational value has gone hand in hand with the profession being dominated by women. But CENTA certification creates large-scale empowerment of both female and male teachers.

Initially formed with Nalini and Anjali, close friends from IIT and IIM, respectively, CENTA began by running an Olympiad for teachers, which also rapidly became international, and led to recognition, awards and new opportunities for the winners. The first few years focussed on building the brand and the test, and reaching individual teachers. The message of a competition—the CENTA International Teaching Professionals' Olympiad or CENTA International TPO—that led to prizes was easy to convey at scale. The competition brought big partners in very early—The Hindu Media Group, Reliance Foundation, Lenovo, Central Square Foundation, EducationWorld, Oxford University Press and, more recently, the universities of Buckingham and California, Santa Cruz, among others. These partners gave big prizes to winning teachers—large cash awards and citations from Reliance Foundation, media profiling by the media entities, summer internships and global trainings at international universities—opportunities that teachers did not otherwise have access to and schools could not create for them. The partners also drove outreach for the initiative in their own ways, for example, ad space in return for brand association, posters through retail outlets and sales forces, millions of messages via SMS on telecom networks and so on. By staying very focussed on this one initiative for the first four years, CENTA was able to reach a large number of teachers and build its reputation with schools without spending much on marketing.

Now—and Ramya calls it 'phase 2' of CENTA—the company works with over 1.5 million teachers, more than 11 lakh on its own platform and another 4 lakh through partnerships, on certification, training as well as career growth. CENTA also works with various state governments and private schools to certify their teachers' skills and competence, and support the upskilling of their teachers. Currently, CENTA is expanding to geographies outside India as well— 140 countries are represented, with about seven of them having a significant number of teachers on the CENTA platform. The first two employees, Priyanka and Kartik, are part of the top team and several others have also joined the leadership over the years. Driving all this has kept Ramya on her toes.

Reflecting on her career journey and those of other women, Ramya feels that if workplaces could reduce travel, it will help women's participation and business economics.

Workplaces that are able to have flexible ways of working automatically end up having women working there. However, there is a caveat. 'I would say an organization should not do that just to have more female participation. Do it because a high-quality resource is going to be unavailable otherwise.'

Additionally, she believes that many of the hurdles women face come from their social and family set-up and mindset. Childcare and home management are still the purview of women in most families and seen as their primary duty. Unless that changes, women will find it hard to cope. This change needs to happen inside families; it cannot be seen as only a workplace issue.

The Modern Family

By the time she was starting CENTA, her friends had gone through their own life changes. Many of them had been married for a long time, and their kids had grown up. Some of them had become single through divorce. Many had seen losses in the immediate family. Ramya found many of her friends going through a mental transition she had experienced too—accepting life in all its forms.

'I realized that I love my work. It gives me a feeling of incredible emotional and spiritual fulfilment, almost a high. I have a very tightly knit family whom I am close to and who understand and give me space for my dreams. I have friends with whom I can share everything in my life.

'And for almost six years, my parents and I were like a gang of three friends living together and having a fantastic time. That experience would have never happened had I been married.'

But the human mind wishes for the next thing. At some point, it became clear to Ramya that, irrespective of marriage, she wanted to experience the joys of parenthood. She decided to adopt a child. She told her parents, 'I'm 38. If I want to adopt a child, I need to apply for it now; otherwise, the deadline will pass. But I want you both on board, because we will all have to raise my daughter together.' Her parents, supportive as usual, were delighted at the thought of a grandchild and assured her they were on board with the plan. The extended family also reacted with unconditional joy when they heard about this.

The only apprehension Ramya had was whether her being a single parent would become an obstacle. However, a professionally run adoption centre recommended by a college senior made the adoption process smooth. Though the interviewers did have questions about her single status, by the end of the interview, they understood that Ramya's immediate as well as extended family could be a lovely place for a child. When the baby, later named Nivedita, came home, she transformed Ramya's life and that of her parents.

As a mother, she tries to pass on many of the things she learnt from her parents. At the same time, she also brings up Nivedita a little differently from her own upbringing. While she teaches her the

---

Ramya's Top Tips:

- Don't define yourself, and do not let anyone define you on the basis of gender. You are a person entering the workplace, your gender does not matter, like your hair colour does not matter.
- Having a set of skills makes the biggest difference in a long professional life for anyone. Focus on building skills. Every six months, get a new skill and get better at it.
- Women tend to cave in communication; it does not help. Making your point and being direct helps a lot.

importance of working hard and being financially independent, she does not put the same emphasis on competitiveness and achievement that her parents did, for example. 'My younger brother Niranjan never imbibed competitiveness or achievement orientation, though he is super successful. That is an interesting role model for me now.

Like many in her peer group, Ramya was well-off by the time her daughter came, and she was keen that the kid should not grow up as an entitled brat. She consciously creates a feeling of scarcity around money sometimes. Despite her work schedule at McKinsey, Ramya had always found time for spontaneity in her life. Now with a fast-expanding business and a daughter's needs to watch out for, she has to run her life by timetables.

Unlike her mother, Ramya encourages her daughter to be interested in cooking, as she considers that a life skill for everyone, regardless of gender. For her daughter, her aspiration is that she should grow up to be an independent, well-adjusted individual.

Though her daughter goes to a fairly traditional school, Ramya has found both acceptance and appreciation for her journey as a single mom. Ramya was not just open with her daughter about her adoption, she turned it into a fun bedtime story. By the age of three, Nivedita looked forward to hearing it every night, with more and more details. At the same time, Ramya had to teach her how to answer questions and drive acceptance of her very modern family among her peers. A few years ago, one of her daughter's friends came home and asked, 'Where is your appa?'

Nivedita replied defensively, 'He is travelling.'

Ramya felt disturbed and, later, asked her, 'Who is travelling?' As Nivedita looked sheepish, Ramya hugged her.

'When someone asks you where your father is, just tell them you don't have one. It's fine. You have a mother. You have a *paati* and a *thatha* and a *mama* and a *mami* and many others. We are a complete family who love you very much.'

At times, parenting does become a challenge, and once in a while, Ramya wishes she had a co-parent to share the joys and burdens. There are little practical issues, like when her daughter wants to climb up high on the monkey bars and Ramya can't reach far enough. But her parents—especially her mother, after the unexpected loss of her father a couple of years ago—have been the pillars of the house. Sometimes, her friends say, her parents have been more supportive than a husband would have been. Living in a complex with some of her closest friends from college has been an unusual support base. This was something she and her friends orchestrated to create another kind of 'modern family'.

Over time, Ramya's definition of success has evolved considerably. Until she was 15 or so, there were many individual things she wanted to achieve. Then it became more about a group's goals and achievements. Over the past 15 years, however, her definition of success has undergone a sea of change. Now she thinks of success as happiness and fulfilment. At the same time, she wants her company to really scale up and create a large impact.

When asked about her life mantra, she says, 'It is my rough understanding of one aspect of the Bhagavad Gita—till you shoot the arrow, put everything into it; but once it is set loose, you have no control over it. So then you just forget about it. It doesn't matter whether it hits the target or not; just move on to the next arrow.'

Hacks to Storm the Norm

Norm: Marriage is the cornerstone of life, especially for women.

Marriage is often painted as the be all and end all of life, especially in India. Even today, it is considered disastrous for women to be single, especially as they grow older. The argument most often used is that marriage prevents loneliness. However, whether you're single by choice or happenstance, research actually proves that lifelong single people become increasingly satisfied with their lives as they grow older, and that their sense of loneliness is not markedly different from that of married people. You can lead a richly fulfilling life as a single person too.

Hacks:

1.   Work on your relationship with yourself
Your lifelong companion, with no strings attached, is you yourself, so it's important to spend time consciously getting to know yourself and being happy about who you are becoming over the course of your life. A deep understanding of your self, what makes you tick and how you want to lead your life will help you shape the life you want.

2.   There are two kinds of families: those you're born with and those you create
Who says the second kind is only born out of marriage? Invest time and emotion in building up a strong and close-knit group of friends-like-family who will be there for you through thick and thin. Make the time for these precious relationships on a consistent basis, because the quality of human connection is one of the best determinants of happiness and longevity.

3.   Make sure you plan for your financial future prudently
As a single person with fewer responsibilities, it can be easy to be profligate with your earnings. But with growing lifespans and a single income that has to tide you over the years after retiring, it's important to think ahead and start early. Get yourself a financial advisor and carefully invest and save for your many needs—which includes fun things like travel and shopping, by the way!

RITU
Aim for the Sky

Introduction

Dr Ritu Karidhal Srivastava is an Indian scientist working with the Indian Space Research Organization (ISRO). Born and brought up in Lucknow, she completed her BSc and MSc in Physics from Lucknow University and went on to pursue an ME degree in Aerospace Engineering from the Indian Institute of Science in Bengaluru. Joining ISRO in 1997, she went on to become deputy operations director for India's Mars Orbiter Mission, Mangalyaan, and mission director for Chandrayaan-2. She was also an integral part of the Chandrayaan-3 team.

A recipient of the ISRO Young Scientist Award from President Kalam, she has also received the 'ISRO Team Award for MOM (2015)', 'ASI Team Award' and 'Women Achievers in Aerospace, 2017' award from the Society of Indian Aerospace Technologies & Industries (SIATI). Dr Karidhal has published over 20 papers in national and international journals. She lives in Bengaluru with her husband and two children.

Why Ritu?

What is the typical image that comes to mind when you hear the word 'scientist'? We can bet it's not a saree-clad woman with flowers in her hair. In fact, most likely, it's not a picture of a woman at all. However, one of the most memorable moments of recent world history is that of a group of saree-clad scientists with bindis and flowers in their hair, clapping wildly and hugging each other in jubilation as India's Mars mission made a successful landing. Around the world, there are far fewer women who pursue careers in STEM as compared to men, and the norm or commonly held belief is that pure sciences are too technical for women to pursue. What drove these women, who looked like the epitome of the traditional Indian woman, to storm the norm and succeed in a career as unique as space research?

That question led us to Dr Ritu Karidhal, one of India's rocket women, who has worked on some of ISRO's key missions, including Mangalyaan. How did a girl born and brought up in Lucknow land up exploring the frontiers of space? How did she avoid the mommy track, bring up her children and launch missions to the moon and beyond?

Passion, Patience and Perseverance: The Girl Staring at the Sky

For a woman instrumental in taking India to Mars, Ritu Karidhal is surprisingly down to earth. While some of the credit surely goes to her upbringing, a lot of it is also down to the person she is—someone who is full of idealism, excited like a child at the thought of exploring space even further beyond Mars, and yet wears her achievements and contributions lightly.

Ritu was born in Lucknow—a city famous for its *tehzeeb*, art and culture, rather than science and technology. However, Ritu remembers always being fascinated by what lay beyond the sky. Even as a child, as she travelled across the city in a typical cycle rickshaw, she would throw her head back and gaze at the moon and stars in fascination. She would wonder how the moon followed them, what made it happen and what lay behind the dark spaces. Watching the night sky, she was intrigued by its vastness and wanted to understand it more. She began collecting news clippings about any space-related activity by NASA and ISRO, wishing she could be part of their efforts.

The oldest of four siblings, Ritu was brought up with a powerful belief in education and hard work. Their father worked in the defence services, while their mother taught at a school. Like most middle-class families, there wasn't much money to spare for anything considered a luxury. But it was clearly understood that achievement and learning should be the driving forces for the children, not money.

Despite the common stereotypes around STEM being difficult for women, Ritu had an avid interest in physics. At times, she found many of the topics difficult to understand. Most of her classmates went to tuitions or coaching classes to do better at school. But Ritu understood that tuition fees would put a financial burden on the family that they could not afford. Determined to do well, she would go over the subject matter time and again until she had mastered it.

STEM was seen as an unnecessary subject for girls to study back then. Although her female classmates compulsorily studied science until Class 8, most of them dropped out after that to study home science or arts subjects, which were considered more suitable for girls. However, unlike most of her contemporaries, Ritu's parents supported her dreams.

Ritu often stayed up until late at night to study, determined to do well. With the whole house silent and dark, the pool of light from the lamp on her desk would be the only illumination. When her enthusiasm was flagging due to sheer tiredness, she'd see her mother walking up to give her an encouraging word, rub her shoulders or offer hot tea to help her stay awake. Despite a hectic schedule, her mother stayed up to give Ritu the encouragement and support she needed.

Studying science and opting for a career was an unusual thing for girls, even within Ritu's family. Most of her female cousins were pushed to study just enough to attract better marriage prospects. The extended family planned to marry the girls off early, as soon as they had completed their college graduation, so they could 'settle down'.

Ritu's parents brought up their girls differently. Not only did they allow the girls to choose what they wanted to study, but they let them travel far from the house for their education, encouraged them to pursue a career and didn't treat marriage as the goal! There was much discussion about the level of freedom given to Ritu and her sister. But, as long as her parents were supportive, Ritu turned a deaf ear to all the criticism.

'Parents' support is very important—sometimes when you are trying to do something and you see your parents having faith in you, that takes you to another level,' she says.

This unconditional support from her parents allowed Ritu to dream different dreams and have the confidence to pursue them. With her mother as a role model, the family thought of teaching as a noble profession. After completing her master's degree in physics from the University of Lucknow, she enrolled in a doctorate course in physics. In the first six months of her PhD programme, she published a paper, began working as a part-time lecturer in physics and cleared the CSIR-UGC exam. But, in her heart of hearts, she knew that her dream job lay elsewhere. She had always dreamt of working at ISRO and finding a way to explore space.

An Eye on the Future

Right from childhood, she tracked what was happening at ISRO, collecting newspaper clippings. As an adult, she kept a keen eye out for opportunities to work there. One day, she chanced upon an ad from ISRO in the newspaper asking for applications from scientists. Excited, she immediately threw herself into the process of applying. There were tough eligibility criteria and a very high marks cut-off to even get an interview, but Ritu managed to clear that stage. Then came the interview—an even harder hurdle to clear.

Ritu spent days feverishly preparing for it with the help of her family. She woke up bright and early on the morning of the interview, the stars still shining in the clear sky. They had always inspired her with huge curiosity. Looking at them, she made a fervent inward prayer that she would do well in her interview. Outside the interview room, she waited impatiently for her turn to come. She couldn't wait to start interacting with scientists from her dream institution. She was so eager to qualify that she raced through answers to the questions they asked. Then began the anxious wait by the gate every morning for the postman, hoping for the much-anticipated appointment letter. The day Ritu received it, she was over the moon!

But sometimes in life, it so happens that when you get what you have longed for, it causes more anxiety. At only 22, it was a big thing for her to let go of a job she was doing well at and move across the country, to a city where she knew no one. Among all the people who had appeared for the ISRO interview, Ritu was the only one who was going to be travelling so far. She wondered whether she was doing the right thing by uprooting herself in pursuit of what might be just a mirage.

'What if I throw up everything here, move across the country and then find out that either I am not qualified enough or I don't enjoy the work? I'll be neither here nor there,' she pondered.

To this day, many parents in India hesitate even to send their sons far off, but Ritu's parents had always encouraged their children to follow their dreams. Their chief concern was that their children should do something good and feel happy. Ritu's mother came to her rescue, telling her that she should give her dream a shot.

'You can always choose to come back in a year if you don't like it. But you will always regret it if you don't give it a chance, this has been your lifelong dream,' she said.

The next complexity to solve was how to get there. A plane ticket was out of the question, it just wasn't affordable. Lucknow to Bengaluru was a complex journey, involving a change of trains. The family decided that Ritu's father would accompany her to Bengaluru, help her move into a home and settle her in.

Ritu was equal parts excited and stressed as the two of them set off—this was the realization of her long-held dream. But within hours of the journey beginning, her father started feeling unwell. He broke into a sweat, eyes glazed over. With every hour that the train took them farther from the comfort of Lucknow, his temperature rose. As she sponged him to try and reduce the fever, Ritu was beside herself with worry. She just couldn't figure out what to do. Should they get off at the next station and go back to Lucknow? Should they stop the journey midway so her father could be admitted to a hospital and get the medical help he needed? They had to get off the train and change to another train at Jhansi anyway. She decided that they would try and get back to Lucknow from there itself. At the back of her mind was the worry whether this meant the end of her ISRO dream.

But her father was determined that he would not get in Ritu's way. He insisted that they continue their journey. Luckily a few army officers happened to be travelling by the same train. When they saw the father-daughter duo struggling, they stepped in. At Jhansi, they made sure Ritu and her father got off the train with all their baggage intact. They waited beside the duo for the train to Bengaluru and ensured that they were safely aboard. Since the two did not have confirmed tickets to Bengaluru, the army officers helped them get their seats allocated so they could travel in comfort. Comforted by the kindness they had shown, Ritu heaved a sigh of relief. Soon they would be in Bengaluru, and her father could get medical help.

The Dream and The Tragedy

Things didn't work out quite as planned. Ritu's father's health didn't improve even after they reached Bengaluru. Far from being able to help her move into a home, he found himself having to be looked after by Ritu. She was already nervous about making a good impression at her new workplace. Added to that, she just didn't know what to do to make her father feel better. Calling her brother to update him on the situation, she broke down, crying uncontrollably. Her younger brother immediately hopped on to the next train to Bengaluru. The two of them found a comfortable accommodation for her and he helped her move in while their father recuperated.

For the first time, she was living away from her family. Ritu had to share a paying guest accommodation with two people she didn't know. She had never tasted the likes of sambar or rasam before and it tasted strange to her. Subsisting on idli-dosa and rice every day instead of rotis, sabzi and dal was a challenge. She missed the familiar taste of comfort food made by her mother, which would have given her a sense of being at home in the midst of so much change. She didn't speak the local language, either.

Between her father's illness and all the new experiences, Ritu was apprehensive—she was in a new city, with a new language, new food and new colleagues. Most of all, she was entering a large scientific establishment , and one she had idealized as a fresher, with little hands-on experience. How would her seniors treat her? Would they wonder why she had been selected? Would she be able to cope with the work she had to do?

But the minute she walked into ISRO, she was welcomed so warmly by her colleagues, junior and senior, that her fears vanished. The culture at ISRO was very friendly and collegial, with seniors making it a point to help their junior colleagues come on board. She found a friend in a female scientist called Devyani Perur, who was almost 15–20 years senior to her. Contrary to the belief that women in the workplace see each other as rivals, Devyani took Ritu under her wing and helped her feel at home. To this day they stay in touch, though Devyani has retired.

At the same time, Ritu was assigned to challenging projects that needed continuous learning and understanding for working out the solution. Being from a pure science background, Ritu did not know computer programming—a key requirement for the work. Borrowing books from the well-stocked ISRO library, Ritu began studying C, Linux, etc. until late into the night to catch up. Her habit of intense study during school and her determination not to give up then was standing her in good stead again.

She began to get accustomed to living in Bengaluru, enjoying the freedom and safety she experienced to come and go as she pleased. She had become friends with the other people living in the paying guest accommodations and they would explore the city together whenever they had the time. Idli-sambar and pongal became her favourite dishes. She found the people of Bengaluru very calm and cooperative, so it was easy to get along with them. And, of course, the famous cool Bengaluru weather helped her feel active and energetic, a contrast to the hot and dusty plains in which she had grown up.

But Ritu was most deeply engrossed in her work. The challenge of it all and the mission they were trying to accomplish fired her up. It was her dream job and she was determined not to get distracted. Her mentor Dr V Kesava Raju was a constant source of encouragement and inspiration. Her first posting was in the Mission Analysis division with Dr Kesava Raju (later the mission director for the Mars Orbiter Mission). Ritu was asked how to manoeuvre a satellite to get a stereo image from the camera. Ritu was happy because this called on both her fields of study, physics and mathematics.

It took her 3–4 months to solve the problem, and her solution was implemented on board the satellite.

A few months later, Ritu entered the office, singing to herself. She finally felt she was gaining a grip over the work she had to do. She had just set down her bag and turned to her desk when the harsh *brr-ing* of the phone startled her. It was a call from her family in Lucknow. She was surprised as they typically called her only at night. But there was an emergency at home. Her father had continued to be unwell since his return from Bengaluru. Now the family felt he was sinking. They asked her to come home urgently. He was keen to see her again.

With shaking hands, for the first time in her life, Ritu booked a plane ticket. She didn't even know how to check in for a flight. Far from enjoying her first time on a plane, she spent the flight feverishly praying for her father. Desperately hoping that he would still be alive when she arrived, Ritu was among the first to deboard the plane. She rushed outside, anxiously looking for the taxi stand when she spotted her brother. Eagerly she looked at him, hoping to hear the answer she had prayed for. He looked back at her gently and then shook his head in denial. Ritu couldn't believe it. Her beloved father was gone, and she hadn't even met him one last time. Even today, she chokes up at the memory of that moment.

Back in Bengaluru, Ritu submerged herself in her work. The excitement of doing something that no one had ever done before, and of doing work that helped the country move ahead in its scientific prowess, helped her to cope with her grief and keep going. Deadlines tended to be short, requiring long hours. Working late into the night, one of the few women at ISRO at the time, she was often one of the last people to leave the campus. But she never felt afraid as she walked alone from building to building or commuted to her PG accommodation.

Ritu's colleagues and supervisors noticed that Ritu brought a touch of passion to her work which helped her surpass her peers. She was driven by such a strong sense of dedication that unless she completed her work, she could not sleep. Not personally overambitious, if she was interested in something she would work on it even if it brought her no personal reward. Recognizing her zeal, ISRO sponsored Ritu to pursue an MTech degree from the Indian Institute of Science.

Studying at IISc was another dream come true; it was the Mecca for Indian scientists and had been set up by the legendary Jamsetji Tata. Stepping into the verdant green campus, though it was close to ISRO's office, was like stepping into another world. The institution, situated in the heart of Bengaluru, boasts 400 acres of greenery with different lanes, all named after trees—Gulmohur Marga, Mahogany Marga, Ashoka Marga, Badami Marga. Stately grey stone buildings in the classical style form the faculty and administration block. The atmosphere of the institute gave off an air of utter tranquillity, making Ritu feel she could tackle even the hardest subjects with ease in such beautiful surroundings. There was ample freedom, with an exhaustive library open at all hours, and high-tech computing labs open through the day and night. These were golden days for Ritu—she was exhilarated at being there, and thrived in the environment and the opportunity to build her knowledge base.

As a Wife and a Mother

Emotional and soft-spoken as she was, she learnt to be forthright and straightforward on technical matters. Several years after moving to ISRO, when she began receiving marriage proposals, she was equally straightforward in her personal life. She made it very clear to prospective grooms that she was going to continue working and that the work she was doing was of vital importance to her and the country. Anyone who married her would not only have to understand that but support her.

She eventually got married to an engineer who worked in the private sector. He sympathized completely with her passion and encouraged her to aspire further, ensuring they shared the home's workload equitably. Even during her maternity leave, Ritu would work from home on her projects. Once they had children, however, the balancing act became more complicated. Her mother and mother-in-law came and lived with them until the kids were a year old. But after that, the two of them had to manage the hectic balance.

Ritu was determined not to compromise either on her work or what she felt were her duties and responsibilities as a mother. Rejoining the office once her daughter was six months old, she was determined to breastfeed her until she was a year old. Every morning she would drop her daughter at the day care. Two to three times a day, since it was only 15 minutes away from her office, she would walk back and forth to make sure her daughter was fed on time.

As the kids grew up, she often faced the tug-of-war that many working women face. On most days, Ritu would ensure she packed the kids' tiffins and saw them off to school. But sometimes PTMs would clash with critical meetings and her husband attended them alone. She would often come home much later, while his work hours were more predictable. But the kids always greeted her with a smile and never complained. Interestingly, Ritu never felt guilty about her long work hours, understanding that doing so would mean she looked down upon herself.

Ritu and her husband shared a very equitable relationship. There was never a sense of competition between the importance of his job and hers. They both relished each other's successes. She looked forward eagerly to sharing news about her day with him and relished the titbits he shared with her. He tracked her missions on the news and was always the first to call and congratulate or condole with her.

A few years later, they bought their first home together. Having accomplished a big milestone in life, Ritu and her husband planned a grand *griha pravesh* or house-warming ceremony. They invited all their friends and family members from across the country to be there on the occasion. Having picked an auspicious date for the ceremony, scheduled a few days after the launch of the satellite, Ritu looked forward to the event with a sense of relish.

Around the same time, Ritu was spearheading the launch of a satellite. Unfortunately, the best-laid plans can often go wrong! As the date for the ceremony got closer, there was a delay in the launch of the satellite. The launch date ended up getting pushed from 2 May to 5 May—the same date as the griha pravesh. Ritu was aghast! As operations director, she could not take leave, she had to take responsibility for a successful launch. Even after the satellite launches, the team has to work for several hours to stabilize it. At the same time, she felt awful about not being able to devote herself to the celebration at home. She knew she could not do any of the preparations for the *puja* as she had to be in the office from 5 a.m.

Once she entered the office, she pushed all thoughts of the ceremony to the back of her mind and focussed completely on her work. There were lots of little operational details she had to sort out, and many small and big issues she had to supervise. Finally, almost three hours after the satellite had been launched, Ritu felt she had done all she needed to. She left for home, for the first time thinking about the puja. What would everyone have thought of her, absent at her own house-warming? How had it gone? She hoped no one had felt offended by her absence.

She walked up to the house to see everyone's footwear scattered outside. As she cracked open the door, she could hear the *pandit* still chanting prayers. Her husband smiled as he caught sight of her and gestured to her to come in. With incredibly fortuitous timing, the pandit was conducting the last *arati* of the puja! She took her place beside her husband, delighted that she had managed to be part of the critical moments of both important events that day.

At times, neighbours or members of the extended family would comment on her hectic schedule and how she was unable to be there for some special occasions. But Ritu turned a deaf ear, having the unshakeable support of her husband and her children. She felt that once they saw the depth, relevance and impact of her work for the country and what ISRO achieved they would change their tune. 'I don't worry about what people say, it doesn't matter to me.'

Mangalyaan and Life After

Mangalyaan was an extremely ambitious project—even for ISRO, which had always set audacious goals. A third-world country launching a mission to Mars was a first. The development of Mangalyaan took a record 18 months from project approval to completion. This was ISRO's first attempt to go beyond Earth. The scientists did not know how to cope when the satellite would go past Earth's gravity. In space, the time taken to communicate goes up from seconds to minutes, so the scientists would not know what was going on with the satellite. So the spacecraft had to be extremely autonomous, intelligent enough to identify and recover from its own problems.

While she had been involved in some aspects of the Chandrayaan, Ritu was appointed Deputy Operations Director of Mission Planning and Operations for the Mangalyaan mission. Her team was assigned to conceptualize and ensure the execution of the craft's autonomous brain—one of the most mission-critical tasks. Ritu was tasked with drafting the autonomy software.

'I had to ensure that it was all executed without any flaw or anomaly. When it comes to launching spacecraft, the slightest anomaly can spell disaster, especially in the case of manoeuvres and Mars orbit insertions, so every single detail had to be thoroughly vetted.'

Ritu's days became even longer. They would start at the crack of dawn and go on until late in the night. Brainstorming meetings, studying, researching, experimenting every single day, hacking away at the problems and finding new solutions. The convivial and cooperative nature of ISRO made for a workplace where gender was irrelevant. What mattered was the person's ability to find a solution and contribute. This attitude created an enriching and fun environment, helping the team stay motivated through late nights and working weekends.

There were many occasions when official duties took precedence over the family. Once, her daughter fell severely ill, her fever spiking to well above 100. Ritu was frantic! Not all the sponging in the world helped cool her daughter down. But she had an urgent mission-critical meeting at the office. Could she really leave her daughter at this moment? Ritu felt torn. But her husband took charge.

'It's just a fever. I'm here, I'll take care of her. Your meeting is very important. Go on,' he said, giving her the strength to focus on her work.

Inspired by her mother's example, Ritu had always taken charge of the kids' education as her personal key responsibility. In the run-up to Mangalyaan, Ritu often reached home much later than the kids' bedtime. But she made it a point to wake up the children and go over their schoolwork. Once they went to sleep, she would begin her second shift of work from home, between midnight and 4 a.m. Even though she barely got 4–5 hours of sleep, this enabled Ritu to feel she was fulfilling her responsibilities both at work and as a mother. It gave her a sense of joy to be able to do both. Her home became an extension of her office for the duration.

Ritu feels that while women have a tremendous amount of mental strength, they often give up physically. Many of them operate by fixed timelines and give up on their own dreams to take care of other people. She was determined to pursue all her dreams, personal and professional. At the same time, the late nights and the workload began taking their toll, leaving her exhausted. Ritu turned to yoga to find the physical and mental strength to cope with everything on her plate. Prayers, meditation, reading and spending whatever time she could find with the kids helped her keep her balance through this and other difficult times.

The launch of Mangalyaan was planned for 28 October 2013. The ISRO telemetry ship steamed off for the Pacific Ocean, to put certain antennas in place. Meanwhile, the finished spacecraft was moved to Sriharikota. Ritu and her team were to monitor and control the satellite's path from the control room in Bengaluru. Everything was on a very exacting schedule. The satellite had to be launched within a certain time window. If not, the entire mission would have to be postponed by two years.

Then disaster struck! Stormy weather set in over the Pacific Ocean. Massive waves roiled the waters. The ship was unable to move ahead. The entire team was frantically biting its nails! Days filled with extreme tension went by. Ritu and the rest of the MOM team wondered if their back-breaking efforts of 15 months would come to nothing.

Finally, on 4 November, they received good news. The storms had abated and the ship was powering ahead. Frenzied work began to ensure the success of the mission—which would be a massive feather in India's cap. It would be the first Asian nation to complete a Mars mission. Ritu felt both anxious and eager—she had been responsible for many of the key innovations that would enable the satellite to succeed, and this was the acid test.

Despite the best efforts of the team, it was possible to launch Mangalyaan only on the morning of 5 November. Then began the process of daily monitoring and regular progress updates to find out whether the mission was proceeding as per plan.

After travelling in deep space for around 10 months, the satellite reached near Mars where the very critical one-time manoeuvre known as Mars Orbit Insertion needed to be performed. At this point in the mission, the satellite was supposed to near Mars and fire an on-board rocket to slow its speed relative to the planet. This was to help it to slip into a long looping orbit around the planet.

Ritu counted down the minutes together with the team, excitement jostling with tension. Slipping into orbit around Mars at the entry point is a tricky proposition. Inaccurate targeting, timing or a flawed engine firing could cause the satellite to be destroyed or to miss Mars completely.

When the satellite sent the signal of correct insertion into Mars orbit, the tension in the control room turned to jubilation. The scientists turned to each other with grins of achievement and started clapping spontaneously. They had done what no other country had done before— completed a successful Mars mission on their very first attempt.

Ritu felt an incredible sense of fulfilment and pride—this was what had driven her to ISRO, this kind of achievement was what she had hankered after! With the success of Mangalyaan, Ritu gained some measure of prominence. When she travelled in India or abroad, she was recognized and feted for her achievements. She felt especially thrilled when people abroad expressed their admiration for ISRO's achievements and the contributions of female scientists towards them. She was invited to speak at various forums, including TEDx conferences and schools and colleges that wanted her to address students. Relatives and friends who hadn't been very interested in what exactly she did suddenly wanted to know more. Her children, especially her 10-year-old son, beamed whenever they saw her on television. The country gave the female scientists at ISRO the epithet of Rocket Women of India.

True Fulfilment

She found the movie *Mission Mangal*, starring Akshay Kumar, to be a good attempt at making the common man understand how an interplanetary mission takes place. Placing the Indian scientists back in the domestic setting made them relatable to the Indian audience, she felt.

Her proudest moment came when she went back to the college where she had completed her bachelor's and the school where she had taken her board exams. When she stepped inside the iron gates of the school, girls lined the entire driveway, eager to see her and reach out to touch her. Later on, when she addressed them at the assembly, there was a long and loud roar of applause. After her talk, many of them thronged to speak with her. They told her they had taken science as a subject because she had inspired them. In fact, they told her that they did not look at it as a tough subject anymore. There was a room where all the girls had made paintings and crafts depicting Ritu and the Mangalyaan. Ritu beamed in delight, awestruck that someone like her, just by the being a part of the Mangalyaan mission, had inspired so many girls to overcome their fear.

'If we stop fearing and take a step, no one can push you back.'

Next, Ritu is looking forward to a satellite that doesn't just orbit Mars but lands on it, and wants to push through more frontiers in space science. She draws inspiration from many sources, including her steely-willed mother who held the family together after losing her husband, her father who always encouraged her to aspire to whatever she wanted, and the scientist Marie Curie, who provided a stirring example of making huge strides in science while balancing her family. She quotes from Marie Curie, 'Nothing in life is to be feared, it is only to be understood. Now is the time to understand more, so that we may fear less.' Her mantra in life is the famous couplet from the Bhagavad Gita, 'Do your duty without thinking about its reward.'

Hacks to Storm the Norm

Norm: A woman's first priority at all times should be her family and home.

The received wisdom of our society is that for a woman, family comes first. It can be hard to constantly balance your professional and personal life and, often, the two can feel like they are loggerheads, competing for your time and attention. However, the struggle to prioritize does get easier.

Hacks:

1. Run a marathon, not a sprint
Remember that life and your career are a marathon, not a sprint. Both are long-lasting and both will take different amounts of effort at different times. There will be times when your career will come first, and other times when life will overtake you. It won't be a consistent 50–50 balance at all times and that is fine.

2. Share the load
Make sure the emotional and mental load are shared equally with your partner, right from the beginning. It's his home and his family too. Make sure your partner is involved in planning and executing the work at home, not just doing it to 'help you out'.

3. Let it go
You can have it all, but you can't do it all! It's okay to let go and not

be perfect at everything. Prioritize what's most important and focus on that. If possible, it pays valuable dividends to over-invest in more domestic help, so that you can cut yourself a little slack.

RUMA
Be Your Own Cheerleader

Introduction

#for the women by the women

Ruma Devi is an Indian social worker, fashion designer and handicraft artist from Barmer, Rajasthan. She began her career fashioning handcrafted bags for an NGO. Eventually, she went on to grow her network and transformed the lives of 30,000 women in rural Rajasthan whose handicrafts now sell across the globe.

Starting with her first exhibition in Delhi in 2010, she and her organization now participate in fairs around the world. She participated in her first fashion show in Rajasthan Heritage Week in 2016, and received great acclaim. In 2020, she was invited to be a panellist by Harvard University, USA. In 2018, she received the 'Nari Shakti Puraskar' award, the highest civilian honour for women in India, and in 2020, an honorary doctorate from Mahatma Jyoti Rao Phoole University, Jaipur.

Dr Ruma Devi is a state brand ambassador of Rajeevika, a rural livelihood mission of the Rajasthan government, founder of the Ruma Devi Foundation and president of an NGO named Gramin Vikas Evam Chetna Sansthan (GVCS).

Why Ruma?

Superwomen don't always come wearing a cape. Sometimes she wears a *ghoonghat* and *lehenga* and comes from a small village in Rajasthan.

Hinduism has a tradition of fatalism—*kismat*. It says that everything that happens to us is predetermined by fate and that one cannot overturn what has been written. Ruma Devi was an illiterate young girl, who was married off at 17 to an itinerant and indigent farmer. She had never set foot outside her little village in Barmer. She was brought up in a highly patriarchal world in which the word of the patriarch was law, and women were only homemakers and mothers.

How could she break the shackles of patriarchy to set her own course? What gave her the courage to be more than a homemaker and mother? What chance did she have to travel the world, to impress international and Indian impresarios, or to help out hundreds of women like herself? Perhaps the anguish of a heartbroken mother spurred her to vow that neither she nor the thousands of women like her would ever have to go through the same heartbreak again.

Ruma Devi was born in Raisar village, a habitation of 5,000 people. Each farm in the village had a *kutcha* house called a *dhanni* and homes were set a kilometre apart. Her one-room hut housed a joint family comprising her grandparents, uncle, aunt and mother. Her father, a BSF soldier, was away on duty most of the time. When Ruma was 4 years old, her mother became pregnant again. Complications set in and her mother was in severe distress. Her father was away and there was no good doctor in the village. Her mother died in the throes of childbirth.

Ruma was made to leave school to help look after the newborn baby. Two years later, her father married again and her stepmother moved into the home. Over the years, there were seven siblings—six girls and a boy—in the house. When Ruma went to her neighbours' and friends' homes, she saw that their mothers gave them good food and made sure that they had enough to eat. Meanwhile, Ruma often went hungry and spent her days looking after her siblings and learning crafts from her grandmother. The only school in the village had classes up to Class 8, and no one bothered to enrol Ruma there.

Ruma felt a sense of responsibility for her siblings. She learnt to cook and manage the household by the time she was eight years old. There was a severe water issue in the village. She was responsible for fetching water in the bullock cart. She also grazed the cattle and managed the home because everyone else would be working in the fields. She missed her mother and craved the kind of affection she would have received from her. She felt ignored and neglected by her family.

Ruma's grandfather had a habit of walking far and wide across the village every day. One day, when she was 12, he went out for his usual walk. Suddenly, he felt overcome with extreme fatigue and wanted to rest. He knocked at the nearest door and asked for water. The people in this home were extremely hospitable and friendly and spoke to him very courteously. He liked the food they served, the atmosphere of the home and the kids he saw running around. He decided then and there that Ruma Devi would get married to the son of the house. Ruma didn't get to ask any questions about who the people were, her future husband—nothing. She didn't even get to meet her fiance until her wedding.

After a five-year engagement, Ruma got married. The wedding was not a fun celebration for her. She was told to sit quietly and given an uncomfortable new dress to wear. But that is how was how it was there. Most children were betrothed in childhood, some soon after they were born. No one got a choice. Grooms were selected based on their property. If there were many girls in a family, or one of the parents had died, all of them were married off in one ceremony, to save money. Ruma and her sisters got married together. At 17, she was the oldest. The youngest was four.

Ruma moved into a joint family with her parents-in-law, brothers-in-law and their family. Her husband had studied till Class 5 and worked as an itinerant farmer. Her in-laws lived off subsistence farming and there was very little money. She hoped for a fresh start and a chance at happiness. She dreamed that she would get the loving care here that she had yearned for since her mother died. But marriage was a continuation of her household duties, with even more responsibility added. It was a hardscrabble world with little room for softness or niceties.

Within a year of marriage, Ruma was pregnant. She was overjoyed. At last, she would have someone who belonged to her and to whom she could feel a sense of belonging. All the affection she had been starving for came pouring out towards her unborn child. She started making grand plans for the child's future.

But her joy was short-lived. Her son was born with a breathing problem and she and her husband were too poor to afford treatment. Within 48 hours, her infant son was no more. Ruma was heartbroken. She felt that there was nothing more left in life. She went into deep depression.

'I couldn't save my child because of money. After losing my child I wanted to kill myself. I felt I had nothing to live for. But I decided to stand again and restart my journey—I didn't give up on myself.'

Nothing to Lose

To find a reason to live and to ensure that she was never in this position again, she wanted to start working.

'It was not planned; circumstances made me decide to work. But this was my first pivotal moment, because where I am today began with this.'

But there was no work available except for construction or domestic service. Then she remembered, 'I have learnt appliqué and embroidery work (*Kashidakari ka kaam*) from my grandmother. At that time I didn't think of using this art as a source of income, but gradually I thought of using these skills. "I have to make my own path," I decided.'

She debated whether she could start making *lehengas* and cloth bags and selling them. She gathered two other women from her village and, with a lot of difficulty, convinced them to work with her.

Her in-laws disapproved of her desire to work and felt that it would bring shame to the family. They delivered an ultimatum: that she must give up all thought of working. But Ruma was determined to work and earn some money, come what may. From craving their affection, she had moved to braving their objections. Shunned by her in-laws, Ruma decided to move out of their home.

Her husband had begun working as a driver by this time, so

the couple used his income to rent a room. He didn't quite believe she would be able to make money, but he went along with her decision. In the beginning, the couple went for days without eating anything, because they didn't have enough money for both rent and food.

There was a lot of talk among the neighbours, but the women braved it out, ignoring the buzz.

'My neighbours used to say, "God knows where their *bahu* is going". My family also said many things but I continued because I didn't do anything bad. What can I do if the people say stuff? They won't look after me when I am hungry.' They earned two rupees and five rupees a day, but it was enough to keep them motivated. Slowly, as her earnings grew, she and her husband baked bricks at night and built themselves a *pakka* room.

While the women could do the initial job of stitching lehengas and bags, they were not able to do the finishing required—for that one needed a sewing machine. Ruma started trying to convince more women from the village to join her little group. She went from house to house, speaking to the women. In many homes, the rest of the family was deeply suspicious. They slammed the doors in her face and refused to let their womenfolk speak with her. But Ruma persisted. Slowly, she convinced 10 women to join her. They all pooled in a little bit of money to buy a second-hand sewing machine.

But there were many difficulties standing in their way, which could make them turn back at any time. Their families and neighbours felt that it was shameful for them to work and they faced objections almost every day. Their precarious financial condition meant that any emergency could crop up and prevent them from showing up to work. Most importantly, they only know how to make things; they knew nothing about selling or marketing them. They didn't even know how to make a bill. Going outside the home had always been a privilege reserved for men. They were not getting enough orders.

A Ray of Hope

One day, through the village grapevine, Ruma heard of an NGO that helped rural women earn a living. Ruma decided to go to their office along with her women. Vikram Singh, the secretary and founder of GVCS Barmer, was surprised to see this large contingent of women who had turned up all by themselves.

'Until now, we have been running around trying to find women like you and motivate them to start working,' he said.

Ruma and her group took out their samples of petticoats and bags.

'Here's our work,' they said. 'This is what we can do, this is what we have been doing.'

He and the rest of the NGO team were surprised. They exclaimed, 'But this is excellent work. Who taught you? What all can you do?'

'Just give us some orders, and you will see what we can do,' Ruma said proudly.

'But we have seen this happen before with so many groups of women. Women take orders but then something happens—a child falls ill, there is some festival or puja and then everything is delayed. How can we trust that you will deliver what you promise?' they asked.

'You tell us what you want, you can test us. We will succeed,' Ruma said with a ring of self-belief in her voice.

'All right, we will give you a trial. We will place an order with you. We will give you the designs and materials. Come back in three days and we will see what you have done till then,' the NGO head said.

Ruma and her group were delighted to have bagged an order. They went back to the village, chattering excitedly. They pulled out the material and turned it this way and that. They held the cloth up, one fabric against the other, figuring out which went with what.

'This is so much fun!' they exclaimed, eagerly creating new colour combinations. They were so excited that they worked through the night. By early morning, the entire order was complete.

Later that day, they walked to the NGO office, eager to show off their prowess. Seeing the group of women walking in the day after they had been allocated an order, Vikram Singh was disappointed.

'What happened? Some problem? You won't be able to do it?' he asked, already resigned. 'This is what happens every time we try to help.'

'Problem? No. We just wanted to show you what we have made.'

With that, the women emptied their sacks upon the table. Skirt after skirt fell out, flawlessly stitched in eye-catching colour combinations. Cloth bags emerged, beautifully finished.

He was too stunned to speak for several minutes, goggling at the merchandise. At last, he said, 'But...but...how? Overnight? Impossible!'

The women giggled, looking at each other. When the work is fun, nothing is impossible, they felt.

They started earning 50 to 75 rupees a day because the women buying their goods also didn't have that much spending money. But even this was more than they had been earning before. Now, no one had to ask for money at home. The women could pay for the education of their children. Nothing stopped them from working, not the heat, nor their various other household chores. If the clothes were not ironed, the women pressed them, struggling with the heavy, coal-filled metal iron in the hot summer. They walked barefoot on dusty, stony, unpaved roads to deliver their orders in the scorching heat, carrying their merchandise in one hand and a jar of water in the other. When they reached the market, they would still hear slurs. But they kept going.

There is a form of traditional folk music called Harjas sung by ghoonghat-wearing ladies in rural Rajasthan. Ruma Devi and her group sang this together every day as they came and went. It gave them new strength and the inspiration to carry on.

At the same time, Ruma realized her problem of money was not unique. There were still so many women in the village who worked hard all day yet didn't have even a rupee to their name. She started visiting their homes to get them to join her. The men in the home resented what they saw as Ruma's interference, and some were quite rude to her. At times, Ruma wondered why she was going to all this effort. But when she spoke to the women, she understood what hope this held for them, and how much they wanted to be able to participate. Ruma increased her attempts to convince the men about the benefits to the family if the women started earning.

'My main agenda was to earn money for my family's livelihood to fulfil basic requirements. And I also wanted to help all those women who [were] suffering with different issues like I have been through.' Once the men in their family saw that the women were earning money, they were more supportive.

From Ruma Devi to Didi

From 10 women, Ruma's gang of women workers grew to 50. Ruma says she knew that there were many other women in the village who wanted to work, and asked the NGO team how she could engage them as well. Vikram Singh told her about exhibitions in the city where they could participate and earn more by selling directly to consumers. The women decided to go to Delhi for an exhibition. This was a very bold move, because, until now, they had never set foot outside their village. And they spoke only Marwari, not even Hindi. They were unsure whether their families would allow them to go. But they resolutely told them that they were going, whether or not anyone approved.

Vikram Singh accompanied them on their trip. He had been a critical mentor and supporter of this group of irrepressible women. He had not only taught them what to make and helped them market their goods, but had also given them the confidence to try out new things.

The women were excited and scared at the same time. When the train arrived, hooting shrilly, at the platform, they jumped back, startled. They had never heard anything so loud. On the train, they looked at the people around them, dressed so differently, and felt self-conscious. They pulled their ghoonghats closer around their faces, hiding behind them as they peered with bright, curious eyes at the changing landscape.

As the train pulled into Delhi, they stared at the tall glass buildings in disbelief. All they had seen till now was their tiny village, which took less than half a day to cover on foot.

'*Yeh shehar khatam hi nahin hota*—this city never ends!' they exclaimed. One of them said to Ruma, 'It looks like the buildings are reaching into the sky and touching the clouds.'

Getting off the train at Delhi station felt like leaving a cocoon and stepping into an alien world. The noise and hustle-bustle of scores of people jostling past made them nervous. They huddled closer together. Vikram Singh led them to the metro station and they stared, awestruck, at a staircase that appeared to move by itself. This was their first encounter with an escalator. They were too scared to attempt to get on it, and looked on with wonder at the myriad people who seemed to treat it as an ordinary thing and not a curiosity.

'Isn't there a real staircase?' they asked timidly.

Vikram Singh encouraged them to try this new experience.

'You'll be fine. It's fun,' he urged.

Finally, one of them mustered the courage and stepped forward, clutching her ghoonghat and bag with one hand, and placed her other hand on the railing. As she felt it move under her fingers, she pulled her hand back in surprise—the sensation felt weird. Then she gathered herself, stepped forward resolutely and jumped on to the first step. As it started moving, she teetered on the edge of step, flailed her arms and almost lost her balance. Her expression was a mix of excitement and terror. Then she planted her feet more firmly. She enjoyed the smooth motion as it carried her upwards effortlessly. A delighted chuckle escaped her. She looked down at where her cohort was waiting and gestured to them, '*Aa jao. Mazaa aata hai.*'

One by one, like a flock of ducklings, each woman took her turn at being brave and hopped onto the escalator. When they reached the last step of the escalator, they leaped off with the agility of deer. When they were all together again on the upper level, they exchanged proud grins of accomplishment.

At the exhibition, they were again bewildered by the crowds and activity around them. They had never participated in an exhibition and didn't even know how to set up a stall. But somehow they managed and began setting out their merchandise so that it looked attractive and colourful. When the first customer walked up to their stall, they felt shy—she seemed so confident, so polished and well dressed. What must she think of them, they wondered. Then the customer spoke to them in a very friendly way.

'*Aap log kahan se aaye ho?* Where did you come from? Did you make this all yourselves? Is this made by machine or do you do it by hand?'

Hearing her tone and questions that they could easily answer, they started feeling a little more at ease. Ruma pulled her ghoonghat back a little and started her sales pitch for the merchandise. One by one, the rest of the women started speaking with the customers lining up to see their merchandise. Soon, sales were humming along. In just three days, they sold goods worth ₹15,000—more money than they had ever seen before!

Back in the village, everyone was astounded to hear how much these women had earned all by themselves. After the exhibition, the women decided that they wanted to enjoy even bigger success in the next exhibition. Rather than spending the money on their homes and families, the women decided to reinvest all their earnings into making more products. They next year, they went back to the exhibition, and, this time, they earned ₹11 lakh! And again, they decided to reinvest the money into growing their business.

They started doing research, trying to understand what kinds of products people wanted and were willing to pay for. They got a master artisan to come and train all the women in producing goods, finishing them at high quality and understanding the market. Concern India Foundation, another NGO, came and trained about 500 women in these skills as well. The group expanded to about 10,000 women across many different villages, while Ruma became a de facto manager for all of them.

Meanwhile, seeing her progress, Ruma's in-laws started respecting her work. She and her husband moved back into the joint family household, and she started taking on responsibility for them. 'My in-laws are not angry with me anymore. They realized that I was only following my passion. In fact, now my entire household, including my mother and sisters-in-law, do embroidery sitting at home. This way, they earn too.'

Ruma's example also set off a chain of changes within the family— her sister earned a master's degree even though she was now a housewife, and her sister-in-law started working at a beauty parlour. Ruma's youngest sister lived with her and wanted to follow in her footsteps. A couple of years later, she and her husband had a piece of personal good fortune—she conceived and delivered a healthy son.

'Ade Rahein Khade Rahein!' (Stand firm)

Ruma and her group of women started dreaming bigger. Ruma Devi heard of something called a ramp show taking place in Delhi during one of her visits to an exhibition in the city. She managed to get admission and was awestruck. The lights, the colours, the pulsating music and, most of all, the frenetic excitement when the models came striding out on the ramp wearing fantastical creations by designers filled her heart with exhilaration. She wanted to participate in the show, too, and wangled her way into a meeting backstage.

'Give us a chance to showcase the work we can do. We can also make clothes like this,' she pleaded earnestly.

But the organizers rebuffed her rudely. 'This is for designers, not tailors,' one of them said with a sneer. Another one just laughed superciliously and didn't even take Ruma's request seriously.

Ruma was incensed. She vowed that she and her ladies would participate in such an event before long, and, what's more, have the crowd eating out of their hands. Through Grameen Sanstha, she heard of an event called Rajasthan Heritage Week. She broached the topic with Vikram Singh ji and convinced him that they could participate. With his help, Ruma approached the organizers, with equal parts hope and trepidation. She explained what she and her ladies did, and showed her work to the organizers. 'But this is not design work, this is just *kashida* and stitching,' one of them objected. Another one was intrigued by the quality of work she saw. She looked at Ruma and saw the pugnacious face peeking out from under the traditional *odhni.* 'But this does represent Rajasthan's heritage handicraft. Let us give these ladies their turn in the spotlight,' she said.

When the rest of the village heard about this, they started laughing.

'Who will want to see clothes made by a bunch of illiterate village women?' said one, while another said, 'Fashion is something for big city people. What do you know about it?'

Ruma wondered if she had made a mistake.

'Will we be able to do this? What if we fail and everyone laughs at us over there?' she thought.

She asked her group of women the same question.

'Do you all think we will be able to pull this off? What if everyone laughs at us? What if our clothes look bad over there?'

They looked at her, thinking the matter over in their own heads. Then one of them said, 'Didi, if we don't try, how will we ever know if we can succeed?' Another said, 'When we started making clothes too, we had doubts. And everyone around us said "You won't be able to do it". But see how far we have come. Did you ever imagine then that we could achieve what we have done till today?'

Ruma saw the immense faith the women had in her and their own capabilities. She also saw their ambition and excitement and felt recharged by it.

'Chalo, let's do it. *Ade rahein, khade rahein!* (keep standing tall and proud),' she said with a grin.

Grameen Mahila Vikas Sadan roped in Bibi Russell, a famed Bangladeshi fashion designer credited with the reinvention of the *gamcha* saree, to help design the clothes, while Ruma and her team, along with Vikram Singh ji, decided how the fabrics, the Barmeri embroidery and patchwork should come together.

The group worked feverishly to design and complete the garments. Everything had to be novel; every stitch, every mirror had to be perfectly placed and sewn. They would leave no room for anyone to pass judgement on their skills, they vowed, often working throughout the night to finish their garments.

At long last, a handful of them set off for Jaipur in an open truck, bags full of their clothes carefully packed to arrive in the best possible condition. They waved at the assembled group that had turned up to wish them good luck, and settled down for the long journey, prayers in their hearts. In Jaipur, the scene was one of hullabaloo and excitement as the venue was being set up. By this time, veterans of many exhibitions, our band of brave women had learnt to take it in their stride, and spent their time finding out about the arrangements for the fashion show.

They met the 30 leading models who were to show their clothes on the ramp. Among India's best-known faces in fashion, some of them were over six feet tall. The diminutive village women looked up at them in surprise. But the models were curious and eager to see the garments that Ruma Devi and her group had made with such love and painstaking labour. The other fashion designers were also interested to see their clothes. Later that evening, the scene backstage was electric—a buzz of activity, music, lights, make-up. Ruma and her group helped the models put on the clothes, pride shining on their faces at the thought of showing off their work to so many people. Their show was titled Handmade in Rajasthan, a tribute to Barmer.

They waited with bated breath as the pulsating folk music set the stage for their show. In the audience were the guests of honour, the then Chief Minister of Rajasthan Vasundhara Raje, the Royal Queen of Bhutan, and the singer Mohit Chauhan. Ruma had decided that the artisans would walk alongside their creations on the ramp. The first model set foot on the ramp, and a spotlight followed her and the artisan as they sashayed down towards the audience. Ruma had her heart in her mouth. She started hearing what sounded like a storm. She took a deep breath and shook her head. Then she realized what the noise was. The entire audience was clapping, their hands making a deafening roar. One of the models came backstage and pulled Ruma onto the ramp. Ruma realized their show was over. And everyone in the audience, including all the other fashion designers, were on their feet, giving her a standing ovation. They cheered for her again and again, and she stood rooted to the spot in amazement. Her heart filled with confidence and joy, and she took from that moment an inspiration that would keep her going in the future.

'We should have trust in ourselves. "Ade rahe khade rahe," this is the slogan I now say every time.'

The World Is Her Oyster

Soon, they were invited to exhibit their products in Germany. Initially, they had a little trouble arranging funds for travel. But, through GVCS, a few organizations came to their rescue, and they travelled to many other countries to exhibit their products. Wherever they showcased their wares, international customers were delighted to find that every piece was handmade, and their goods sold out in no time. Slowly, the women expanded their product line into bedsheets, dresses and more. They got invited to do fashion shows at Lakme Fashion Week.

Ruma's network of women artisans expanded to 30,000 women across 250 villages. Her natural leadership skills and courage helped her keep this large group motivated and working cohesively. She made the office feel like a family space so that the women could enjoy spending time there together. She also learned to speak up for their rights.

'The art of self-advocacy is crucial for our success in all areas of life, but especially in the workforce. Whether we are just starting out or well into our career journey. It was important for me to make sure my voice was heard so that I could amplify my accomplishments and get the help we needed to empower women.'

Ruma received the Nari Shakti Puraskar in 2018 from the president of India, one of India's most prestigious awards. A few years later, she received an invitation to speak at a conference. It was from Harvard University, one of the world's most prestigious universities! However, Ruma had never heard of it. She took the letter to Vikram Singh, who told her what it meant. Ruma Devi was not just surprised but shocked at the invitation. 'Why do they want me to speak? I'm just an illiterate village woman. What have I done that is so great?' she questioned. She couldn't even believe it was a real invitation and was hesitant to send an acceptance. A month later, she got a follow-up letter from Harvard.

That was when she realized she owed it to not just herself but all the women she represented to take the opportunity to showcase their grit.

'When I started doing this work, no one supported me, and people started taunting me, but I didn't look backwards and kept growing. Now all those people who discouraged me are following me.'

Now, she is invited by many different countries around the world to speak about microenterprises and empowering women. As a mother of a young son, she regrets that she doesn't manage to spend as much time with him as she wants. But she is keen on giving him the right upbringing and ensuring he grows up to be a good human being.

Ruma believes that women are each other's biggest strengths and should stand together to fight against a patriarchal society. She still stays up at night wondering how she can empower more women and make them financially independent.

'All individuals have talents. We just have to find out what we are good at and make ourselves independent. Women should step out of their house and make their own norms,' she says.

If she could speak to her younger self, she would like to tell her, 'Other people's opinions are a reflection of their limitations and boundaries. So, be limitless and don't get affected by the negative society. Be grateful every day, build a solid foundation in yourself, listen to your gut and achieve your goal.'

Hacks to Storm the Norm

Norm: You can never rise above the circumstances you are born in.

Sometimes, the circumstances in which we find ourselves can seem so difficult that we come to believe they will be impossible to overcome. Poverty, lack of education and lack of visible opportunities can all seem like mountains to climb. Yet, many people have successfully transcended the limits prescribed for them. One of the biggest predictors of success in life is resilience—your ability to pick yourself up and move on after you fall after you fail. And this is something you can learn.

Hacks:

1. Be the heroine of your story

Think of your life story so far. What is the story that you tell yourself? Are you the victim of circumstances or are you the master of your own fate? The stories we tell ourselves have a defining impact on how our life plays out. Be the heroine in your story and decide that your circumstances and your story can both change. Think of a thing you can do to change the circumstances and take the first step.

2. Have faith in your dream

There is great power in the imaginary; a yearning for a utopian future. This approach works more on the power of yearning than the actual specifics of a plan or tactics. It's the strong desire to break free that gives you the power to imagine the impossible without really having the nuts and bolts in place. All you have at this stage is a beautifully vivid, clear visualization of what you want to create; a picture so sharp that, once you have seen it, you cannot unsee or get it out of your head.

Do not look to other people for validation because at this stage you will only get raised eyebrows and crazy looks. Learn to rely on your dream and believe in it rather than the opinions of those around you.

3. Be your own cheerleader

Sometimes when you're facing difficult circumstances, yet have an aspirational dream, it's difficult to find support from other people around you. Bound by the same circumstances, they can feel hopeless, bitter or even resentful that you think you can rise above. If that happens, become your own cheerleader. Give yourself daily affirmations—'I am good enough', 'I am capable', 'I can do this'. Become your own best friend and cheer yourself on for the tiniest of victories. Each of these helps you keep alive the flicker of optimism that can help you to keep moving forward.

SUPARNA
Do It for the Right Reasons

Introduction

Suparna Mitra is the CEO of the Watches & Wearables Division of Titan Company Limited. She holds a degree in electrical engineering from Jadavpur University (JU) and an MBA from IIM Calcutta. She has extensive business experience, mainly in the lifestyle and marketing fields. She started her career as a management trainee at Hindustan Unilever Limited (HUL). Subsequently, she joined Titan, where she worked in several roles in marketing, both international and domestic. Her next stint was at Talisma Corporation Private Limited as a director of product marketing. She moved on to become business head of Lee in Arvind Brands Ltd.

She rejoined Titan and became the global marketing head, where she was responsible for all marketing in Indian and international markets. After this stint, she was the regional business head of South for Titan Company Ltd, where she headed all businesses of Titan Company Ltd, including watches, jewellery and eyewear for the southern region. Her last assignment was as the chief of sales and marketing officer for the Watches & Wearables division.

A mother of two daughters, Suparna is an avid reader, music enthusiast and firm believer in the power of 'me time'.

Why Suparna?

Suparna was Priyadarshini's classmate in business school—articulate, passionate, sharp as a tack and luminously beautiful, yet understated about her achievements. Over the years, Priya saw her through every step of her personal and professional journey and marvelled as she negotiated so many turns with seeming ease—starting as a management trainee in one of the most coveted campus placements to becoming a young married professional. Suparna later chose to be a trailing spouse and mother who followed her husband overseas. Coming back from a break to a fast-paced corporate career, she went on to become the CEO of one of India's best-known brands. What intrigued Priya was that she had the same building blocks as all the women in the batch, and indeed, as all the men. Yet few of them have achieved what she has. What, then, made the difference?

Working women are torn between two role models—the father who went out and earned a living and the stay-at-home mother who ran the home smoothly and spent her time bringing up the children. Thus, they constantly feel guilty, like they are compromising one for the other. How did Suparna negotiate this? And, given the twists and turns in her professional journey, was her success a series of smoothly planned moves, or was it, as the social norm about successful women goes, luck by chance?

To Thine Own Self Be True

Suparna remembers the moment when her life took a very intentional pivot. She was 11 years old, and living in Durgapur. It was a hot, sunny, sticky day. Her father was at work, and her mother was busy with the two older girls. The youngest of three sisters, Suparna wandered out into the garden of their home. The overgrown grass scraped at her legs as she walked round and round in aimless circles. She stared up into the sunlight, watching a flock of birds fly past. Thoughts drifted in her brain like clouds across the clear blue sky. And suddenly, there popped in a thought that seemed to be written in letters of fire—when she grew up, she would have a job, and what's more, not just a job, but a career! It would not be something she did just to earn a salary, but much larger, something that would give her mental satisfaction and challenge, something that she would enjoy doing all her life, something she would build her life around.

The thought came out of nowhere because in the small steel

township of Durgapur, families were more traditional. Life centred around home and school. Suparna's limited exposure to the world outside had come mostly through books and international magazines like *Time* and *Newsweek* that her father brought home. The men worked at the steel plant, and very few women that Suparna encountered were working women. In fact, working women were mostly gossiped about as mothers who neglected their children.

But once the thought sprang into her mind, it took root as a life ambition. She was determined to live the lives of her father—a successful professional, and her mother—a warm homemaker—the same lifetime.

Starting Anew

Suparna's father was born into a large family of seven children. He was the first one to go into engineering. Suparna's father was a highly distinguished metallurgist, rising to become the managing director of Bhilai Steel Plant. Her mother, too, was a postgraduate— Suparna's grandmother had insisted she complete her education before marriage. The family moved across different towns over the years, from steel plant to steel plant. Suparna and her two older sisters, Sonali and Barnali, had to repeatedly change schools and make new friends. This built Suparna's skill to quickly find her feet and mix with different people. At the same time, it meant forming new relationships rather than the tightly knit, exclusive relationships that are the norm during one's teenage years. Suparna grew up with a rich inner life— daydreaming and contemplating life. She read every book she could lay her hands on and, from an early age, developed a clear idea of equity and fairness. Some of these ideas were picked up from books and some from her own intuitive sense of what seemed right.

With the many disruptions of postings, the family became the backbone that supported each other, as opposed to the peer group. While seemingly docile, Suparna's mother was a forceful personality in her own right. One of the skills the girls gained from her was the ability to point things out without making a big deal out of it. Another value they learnt from both parents was to stick to their beliefs, even if people were unhappy with them.

Sonali, the oldest sister, was somewhat of a rebel, often questioning and breaking the rules. The taboos she broke smoothened the road ahead for the two younger ones. Sometimes, she and Barnali would go on hunger strikes at home to protest what they thought of as unfair behaviour by the parents. Independent-minded Suparna would make her own decision on whether or not to join the strike depending on how hungry she was feeling at the time. While she was close to her sisters, she thought for herself right from childhood, instead of blindly following their lead.

The Seeds of Change

When Suparna was 15, after spending almost 30 years in Steel Authority of India Limited, her father resigned due to differences of opinion and joined a private sector firm in Kolkata. Wanting his family to remain independent, he chose to move them into a flat in Kolkata rather than move back into the home where his extended family still lived.

In Kolkata, 15-year-old Suparna found that there were two distinct groups of students in school—girls who were looking forward to getting engaged or even married, and a handful of girls who were ambitious and discussed career plans. Luckily, teachers were quick to spot the bright sparks, support their ambitions and widen their exposure to the world. But it was a constant push and pull on whether to merge with the larger herd from the social point of view or retain her ambition and stand apart a little.

Sonali and Barnali had arranged marriages in their early twenties and completed their postgraduate degrees after getting married. Suparna consciously chose a different path. Bhilai had been a hotbed of ambitious youngsters wanting to get into IIT. Many kids ended up becoming JEE toppers. This ambition had infected Suparna as well. Very good at science, especially physics, it seemed a natural progression for her to aim at going to an IIT for an engineering degree. However, when she began preparation for the entrance exam, she realized that many subjects in the JEE syllabus had not been taught in school. Back then, there wasn't easy access to coaching classes. Suparna struggled to teach herself those subjects, going through the subject matter over and over again. But it was hard because she didn't just have to grasp new topics, but excel at them in the highly competitive entrance exam.

The morning of the entrance exam, while she was on her way in the car, she mentally pored over the new topics again, trying to do one last revision. She was not feeling confident about how she would perform. With a fervent prayer that she would be able to do her best, she entered the classroom, picked up the exam paper and took her place on the hard wooden chair. All around her were serried rows of studious heads bent over the wooden desks industriously. The three-hour exam flew by, Suparna hardly noticing the humid heat as she scribbled away furiously in the answer book. It came as a surprise when the bell rang to announce that the exam had come to a close. As she gathered her pens and her bag, Suparna knew that she had not done her best. She could feel in her bones that she would not qualify. With a sinking feeling in the pit of her stomach, she slowly made her way back home. Used to superlative academic performance, it felt like the end of the world!

However, she ended up qualifying for electrical engineering at JU in Kolkata. While it was not an IIT, Suparna found some consolation in getting admission into this prestigious engineering college, which saw heavy competition for the limited number of seats.

But while the family celebrated, there were some naysayers. Both among the extended family and the neighbours, she faced sexist comments. Some people felt she had 'taken away' a seat in engineering from a boy who needed it more. Others claimed she was becoming masculine because she had chosen engineering. But, with an independent streak from childhood, Suparna had learnt not to look for external validation. She had what she calls a 'Teflon' attitude towards rude comments. The only people whose words meant anything to her were those whom she knew had her well-being at heart—her parents and siblings.

She knew that her parents would let her follow her heart when it came to career choices. Being a 'good girl' and helping around the house, being respectful and obedient and not having a boyfriend got her brownie points that she could trade off. 'It was like a pact—I was allowed to do some things, like go for my dreams, as long as I stayed within the general norms of appropriate behaviour.'

JU had a much more relaxed atmosphere with a better gender ratio than IIT. Suparna found a group of friends with whom she enjoyed her four years on campus without facing the kind of pressure that would accompany an IIT. However, while she liked her course, she realized that she could not work in engineering for the rest of her life. She had a strong creative orientation around art, music, literature and psychology, all of which were missing from the world of engineering.

Suparna wasn't clear what an MBA meant but it seemed to offer more interesting career paths. She decided to appear for the CAT (Common Aptitude Test) and got through the rigorous entrance process with admission to two prestigious IIMs—Bengaluru and Calcutta. Having always lived at home, she was keen to try her wings and live away from home. However, IIM Calcutta was rated higher than IIM Bengaluru, so she reluctantly chose to stay in Kolkata. Luckily, the MBA was a residential course, so she got to stay on campus and experience independence to some degree.

On Her Own Two Feet

Until then, Suparna had done well in academics without too much effort. IIM Calcutta came as a huge shock. The stakes were much higher, and the class was diverse, with people from across India. There was just a handful of women at the institute, and they were met with a strange combination of admiration coupled with not being taken seriously. Some of the boys had a slightly patronizing attitude and admitted very few girls to their friend circle. For a long time, Suparna continued to hold the belief that it was a badge of honour to be considered one of the boys and was delighted to be considered worthy.

IIM Calcutta was like a cocoon, a verdant, lake-filled world within itself. On the outskirts of the city, without easy access to transport and phone lines that rarely worked, students were cut off from the world outside to a large extent. Life was very busy with a plethora of curricular and extracurricular activities—new friendships, projects and events to be organized. On campus, Suparna learnt to make choices without any input from the family. Be it something like which courses to opt for, what extracurriculars to participate in or whether to stay up partying with classmates through the night—these decisions and the consequences of those decisions were now wholly her responsibility. She became a fully independent adult over those two years.

At placement time, she landed the marketer's dream job as a management trainee at HUL and was assigned to Brooke Bond. The traineeship stint was rigorous. Her job involved grassroots marketing, with sales calls in rural India, and the pressure of achieving sales numbers. Living in a company-assigned chummery with six male trainees, she was allotted a tiny storeroom with little ventilation.

After two months of travelling by government bus to outstation locations like Tumkur, she fell sick with typhoid. Her father flew down to take care of her and was horrified at her living conditions. He told her, 'Come back home. I can find you a far better job. You can't live like this.' But she was adamant. 'I want to make my own way, Baba. I want to build my career the way I want,' she insisted.

Her work required her to visit the factory in Coimbatore and stay in the city for six weeks. But in that small, conservative town, no one was willing to rent a room to a single girl. She struggled to find a decent place to live. Later, she was posted to Vellore, with an option to stay in Chennai. Again, finding a place to rent was a problem. In Chennai, many landlords refused to rent their rooms to anyone who ate meat. She eventually ended up staying in a guest house. Overcoming such hurdles and learning to ignore them in pursuit of her ambitions was a lesson for life.

In a Man's World

Soon, as per custom in HUL, Suparna was assigned to lead a sales team. The team included men much older than her—her second in command was 55 years old, while she was barely 25. While sales teams were used to young MBAs coming in from the head office in positions of leadership, young women MBAs were a rarity. In the beginning, dealers and distributors too found her an oddity—there were relatively few women in marketing, that too doing sales stints in small towns. Once a salesman said, 'Ma'am, are your family circumstances in such a bad state that you have to work?' People weren't used to the idea of a woman who was career-minded. The general perception in the company was that female management trainees were a bother. A senior leader actually asked Suparna, 'Why are you working so hard to succeed at your job considering you will soon get married and leave?'

When she visited small towns, distributors would invite her to their homes. Once, one of her key distributors invited her over for a meal. Suparna went along, wondering what they would chat about. When she reached his house, she was effusively greeted by his wife and daughters. They asked her to sit down on a ceremonial stool and held out a steel tray on which stood the traditional tiny containers of *haldi* and *kumkum*. On the side were two betel leaves along with two areca nuts and the customary blouse piece—a symbol of *lakshana*. Suparna was touched by this gesture—they were treating her like a family member. After a sumptuous lunch, the distributor's wife took her inside, and then she and her daughters began an intensely feminine conversation, excitedly pulling out their sarees and jewellery and showing them to Suparna. They asked her personal questions about her family and how she ran her home. It was a far cry from the professional conversation Suparna had imagined she would have with her distributor.

Fortunately, the interest around gender soon gave way to a conversation based on her work—when would the stock arrive, for instance. Once she established her desire to work alongside the team, she faced no problems from them. There was a sense of fascination that a woman was working in sales. Over time, as she proved her mettle in successfully delivering sales targets, the team began taking pride in her. They would refer to her as '*our* Suparna madam' and revel in the fact that she was doing so well.

While the sales stint was a good learning experience, it did not appeal to Suparna's core interest and strength in marketing. She got married to her IIM batchmate around this time and decided to move to a marketing role. She landed a role as brand manager in Titan, a thoroughbred marketing company. Assigned to international marketing, she had frequent access to legendary leaders in Titan and gained immense exposure to marketing, decision-making, aesthetics and developed an eye for finer details.

The Guilt Factor

While there were a few sneaky snide comments about women, for the most part, men and women worked amicably together at Titan. Suparna thrived at the company. However, when she had her first daughter, Suparna found it hard to go back to work after maternity leave. She felt guilty when she left her daughter to go to work, and then would feel guilty that she wasn't focussing on her work with the same undivided attention as before! Struggling with the balancing act, it came as a relief when her husband's job transferred him to Europe. Now she felt she had a legitimate reason to resign and be with her baby.

At the same time, she knew she wanted to get back to working eventually, though she wasn't sure what path that would take.

After three years overseas, Suparna and the family moved back to Bengaluru. Finding a job after a career break was not as hard as she had thought it would be. 'I had drawn up a list of companies in different sectors and I kept applying. Persistence has been a trademark quality for me and has served me well in all these years.'

She decided to take a chance in the burgeoning world of technology and joined Talisma as director of product marketing. This was the first time she had worked in technology. Within six months, however, she realized that the core of the company was coding. Since she wasn't a coder, she faced an inbuilt glass ceiling she would not be able to shatter. However, the Talisma experience helped her get back into the workforce. She then began working with Arvind Brands in marketing.

As her daughter was still quite young and both her parents and her in-laws stayed far away, Suparna would ensure she was home by five or six p.m., so she could give her daughter the time she needed. She tried to keep work travel to a minimum. But no matter what she did, Suparna heard a voice at the back of her mind telling her she was not doing enough for her child. It became an exhausting treadmill to cope with the demands of a full-time, fast-paced career along with the kind of care she believed it was her duty to provide her daughter.

When she had her second daughter, Suparna decided to take another break. Being a full-time mom helped her feel she was doing justice to her role as a mother. It also helped her gain some much-needed perspective so that she felt replenished and ready to go back to work.

However, she felt responsible for everything to do with the kids, from their physical and emotional well-being to school activities and more. She overcompensated at the workplace on occasion because in her mind this would cancel out the times that she prioritized her children's needs. 'Mommy's guilt' was constant, especially when she had to travel and her daughters would wail and wrap their little arms around her legs to keep her from being able to move. Even though she knew that they would be playing happily moments later, she found it hard to wrench herself away. 'I agonized over decisions on whether to travel to work or not when one of the children had a fever or an exam or something else that needed my attention. In later years, I learnt not to feel guilty—there are many people in the office to manage work, but I'm their only mother—that was how I'd explain myself.'

To help balance out family life, she hired a helper who is still with the family, to stay with the kids from morning to evening. She and her husband ensured they did not travel at the same time so one of them could always be around for the kids. Often the hand-off would take place at the airport, with one of them flying in and the other flying out.

Only years later did Suparna realize she had a gender bias that it was okay for a man to prioritize his career over children but not for a woman. 'Once, in a diversity workshop, I took the Harvard implicit bias test on gender and realized that the ingrained conditioning in me was that the raising of children was primarily the mother's job.'

Reclaiming Her Space

After her second break, Suparna rejoined Titan as marketing head, where the meritocratic yet nurturing culture suited her. 'Organizational culture is probably the single biggest factor in women making it to the top. I chose culture over every other factor, and it really paid off for me.' Though, at that time, Titan did not have specific diversity and inclusion policies, the inherent culture was fair and equitable.

Between 2006 and 2013, Suparna worked in marketing—a big challenge considering she was helming one of the country's most loved and known brands. In 2009, due to organizational restructuring, the international division also became part of Suparna's responsibility. She now had to grapple with the nitty-gritties of understanding new customers in each country. This was a time of huge learning and development as she had to understand diverse consumers and develop different marketing strategies to target them. The period involved intensely creative work that she loved, relaunching the beloved Raga brand and launching new brands like Zoop. This was where she found her ikigai—doing work that she loved and that was needed.

Around this time, Suparna became the first woman to become part of the Titan management council—the leadership team. This time, being the only woman in the room didn't thrill her. 'To be the only woman in the room seems like an honour and privilege till one realizes how entrenched the social conditioning is about women and their place in the larger world.' She began thinking about how she could get more women into the conversation. From then on, 'Whenever I am the only woman in the room, I think of it as, "I'm the first woman in the room," and I start thinking about how I can open doors for many more.'

In 2012, she was selected to be the regional business head of South. However, she was unsure whether she would be able to do justice to it. From managing a small marketing team of 12 people, she would now be responsible for 978 people and thousands of crores of turnover. She would be looking after not just marketing but sales and business.

'I'm not sure I can do this role. So far I've been a marketing specialist—this involves so much more,' she said to Bhaskar Bhat, then managing director of Titan. But he refused to listen to her excuses. 'Suparna, I firmly believe that if anyone can take this on, you can. It's a very critical role for the company, and it's something we believe is going to help you grow professionally. Take it on, you'll learn a lot from it,' he shot back.

Having taken on the challenge, 'I surprised myself and many others in the company that not only did I do it, but I thrived and blossomed.' One of the factors she attributes her growth to is her team. 'The young people in my team challenged me to become somewhat of a paranoid professional who always feared that I would get outdated if I did not make the effort to learn and grow.'

Starting a New Chapter

Over time, while her early career ambitions had been about financial independence and enjoying her work, she began to see that the CEO position was within reach and that she was a strong contender for the job. 'It isn't a one-day story. Every decision counts. Every move counts. Every day and every day's work counts. You have to grow and get the breaks and promotions. You create your destiny every day.'

Very few people in the corporate sector go on to become CEOs. Fewer still are women, especially in India. It was a rare chance, but Suparna wasn't completely sure she would be able to do the job. One of the smartest yet most difficult things to do is ask for help when one needs it. There was a leadership development programme at the company. Suparna asked for a coach to work with her. The coach was able to pinpoint things that were holding her back and help her move from being a marketing leader to an enterprise leader. 'I felt mentally, emotionally, physically, intellectually and spiritually that this is a big responsibility and one needs to be prepared, and this was my prep for that position.'

With her years of experience at Titan and solid credibility in the company, Suparna was announced as the CEO-to-be in March 2019. The incumbent was retiring in March 2020. The company created a mezzanine role—chief sales and marketing officer—so Suparna had a year to shadow the previous CEO and the company could transition easily.

Suparna was slated to take over as CEO in April 2020. On 24 March 2020, the Indian government announced a complete lockdown

Work-life balance: a possibility or a myth?

I think, for many of us, work is an integral part of life and life is everywhere. It is not even just work and life; it is work, family and self.

Two or three tips for women suffering from mid-career crisis.

One thing is that women think they are the only ones and they have to fix everything. That isn't necessary.

Two people wearing the pants at home is clearly a form of conflict. Yes or No?

I don't think the expression is proper. It makes me feel as if an independent woman is masculine in nature. I reject this idea.

What do you wish you would have known at the beginning of your career?

I wish I knew that no matter what turn or move I was making, if I made it for the right reasons and am living up to my fullest potential, it's the right one.

for 21 days, limiting the movements of 1.38 billion people to slow down the Covid-19 pandemic. On 14 April, the prime minister extended the lockdown till 3 May, and later, to 17 May. Eventually, the lockdown was only lifted on 31 May.

Titan's business depended on retail sales, and people walking into stores. Once the lockdown began, people were worried about the essentials—groceries and medicines. With pyjama dressing becoming a fact of life at online offices, no one was thinking of investing in watches. As a company, Titan didn't have a consumer raison d'être. At the same time, there were thousands of employees, hundreds of franchises and distributors who needed to keep their home fires burning.

Anyone in Suparna's position would be forgiven a moment of self-pity and wonder why it had to happen on their watch. However, she believes that no one is given something beyond their ability to handle and persevere through. There were no playbooks on what to do in such an unprecedented time. As a result, she was able to invent the role for herself, without any comparisons.

Suparna and her team spent hours in online meetings, brainstorming how to cope with this challenge. As a large, responsible corporation that believed in stakeholder welfare, Titan chose to look beyond its losses at that time and gave loans and grants to franchises, distributors and vendors so that they could pay salaries to their employees during the lockdown period. This support cemented the company's deep relationships with its partners. The company also decided to use this enforced downtime to begin a process and systems overhaul to build efficiencies for a post-Covid future.

In addition, Suparna decided to brave her fear of contracting Covid-19 and travelled extensively. Being visible in the trenches was something she believed was critical to show solidarity and support to front-line workers and factory employees who had no choice but to work from home. 'The main agenda for me was to keep spirits high, to maintain optimism while being seen as realistic and grounded.' In addition, her travels gave her ideas on what she could do to bring business back. By July, green shoots were visible among consumers, and by October, the company was humming again.

Staying True to Herself

Looking back at her journey, Suparna feels that gender has made it more interesting and unique. One of the things that has helped her succeed is her ability to drop her ego. This enables men to drop theirs too and she is able to sidestep the minefield of ego battles.

She acknowledges that for her generation of women at the workplace, the way to get ahead was often to ignore bias and criticism and work harder than anyone else at their job. Now with a seat at the table, she is no longer diplomatic and prefers to say it straight. In a way, she wants to pay it forward to the next generation of women, as well as pay back her mentors for having had faith in her all along.

As chairperson of the DEIB Council, Suparna leads DEIB (Diversity, Equity, Inclusion, and Belonging) initiatives at Titan. The company wants to actively increase the percentage of women at both senior leadership and middle management levels. The latter is particularly important, as this forms the funnel for future leaders, and also tends to be the stage where many women drop off the career ladder, stymied by the challenge of managing a young family. The DEIB initiative focusses on grooming both internal talent and lateral hires in the critical sales and retail functions. In addition, Suparna is personally mentoring a woman who is on the cusp of an enterprise-wide role in the next few years, and finding the mentorship journey rewarding not just for the mentee but for herself as well.

One thing Suparna has done consistently throughout her journey is self-care. Even from a time when the term was not commonly used, she was very careful to preserve her me-time for exercise, meditation, hobbies and most importantly, time for sleep. Very early on, she realized that it's not about managing time, it's about managing energy. She stays away from activities or people who are energy vampires and adds activities and people that make her feel energized. 'For instance, I don't watch TV—haven't watched it in years; but I'm always up for meeting friends, especially old ones! They fill me with joy and playfulness that uplifts my mood instantly.'

Suparna defines energy vampires as people who are either

grandiose and boastful and leave one feeling inadequate and small, or those who complain and are self-critical and divert your positive energy to replenish their own self-esteem. Her way of dealing with such people (as one can't really avoid many such people in life and at work), is to keep engaging but remaining aware and not getting hooked on to their drama. 'Retain your inner poise and protect your energy,' she says with a smile.

Interestingly, this is a skill her daughters would like to emulate in their own lives. 'Her interest in art and music, her focus on mindfulness and health, and her ability to dedicate parts of her day to just herself—that's something special.'

Someone who invests in thinking deeply about people, networking for the sake of it feels artificial and she prefers to look for heartfelt connections. She owes many unexpected opportunities to having made a genuine connection with people. For example, trying to plan what she would do after retirement, she interacted with a philanthropic volunteer organization. That led to many new connections and possibilities in the social impact space that she is keen on exploring later on. Going forward, she wants to create an organization that helps women to become more financially intelligent and independent.

As a mother of two daughters, Suparna has taught them by example how to be fiercely independent, yet individualistic. Among the core lessons her older daughter Shreya has drawn from observing her mother are:

1. Kill 'em with kindness but stand your ground.
2. You get to choose your own metric of success, and happiness is when it rings true to you.
3. You become who you choose to surround yourself with; working with good people always pays off!

Hacks to Storm the Norm

Norm: Women tend to assume the 'corner office' is a responsibility too tough to manage.

Research across the world shows that men are far better at clinching promotions, while women tend to be much more cautious and underestimate their own capabilities and readiness for the next level. Very often this is fed by the imposter syndrome that seems to affect women disproportionately.

Hacks:

1. Ask for help
Seek feedback; ask the boss what he found most challenging, and what challenges he foresees in the next five years. Look for external leadership coaching. Ask your organization to invest in it for you.

2. Put your hand up
Ask for challenging assignments early on in your journey. These will not only be valuable learning opportunities but will afford you visibility, too. Moreover, knowing you can punch above your weight gives you a level of confidence nothing else can.

3. Understand your career DNA
What are the unique skills, knowledge and value you bring to the organization and the team? What do people rely on you for? Ask your boss, your peers and subordinates for their input to get a clear vision of what you bring to the table like no one else can.

VINEETA
Act Fast and Analyse Later

Introduction

Vineeta Singh is the co-founder and CEO of SUGAR Cosmetics, India's fastest-growing beauty brand, available across more than 50,000 branded retail outlets in more than 550 cities. One of the sharks on the reality show Shark Tank India, she is committed to creating products that allow every Indian woman to find a favourite, and inspiring them to start their own entrepreneurship journey. An alumna of IIT Madras and IIM Ahmedabad, she is famously known for declining a ₹1 crore job offer from a leading investment bank to follow her heart and dive into entrepreneurship. Also a triathlete and ultra-marathoner, her passion for running has helped her challenge her limits time and again.

She has been featured in *Fortune's* and *The Economic Times'* 40 Under 40, *GQ India's* Most Influential Young Indians and *Business Today India's* Most Powerful Women in Business lists, and on the covers of *Business Today, Forbes* and the *Entrepreneur* magazine.

Why Vineeta?

While India now celebrates its many unicorns, too few of them have women at the helm. Is it a lack of confidence or a fear of failure that keeps women from entering the high-stakes field of entrepreneurship? Becoming an entrepreneur takes a different skill set than being a successful employee even at the highest levels. At times, it could mean being okay with being disliked or going against accepted wisdom. Women are typically brought up to be agreeable, to be liked and to colour within the lines.

Can women cope with the key task of being a founder, which is to constantly raise more money? Can they overcome imposter syndrome to lead hundreds of employees into a tabula rasa? Vineeta Singh is one of the few examples of female entrepreneurs who have done just that, creating an Indian cosmetics brand from scratch. Did she face these challenges or were there others she overcame to be where she is today?

Vineeta Singh

In 2012, Vineeta Singh was raising funds for her second start-up. She found it extremely difficult. Some investors told her, 'We don't invest in solo women founders because they have families and stop focussing on business.' Others said, 'We would put in the money subject to your husband coming into the business full-time.' With her husband on board, they then turned to her and explained that, 'Husband-wife teams are a big red flag for us.' It didn't look like she was going to be able to succeed in getting her company funded. She and her husband decided to break their last fixed deposit of 30 lakh to keep the company going.

Seeds of the Future

Vineeta grew up in a household where it was not just accepted but expected that she would grow up to have a thriving career of her own. Work and career were important parts of her parents' lives. Her father is a scientist with his own lab at AIIMS. He worked around the year to discover protein structures and added them to the global database so that they could be used for essential drugs. He had set himself a target of discovering 600 protein structures in his lifetime, to be the world's greatest contributor to protein structures. That set a high benchmark for Vineeta to follow.

At the same time, she saw that his obsession with work meant that he sacrificed all his personal time for this pursuit. He didn't have enough time for the family. She vowed that her life would have a better balance between work, her own interests and hobbies and family.

'But I would always err on the side of being 'overambitious' because the concept of aiming to be "world class", staying focussed on the long term and choosing delayed gratification over short-term wins was drilled into my head over and over.'

Her mother too is a PhD holder. She continued working after marriage and had a kid and is one of Vineeta's role models. Her father said appreciatively, 'So many of the women at AIIMS lose interest in their work after they have kids. They slow down and are just not that ambitious anymore. It's very sad. See your mother, on the other hand, who chose to never bow out.' Vineeta grew up with the ambition to not slow down and was paranoid about not derailing the 'career track'. It was only much later that she learnt to appreciate women for all the choices that they make, including being homemakers or those who work outside the home.

Vineeta was brought up to strive hard in school. Her parents actively discouraged her from doing domestic chores or anything that could distract her from study time. In her own words, she was 'raised like a boy'. Her parents wanted her to excel at everything. They would have preferred that she went into medicine. But when she picked engineering instead, they were clear that she had to study from the best, i.e., an IIT. They showed her many examples of IITians who had gone on to achieve great things. It was another story that those all happened to be men, since there were very few women at IIT.

The First Taste of Patriarchy

It was only once she got to IIT that Vineeta came across ingrained patriarchy. There were only 24 girls in a class of 400! Some classmates commented about girls having gotten in because of an unsaid women's quota. Others sneered that girls wouldn't be able to handle the difficult coursework. For the first time, Vineeta started doubting herself and her capabilities. She fought back by working harder than ever to prove that she deserved her place.

Like many of her peers, while she was bright and ambitious, she was still trying to figure out where her passion lay. She was unclear about what she wanted to achieve in life. Post IIT, Vineeta knew that she didn't want to work as an engineer. She qualified for admission into IIM Ahmedabad.

At IIM Ahmedabad, she met the man she would go on to marry, Kaushik Mukherjee. She also did a summer internship at Deutsche Bank in investment banking and ended up with a PPO—Permanent Placement Offer—paying her a salary of ₹1 crore. But she took the bold decision to turn down the job to co-found a start-up with three of her batchmates. At the same time, with her mother as a role model, she was also clear that having a family and a child was part of her life plan.

'I was always quite certain that, irrespective of my career choices, I'd be someone who would get married and have children because I saw that my mom, in spite of having a fabulous career, got her greatest happiness from raising her daughter.'

She was surprised and shocked at the very different way in which people reacted to her dreams versus her co-founders'. They were all men, and everyone seemed to think they were doing something brave and wonderful by becoming entrepreneurs. There was encouragement and praise coming forth for them. For her, there was caution and a warning that she would not be able to manage being an entrepreneur and having a family.

'I got so much advice at 23 about potentially derailing my plans of having a happy, married life with kids by choosing such a difficult career option that would require me to work long hours. Even my greatest mentors were concerned that starting a business would make me so obsessed about it that I'd miss out on the joys of raising a family!'

While her male co-founders were being encouraged to go all out, she was being asked to rein in her ambition, consider finding a life partner early and move cities and careers to be with him!

Run, Vineeta, Run

Vineeta wanted to do something fun, quickly scale the business and do an IPO. She and her co-founders planned to build a background verification check service for employers. She started her career with a meagre salary of ₹10,000, in Mumbai, one of India's most expensive cities to live in. The rent itself consumed half of her salary, for a measly one-room dwelling that dripped in the monsoon.

Once she began her entrepreneurial journey, Vineeta found the road to success quite difficult. Some of it was on account of gender. At this point, she didn't have the confidence to run the business the way she wanted. Business development was hard for her to master. Some potential clients either patronized her or were arrogant and shady. Her co-founders were batchmates she looked up to. Her need for the crutch of her co-founders was very strong, so she kept hustling to make this start-up work. She ended up taking on small-time contracts just to keep the wheels rolling. Despite all the hard work she was putting in, she didn't see any progress. Ignoring her frustrations, she continued working on the start-up for several years.

Adding to her disappointment were the unavoidable failures. Like many intelligent kids, she had grown up knowing her strengths. She ensured her work centred around things she knew she would be good at. She hadn't taken a chance on things she wasn't sure she could do. As a result, she had rarely had to deal with failure.

'I grew up being great at certain things and not so good at others, so I would very carefully craft my goals and dreams and aspirations around the things that I felt I could accomplish! I think it was a creative way to avoid failures and not take risks. It almost led me to feel like I could get through most of life without having to learn how to deal with massive failures and rejections, but entrepreneurship was extremely humbling.'

That made it much more difficult for her to come to terms with failure. It affected her self-confidence for years before she understood how to cope.

Upset with what was happening on the professional front, she knew she needed to find an outlet and an escape. She took to running. True to her personality, she was not content with mere jogging. She trained for a marathon and then went on to become a regular marathoner. Challenging herself further, she then ran ultra-marathons and participated in triathlons. The races and the medals she won gave her a feeling that something, at least, was going right.

Each little win gave her a welcome boost of confidence while she continued to struggle at the workplace. A few more years down the line, her ambitious nature would lead her to take on one of the hardest endurance tests in the world—the Ironman challenge.

After five years of slogging, she decided that the start-up was not working for her. She realized that Quetzal was a 'spectacular failure', as she described it. It was a commodity business with no differentiation; hence price undercutting was the only way it worked. 'Such businesses just don't work in India because there will always be someone who can do it for a lower cost,' Vineeta says.

When she exited her business, she started questioning her decision to become an entrepreneur. Looking back at her failures, she doubted if anyone would be willing to pay her even ₹50,000 a month. She wondered if she had any skills that were valuable. In hindsight, she says, 'I wish I had known earlier that there would be absolutely no avoiding failures.'

Her self-belief was at rock bottom, even though she had competed in some of the most gruelling physical challenges in the world. It was going to take years of hard work and scaling up two other businesses to rebuild her confidence. But each time she failed and built herself back up, she felt she had cracked open the door wider. She was able to make bigger and bolder moves and take decisions her younger self would not have been able to. Failure ended up being a better teacher than success.

Milk for the Baby and Sugar for Me

Vineeta and Kaushik get married in 2011, around the time she was winding up her start-up. She realized she enjoyed experimenting with international cosmetics brands and decided to start a cosmetics subscription business, Fab Bag, with her husband, in 2012. She was truly passionate about this and started enjoying coming to work every day, for the first time in a long time. Over time, she built up a subscriber list of two lakh customers. From listening in on their conversations and her own experience growing up, she realized that young girls have very little access to make-up, especially if they are from middle-class families. Most brands didn't market affordable cosmetics designed for India's younger generation. In addition, many international brands just did not cater to Indian skin tones, the type of Indian skin or the way of life. For instance, make-up needs to be long-lasting while a woman commutes to her workplace by public transport in a hot and humid climate.

Armed with this insight, in 2015, she started SUGAR Cosmetics—a range of affordable cosmetics designed for young Indian women. While both these businesses were not easy to run, she was very passionate about them and had fun building them up. Indian consumers until then used minimal make up on a daily basis. Educating the consumer and inspiring them to have fun experimenting became part of the brand's DNA and they used emergent digital platforms like YouTube, Instagram and the SUGAR app to embrace this. They also decided to be omni channel and be present wherever consumers shopped, be it online or offline.

'When you get to build something you truly love, the rejections and failures en route feel disappointing but never exhausting! You somehow gather the enthusiasm to keep going back to your mission and finding smaller milestones to celebrate and keep yourself going.'

One of the life lessons she took away from this experience was that she should follow her passion rather than think, 'Let me do work I hate for X years and then I will follow my passion.'

Coincidentally, 2015 also happened to be the year she started a family. With the start-up in its most intense phase, it took courage to go ahead with parenthood at this time. She knew investors were unsure of her ability to succeed. But she felt so strongly about becoming a mother that she wanted to go ahead.

'When I had my first baby in 2015, our start-up was going through its hardest patch and we had investors on board who were obviously doubtful of our abilities as founders to turn this around. I had thought long and hard about whether I wanted to jeopardize my future fundraising options by having a baby at a time like this, but I was so clear about not letting my career ambitions take away from my dream of being a parent that I decided to have a baby; and I can't even put to words how much courage this took, back in 2015.'

However, in her head she heard the naysayers, the ones who passed sexist comments about women's ability to succeed at entrepreneurship. As a result, she felt the need to keep proving her worth to them. She dressed in clever layers to hide her pregnancy during investor meetings. Only when she was in her seventh month and it was no longer possible to conceal it did she break the news. Hesitantly, she said, 'As you can see, I'm expecting my first baby. But you can rest assured—my pregnancy or becoming a mother won't get in the way of my business. I will ensure that we meet and beat the targets we have committed.'

There was a stunned silence from the investors before they said, 'Congratulations, that's great news. And don't worry, it's fine to take the time to enjoy this phase of life. Don't get stressed about the business at this stage.'

Vineeta was taken aback, but still didn't get the message. Soon after her son was born, she called each one of them up.

'I have a great support system lined up, between family and qualified nannies. Don't worry, I'll be back at work within a month,' she told them brightly. One of her investors came over to visit, carrying a gift for the baby. As he cooed at the baby, Vineeta felt compelled to launch into her reassuring message yet again.

'Stop it, Vineeta,' he chided her. 'This is a very important time in your life. You must ensure you take the time to bond and really be present for your child at this point. Work will always be there. Life is about more than just work, you know.'

That's when Vineeta had an epiphany. She realized that she felt guilty about pursuing her personal goals over her professional ones, like many ambitious women. That made her rethink the need to separate her personal and professional life. She realized that if she was open about her personal life, her baby could be included in her busy schedule.

She decided to embrace the twin identities of being an entrepreneur and a mother. That meant she could travel with her son, take breaks to feed him and so on. This gave her a new sense of freedom and flexibility.

'Just the openness that this part of my life was as important as the other part gave me so much power and conviction.'

So much so that a few years later, she would take her second child along to investor off-sites quite happily. This helped build a company culture where her employees, both men and women, could embrace their whole lives instead of having to compartmentalize.

'Our senior designer brought her 11-month-old to our company off-site after she got back from her maternity leave, and it just became more and more common with every passing year for women to be comfortable with the struggles of managing work and their little ones whenever they came back from maternity leave. They'd openly share and discuss their problems rather than being secretive about them out of fear of that putting them on a mommy track.'

> **Top Three Takeaways**
>
> • Visualize your best life and fight for it! Be patient with outcomes but don't settle for anything less than your best life!
>
> • Be the most ambitious person you know! It's very hard because we are brought up to downplay our ambitions, so overcompensate for that consciously by boldly sharing your ambitions with people you know—enough to make them laugh at how crazy you are!
>
> • Being passionate about your work is a competitive advantage because you end up spending more than a decade to become exceptional in your field. So, take the first four-five years to discover what's right for you and what you would truly enjoy doing.

Shattering Mental Glass Ceilings

Coping with a child and a busy workplace, she found a newfound appreciation for housewives and women who voluntarily put their careers aside to focus on their families. Getting positive feedback at work made one accustomed to expecting it in personal life as well, and not getting it could lead to anxiety. Recognizing her guilt and her low self-confidence as a mother, she told her husband to periodically remind her that she's doing alright. In fact, alternating between self-doubt and working her way back to self-belief is a pattern one observes throughout her journey.

At work, she chased the goal of hitting a ₹4,000 crore valuation with all intensity. While some of it was driven by her own ambition, it was also born out of her fervent need to prove to her investors that they were right in backing her. It was only after the company reached the ₹4,000 crore valuation that she began to re-evaluate what was important. She felt that the valuation, while important, was just a number.

Despite her success, the sexism didn't stop. During an interview with an author who was featuring IIT Madras entrepreneurs, she was aghast when he casually asked her, 'Isn't it stereotypical that the only woman founder in the list runs a cosmetics company?' People commented on social media that her success isn't deserved or worth celebrating because she made 'a frivolous product' or because she 'wasted' her engineering degree. She fumed about sexist attitudes and wondered when it would ever end. She realized that, in some way, she would never measure up, could never prove herself 'worthy enough'. Stereotypes would continue to exist and there would always be some requirement for her to justify herself.

'That's when it hit me that this fight to prove myself "worthy"—I just could not win it—it didn't matter if I was the one who got the best job on campus or the one who built a large, highly valued company. There would always be something "stereotypical" to explain that success and I'd always still be "trying to prove I'm equal". I had a paradigm shift in the way I started thinking from that day onwards and so I don't like to talk about "glass ceilings" and "gender equality"—I just build the way I enjoy building, empower thousands of women through my work. I feel that just having millions of empowered women everywhere is the best answer to these age-old questions and I feel so fulfilled by finally focussing my efforts and energy there.'

That was the day she decided to stop thinking about stereotypes and just enjoy her work completely. What gave her satisfaction and fulfilment was being able to create impact on scale, both among consumers and employees. She wanted to empower millions of young girls to feel confident, and to create a company firmly founded on equality. With several women in leadership positions at her firm, the company had redefined traditional leadership skills. Attributes like kindness and empathy walked hand in hand with excellence and growth. She also began her journey in philanthropy, giving back 10 per cent of her earnings. In the future, she wants to give back not only in terms of money but also her time and attention.

SUGAR Cosmetics now employs 3,000 women and 1,000 men and a leadership team with diverse experiences. With many of them more senior to Vineeta in years of experience, it had been challenging to cope at times. One of the critical life skills that Vineeta has learnt over the years—something women generally tend to be poor at—is taking help when needed and practising self-care. She worked with a coach to help her lead a fast-scaling business. She also ensured she made time for herself—to read, run or just relax.

The Marathoner Who Wouldn't Quit

As in any profession, there were the inevitable bad days that made her wonder if it was worthwhile. Vineeta had found a mantra to help her get through it. The first thing she did when facing a crisis was to take a break and do something that made her happy—go for a run, have a cup of coffee or a glass of wine or talk to a friend who could put things in perspective. She remembered to be grateful for how far she had come from the days of being a struggling entrepreneur who had to think a lot before paying for a cup of coffee to employing thousands of people. And the thing that always put a smile on her face was reading the comments on social media from millions of young girls who bought her products, reminding her why she had started this business.

Amongst the things that she brought to her work, she counted perseverance as her biggest strength.

'I'm the marathoner who doesn't quit.'

She loves inspiring her team to do better in terms of building great products, growing faster or just creating small moments of consumer happiness. She values the principle of compounding—as she puts it, once you start getting good at what you do, the value you bring just multiplies manifold.

Looking back at her journey, she wishes she had given her 23-year-old self more credit and backed herself more. While her decision to go into entrepreneurship seemed bold and brave at the time, now she wishes she had stuck to her guns and found something she was passionate about from the beginning, rather than getting stuck in businesses that weren't meant for her.

'When I see women in their early twenties today, I'm so happy that they don't receive a ton of this unnecessary advice about "not forgetting what's most important for a woman"!'

With two young children and a fast-growing company, she prefers viewing work-life balance as a fluid concept. Each day doesn't have to be a perfect balance. Her mother has been a backbone of support by coming to stay when the kids were younger or by seamlessly taking over when Vineeta has to travel for work, while her husband has been her trusted sounding board.

Throughout her journey, Vineeta has faced several situations where she doubted herself and had to fight her way back to self-belief. Today, finally, she is at a stage where she says without any hubris that the only thing that keeps her up at night is her babies.

Hacks to Storm the Norm

Norm: Women entrepreneurs are less likely to succeed.

A majority of women across the world face multiple barriers like lack of family support, lack of capital and lack of self-confidence that act as hindrances in their entrepreneurial pursuits. From being the perfect mother to running a business, women have the power to balance work and family, yet somewhere they are being held back from fulfilling their dreams.

'When you think the possible is impossible, it is. When you're constantly told you are at a disadvantage, you start to believe it. The truth is, we can achieve whatever we put our mind to, regardless of sex, race or religion.'

Hacks:

1. Figure out what success means to you

Women can be their own worst enemies. Their sense of responsibility makes them do the 'right' thing for everyone else but themselves. Entrepreneurship is a risky step that requires getting support from lots of people around you, and taking it abundantly without guilt is the key to success. If you want to strive for success as an entrepreneur, you need to fully believe in yourself and that you deserve a fighting chance at success. Success means many different things to different people. You need to figure out what it means to you before you allow yourself to run after the wrong thing. There is no room for self-doubt in this journey.

2. Be overconfident

To be a successful entrepreneur, you have to be overconfident. You have to believe that you're better than everyone around you. Having misplaced confidence in yourself and thinking you can win when other people always lose is a strong determiner of entrepreneurship. The aspect of overconfidence, though, is an interesting one—because a lot of people assume that being overconfident is a negative, yet, in some of these cases, overconfidence is actually a positive. Women tend to be more humble and self-effacing, and even in the face of actual success, they end up attributing it to everything else and a lot less to themselves; instead of leveraging and taking advantage of it.

3. Simplify

Women have a tendency to overthink things. They get into their own heads. Where men will usually just make a decision and go with it, women will look at the situation from every possible angle. The female over-analytical brain sometimes restricts women from making quick, bold decisions that are the hallmark of successful entrepreneurs. So, women need to act fast and analyse later.

Acknowledgements

First and foremost, this book would not have been possible without the time and patience of all the wonderful women we have featured. They were extremely generous with both as we understood their stories, crafted out the narrative and went back to them time and again for clarifications, more information and for more nuance. And of course, as we got to know them better through the course of writing this book, they inspired us even more.

Special thanks to Kiran Mazumdar-Shaw for believing in the book and helping set the right context with the foreword.

Amrita Bansod, design entrepreneur, co-founder of Studio ABD and the best in her craft. After the much-acclaimed first book cover by her talented spouse Abhijit, it is Amrita this time who has excelled with our new book cover. Truly indebted to both of them for being our design partners.

Rajeev Chaba, CEO and MD of MG Motors has raised the bar and walked the talk with his game-changing diversity interventions in a male-dominated industry.

Archan Kundu, journalism student and researcher, helped us enthusiastically with the background research, sat through many of the interviews, transcribed them all and gave us fresh insights into the stories.

Pervin Saket, our first editor, helped us bring the stories to life with her clear-eyed insights into pace, narrative style and the ordering of the story, tone, voice and grammar.

Dibakar Ghosh from Rupa Publications who enthusiastically said yes and helped steer the book to its final publication.

Our families, who saw us through endless delayed meals, late nights, zoom calls and more through the writing of the book.

And all the inspirational women, and men, who were our role

models, allies, friends and cheerleaders as we strove in our own ways, to Storm the Norm.

ACKNOWLEDGEMENTS
BY PRIYADARSHINI NARENDRA

To all the wonderful, fierce, feisty and warm women who nurtured us, supported us and inspired us to Storm the Norms, and who would be very surprised to be described as giants!

Premalatha, my mom, who has been a passionate champion for me through my professional and personal decisions, and without whose advice I would never have set off on my career journey. Whose wholehearted care for my children gave me the freedom and peace of mind to continue my career journey.

Subhadra Bai and Shanti Bai—my grandmothers who were living proof that wearing a saree and looking delicate is no indication of the steel inside.

Champa, Vasanthi, Brinda—my aunts. Career women who inspire me every day with their confidence, style, zest for life and sheer grit; who stormed the norms to live life to their own beat.

Aliya, my mother-in-law. She took incredibly bold decisions for her time, lived life on her own terms without wearing it on her sleeve and raised a feminist son whom I'm proud to call my husband.

Masooma, my aunt-in-law. A tour de force, a combination of roots and cosmopolitan elegance. Someone with whom I could discuss family matters and world affairs with equal comfort.

Mrinalini, my sister. Perfectionist whether at work or at home. Setting new benchmarks and inspiring me constantly. My first critic whenever I write something. All-round badass.

Fatima, my sister-in-law. Warm-hearted and generous, she welcomed me into the family and is truly a sister of the heart.

Mimi, my soul sister; the first person to hear my good and bad news, who is equally ready with hugs or champagne as the situation warrants.

Parvati and Anurupa, my housekeepers, nannies and domestic mainstays. Who gave unwaveringly not only of their time but dedication and love, and look after my children and home as their own, letting me have it all without doing it all.

ACKNOWLEDGEMENTS
BY ANISHA MOTWANI

To the graceful feminine pillars of my life:

This book is heartfully dedicated to my three mothers, whose presence has been a constant source of strength and inspiration.

First, to my mother, Champa Chandwani, whose unwavering positive outlook has been my guiding light. Her ability to remain optimistic and empathic in the face of life's trials has taught me invaluable lessons about resilience and compassion.

I extend my deepest gratitude to my late mother-in-law, Mohini Motwani. She was a beacon of support, joyfully sharing the responsibility of caring for my children, allowing me to pursue my career with peace of mind. Her memory continues to be a source of comfort and motivation.

And finally, to my aunt mother-in-law, Dr B.G. Kotwani, a remarkable 95-year-old practising gynaecologist at Gangaram Hospital. Her zest for life and unwavering passion for her profession defy age and continue to amaze and inspire me every day. Her journey is a testament to the enduring power of dedication and love for one's calling.

To these extraordinary women, I owe a debt of gratitude that words can barely express. This book is a tribute to your enduring impact on my life.

With love and admiration,
Anisha